MW00335097

.
.
.
.

KEN SCHULTZ'S
Field Guide to Saltwater Fish

KEN SCHULTZ'S
Field Guide to Saltwater Fish

by Ken Schultz

WILEY

JOHN WILEY & SONS, INC.

Published by John Wlley & Sons, Inc., Hoboken, New Jersey
Published simultaneously in Canada

Design and production by Navta Associates, Inc.

For general information about our other products and services, please contact our Customer Care Department within the United States at (800) 762-2974, outside the United States at (317) 572-3993 or fax (317) 572-4002.

Wiley also publishes its books in a variety of electronic formats. Some content that appears in print may not be available in electronic books. For more information about Wiley products, visit our web site at www.wiley.com.

Library of Congress Cataloging-in-Publication Data:

Schultz, Ken.
  Ken Schultz's field guide to saltwater fish / by Ken Schultz.
      p. cm.
  Includes index.
    ISBN 978-1-63026-126-9
  1. Marine fishes—North America. 2. Marine fishes—North America—Identification. I. Title: Field guide to saltwater fish. II. Title.
    QL625.S42 2004
    597.177—dc22   2003015773

Printed in the United States of America

10 9 8 7 6 5 4 3 2 1

Contents

Glossary   265

Introduction

This guide is derived from the widely praised and award-winning volume *Ken Schultz's Fishing Encyclopedia.* Weighing nearly 10 pounds and containing 1,916 pages of information in an 8.5- by 11-inch format, it is hardly a book that can be taken afield or casually perused.

Among the many virtues of the encyclopedia is its detailed information about prey and predator species worldwide, which many people—including numerous lure designers, scientific researchers, and anglers—find very valuable and which is available nowhere else. To make it easier for people interested in the major North American fish species to reference this subject matter, that portion of the encyclopedia was excerpted into two compact and portable guides, *Ken Schultz's Field Guide to Freshwater Fish* and *Ken Schultz's Field Guide to Saltwater Fish.*

These books are primarily intended for the angler, placing major emphasis on gamefish species (nearly 260) sought in the fresh- and saltwaters of Canada, the United States, and Mexico, and on the prey species that most gamefish use for forage. Although many hundreds of species are included here, such compact books lack room for detailed information about many of the lesser species; however, they are well represented in the information that exists under certain groupings. For example, there are more than 300 species of "minnows" in North America, and much of what is said about them as a group in the freshwater guide pertains to the majority of individuals. Profiles are provided, nonetheless, of some of the more prominent members of this group.

The same is true for some larger, more well-known groups of fish, like sharks. There are at least 370 species of sharks worldwide and dozens in North America. The saltwater guide provides an overview of this group, as well as specific information about the most prominent North American members. And, of course, color illustrations help identify the individual species profiled.

There is a slight but deliberate content overlap in both books, as some species occur in both freshwater and saltwater. This is primarily true for anadromous fish like salmon, shad, and striped bass. However, a few saltwater species, such as snook, mullet, and ladyfish, are known to move into freshwater for part of their lives, even though they are not technically anadromous, and thus are also represented in both volumes. In this sense, certain species were included in both books for practical reasons, as opposed to purely scientific ones.

At the end of the book is a glossary that explains the terms used in the species profiles, and following this introduction are two chapters of information invaluable to anyone who desires to know more about fish in a broad general sense. The Overview and the Fish Anatomy chapters are written in layman's terms and provide concise information about fish that is useful to the angler, the naturalist, and even the aquarium hobbyist—all of whom share a passion and a concern for some of the most remarkable creatures on the planet.

An Overview of Fish

FISH

The term "fish" is applied to a class of animals that includes some 21,000 extremely diverse species. Fish can be roughly defined (and there are a few exceptions) as cold-blooded creatures that have backbones, live in water, and have gills. The gills enable fish to "breathe" underwater, without drawing oxygen from the atmosphere. This is the primary difference between fish and all other vertebrates. Although such vertebrates as whales and turtles live in water, they cannot breathe underwater. No other vertebrate but the fish is able to live without breathing air. One family of fish, the lungfish, is able to breathe air when mature and actually loses its functional gills. Another family of fish, the tuna, is considered warm-blooded by many people, but the tuna is an exception.

Fish are divided into four groups: the hagfish, the lampreys, cartilaginous fish, and bony fish. The hagfish and the lampreys lack jaws, and as such they form the group called jawless fish; the cartilaginous fish and the bony fish have jaws. The bony fish are by far the most common, making up over 95 percent of the world's fish species. Cartilaginous fish, including sharks, rays, and skates, are the second largest group, numbering some 700 species. There are 32 species of hagfish and 40 species of lampreys.

Overview

Body of the fish. The body of a fish is particularly adapted to aquatic life. The body is equipped with fins for the purpose of locomotion. Scales and mucus protect the body and keep it streamlined. The skeleton features a long backbone that can produce the side-to-side movements needed for forward propulsion in water. Since water is 800 times more dense than air, fish must be extremely strong to move in their environment. Fish respond to this condition by being mostly muscle. Thus, muscles make up 40 to 65 percent of a fish's body weight. Many fish have air or gas bladders (sometimes called swim bladders), which allow them to float at their desired depth. Fish also have gills, their underwater breathing apparatus, located in their heads. Most fish have only one gill cover, although some, like sharks, have gill slits, some as many as seven. The gills are the most fragile part of the fish; anglers should avoid touching the gills on fish that they plan on releasing.

The limbs of a fish come in the form of fins. A fin is a membrane that extends from the body of the fish and is supported by spines or rays. Because the number of rays is usually constant within a species, a ray count is often used by scientists to determine the species of a fish. Each of the fins on a fish has a name. Since these names are used in almost all descriptions of fish and are used in this book, it is worthwhile to become familiar with the different fin names.

Moving from the head toward the tail, the first fins are the pectoral fins. The pectoral fins are used for balance and maneuvering in many species and in a few are used for propulsion. Farther down the underside of the fish are the pelvic fins, located beneath the belly and used for balance. On the back of the fish is the dorsal fin. Some fish have more than one dorsal fin; in this case, the dorsal fins are numbered, with the fin closest to the head called the first dorsal fin. Behind the dorsal fin on the top part of the fish there is occasionally a smaller, fleshy fin called the adipose fin. Back on the underside of the fish, behind the pelvic fins and the anus, is the anal fin. The final fin, usually called the tail, is known scientifically as the caudal fin. The caudal fin is the most important fin for locomotion; by moving it from side to side, a fish is able to gather forward momentum.

The scales of a fish form the main protection for the body. Fish scales are kept for the entire life of a fish; as a fish grows, the scales get larger, rather than growing anew. Scales are divided into several types. Most fish have ctenoid or cycloid scales. Ctenoid scales are serrated on one edge and feel rough when rubbed the wrong way (largemouth bass have such scales). Cycloid scales are entirely smooth, like the scales of trout. More rare types of fish have different types of scales: Sharks have more primitive placoid scales, which are spiny; sturgeon have ganoid scales, which form armor ridges along parts of the body. Some species, like catfish, have no scales at all. Fish scales can be used to determine the age of a fish. A fish scale will develop rings showing annual growth, much like the rings of a tree.

Many fish also have a covering of mucus that gives them a slimy feel. This covering helps streamline their bodies and prevent infections. The mucus covering will rub off onto a person's hands (this is the slimy substance that you can feel on your hands after handling a fish). Since the loss of mucus is detrimental to the fish, it is better to wet your hands before handling a fish that will be released to minimize the amount of mucus removed, being careful not to harm a fish by holding it too tightly.

The skeletal and the muscular systems of fish work together to maximize swimming power. The serially repeated vertebrae and the muscle structure work together to create the shimmering, undulating muscle movements that allow a fish to move forward quickly. This structure is particularly evident in a filleted fish, where the muscles show themselves in their interlocking pattern. The muscular nature of fish is the reason why fish make such good eating and is also a factor in making fish a high-yield food source.

Bony fish have developed an organ called an air bladder, which acts as a kind of flotation device. A fish's body is naturally a bit more dense than water, but the air bladder, filled with gas, increases a fish's ability to float. Fish can change the depth at which they float by varying the amount of gas in their air bladders. This allows a fish to float at any depth it desires without expending any effort. Fish that do not have air bladders, such as sharks, must continually move in order to avoid sinking.

Like virtually all animals, fish need oxygen to survive. However, a fish can get all the oxygen it needs from water by use of its gills. Water entering through the mouth of the fish is forced over the gills, and oxygen is removed from the water by the gills. In order to breathe, fish must constantly have water passing over their gills. However, in order to get enough oxygen, certain fish must either move continually or live in water with a strong current.

Although most fish are referred to as cold-blooded creatures, this is mostly but not entirely true. Some species are called warm-blooded, yet they cannot sustain a constant body temperature as humans do. Instead, the body temperature of fish approximates that of its surrounding medium— water. Certain types of fish, such as tuna, by their constant vigorous propulsion through the water, sustain high muscular flexion that creates heat associated with rapid metabolism. Through built-in heat conservation measures, the fish is capable of maintaining a warmer body temperature than the medium that upholds it; for example, a bluefin tuna's fighting qualities are not impaired physically when it suddenly dives from surface waters where it was hooked down to the colder depths.

Fish Shapes

Fish shapes have also uniquely evolved to suit the needs of their aquatic lives. The body shapes of fish fall into general categories: Some are narrow, with bodies that are taller than they are thin, like sunfish, largemouth bass, or angelfish. Some are flat, with bodies that are shorter than they are wide, like flounder. Some are torpedo-shaped, like tuna or mackerel. Some are tubular and snakelike, such as eels.

Shapes tend to be related to a fish's habits and habitats. Narrow-bodied fish are extremely maneuverable and tend to live in reefs or densely weeded ponds, where the ability to maneuver between rocks or plants is essential. Flatfish tend to live on the bottom, where their low profiles prevent recognition. Torpedo-shaped fish are built for speed and are found either in open water or in strong currents where less streamlined fish would be swept away. Tubular fish often live in small crevices and areas that are inaccessible to other animals, rather than in wide-open ocean waters.

Fish Color

The amazing variety of colors that fish display clearly demonstrates the importance of color in the fish world. Most fish are colored for purposes of camouflage. When viewed from above, fish tend to be dark in order to blend in with the dark bottom of the water. When viewed from below, they look light in order to blend in with the sky (this is called countershading). Fish have developed a huge variety of colors and markings that allows them to escape detection in their own environments. Color is also used for mating purposes. Certain fish have special breeding colors, usually brighter than normal colors. Many reef fish have brilliant colors year-round. The wide variety of colors of reef fish helps to differentiate between the many species that live on the reef.

Fish Senses

Although some fish rely more on certain senses than on others, there are statements about senses that apply to all fish.

Fish hear very well. Sound travels five times faster in water than in air, and fish are quite sensitive to loud noise (which is why you should not tap on fish-tank glass). Fish can be scared off by the noise from people banging around in a boat, loud talking, and motors. Although fish do not have external ears, they do have internal ears. These internal ears, set in the bones of the skull, hear very well. The role of sound in the lives of fish is not entirely understood, but many fish are known to be noisy; fish have been recorded grunting, croaking, grinding teeth, and vibrating muscles. The importance of these sounds is not yet fully known, but what is known for certain is that hearing is an important sense for fish.

A fish's sense of smell is often very good, but the importance of this sense varies widely among species and may be subordinate to other senses, especially vision. With olfactory nerves in their nostrils, fish can detect odors in water just as terrestrial animals can detect odors in air. Some fish use their sense of smell to find food, to detect danger, and perhaps also to find their way to spawning areas. There is evidence that a salmon's keen sense of smell contributes to its ability to return to its birthplace. Certainly, a salmon's sense of smell must be considered incredible: Salmon can detect one part per billion of odorous material in water. They may refuse to use fish ladders if the water contains the smell of human hands or bear paws. Salmon will panic if placed in a swimming pool with one drop of bear-scented water.

Sight varies in importance for fish. Most fish are nearsighted; although they can see well for short distances, their vision gets blurry past 3 feet or so. Some fish are exceptions to this rule; brown trout, for instance, have excellent vision. An important fact to realize about most fish is that they can see almost 360°; the only space they cannot see is a small patch directly behind them. Fish can also see color. In laboratory experiments, largemouth bass and trout have been able to identify red, green, blue, and yellow. Some fish have demonstrated preferences for certain colors, and red has long been considered a foremost attraction, although this is subject to a host of variables, as well as to disagreements among anglers.

The sense of taste does not seem to be as important to fish as are other senses; taste buds are not as well developed, although there are exceptions, especially among bottom-scrounging fish. Some species, like catfish, use taste to find food and utilize this sense much more than do other species of fish. Catfish even have taste buds on their barbels, and certain species have them on the undersides of their bodies.

Fish have an additional sensory organ called the lateral line. Visible as a line running along the length of the bodies of many fish, the lateral line is used to detect low-frequency vibrations. It acts like both a hearing and a touch organ for fish, and it is used to determine the directions of currents, the proximity of objects, and even water temperature. The lateral line is sensitive to water vibrations and helps fish to escape predators, locate prey, and stay in schools.

Reproduction

Fish reproduce in many different ways. Most lay eggs, but some bear live young; most eggs are fertilized after they are released from the female's body, but some are fertilized inside the female's body. Since almost all game-fish are egg layers (sharks being the main exception), the reproductive habits of egg-laying fish are the most important to the angler. Mating, called spawning in egg-laying fish, usually occurs once a year at a particular time of year.

Each species has its own spawning habits, which have a great influence on behavior. Some fish do not eat when they are in a spawning mode; others are voracious prior to spawning. Some migrate; some build visible nests, and others have no nests; some move to the deep water, and some move to shallow water. Once a site is chosen for spawning by fish, or the time is right, they begin to mate. Sometimes the mating is an elaborate ritual; sometimes it merely amounts to the female scattering the eggs and the male fertilizing them.

After the eggs are fertilized, some fish guard and care for the eggs, and some do not. The eggs hatch fairly quickly, at times in as little as 24 hours, although the time is influenced by such factors as water temperature, turbidity, sunlight, salinity, and current. The young fish just out of the eggs are called fry. Fry are usually so much smaller than their parents that they are not recognizably similar. Fry live on microorganisms in the water until they are ready for larger food. In certain species, each spawning pair can produce thousands of fry, but only a few grow to adulthood. Most fall victim to predation; fry are eaten by many predators, including other fish and, in some species, their own parents.

Certain types of fish spawn in habitats other than their normal ones. Some fish that live in the ocean spawn in rivers, and some fish that live in rivers spawn in the sea. Fish that live in the ocean yet spawn in freshwater are called anadromous. The most prominent examples of such fish are salmon. Fish that live in freshwater and spawn in the sea are called catadromous. The most prominent examples of such fish are eels.

Fish Food and Feeding

Fish have evolved to fill almost every ecological niche. Many fish are strictly herbivores, eating only plant life. Many are purely plankton eaters. Most are carnivorous (in the sense of eating the flesh of other fish, as well as crustaceans, mollusks, and insects) or at least piscivorous (eating fish), and some are among mankind's most feared predators in the world, although their danger to humans is oversensationalized.

Almost all species that are considered gamefish are predators because their eating habits and aggressive behavior lead them to strike bait or lures that essentially mimic some form of natural food. Many predaceous fish eat other fish, but they also eat insects, worms and other invertebrates, and other vertebrates. Some fish will eat almost anything that can fit in their mouths and is alive. Some fish are scavengers and will consume dead fish or parts of fish. Many fish fill only specific niches and have very specific diets. Knowing the natural food of a gamefish can be important for anglers.

Fish Growth

Growth in fish is affected by many factors; especially important are heredity, length of growing season, and food supply. Although each species can be expected to reach a predetermined size, the length of time required to reach this size is extremely variable. The growing season is the time during the year when a fish will actively feed and grow. Generally, fish living in northern latitudes and colder waters have a shorter growing season than do fish living in southern latitudes and warmer waters. If all other growing factors remain the same, the fish with the longer growing season will reach a greater size over a given time period.

In addition, a fish that has optimum food and space conditions will grow more rapidly than one that must compete more heavily for food and space. This in part explains why fish of the same species in the same latitude and growing seasons, but in different bodies of water, may have different rates of growth.

The Diversity of Fish

Fish are the most diverse class of vertebrates. There are more fish species than all other vertebrate species combined. Fish live in almost every aquatic environment in the world, from lakes 14,000 feet above sea level to 36,000 feet beneath the ocean surface. Fish are found in desert pools that are over 100°F and in Antarctic waters that are only 28°F (water freezes at less than 32° there because of the salinity; the fish do not freeze because they have a special biological antifreeze in their bodies). Some fish can survive for entire summers out of water by hibernating; others can glide out of the water for several hundred feet; a few can produce their own electricity or their own light. Some can achieve speeds of 50 or 60 miles an hour, and some live immobile, parasitic lives. In terms of biological and habitat diversity, no group of animals can outdo fish.

Fish Anatomy

ANATOMY (Body, Function, and Relation to Angling)

Size

Fish range widely in size. On the bantam side of the spectrum are tiny Philippine gobies less than half an inch long, the smallest of all animals with backbones. They are so diminutive that it takes literally thousands of them to weigh a pound, yet they are harvested commercially for use in many foods. At the behemoth end of the spectrum are giant whale sharks 65 to 70 feet long. The largest whale sharks can weigh as much as 25 tons, but they are so docile, they may allow inquisitive scientists to pull alongside them with boats and then climb aboard to prod and poke as they give the big plankton-eaters a close examination. Between these extremes are seemingly limitless shapes and sizes among an estimated 21,000 species. This number exceeds the combined numbers of species of all other vertebrate animals—amphibians, reptiles, birds, and mammals.

Another giant of the sea is the mola, or ocean sunfish, which also goes by the name of headfish because its fins are set far to the rear on its broad, almost tailless body. The mola, which has the unusual habit of basking at the surface, lying on its side as though dead, may weigh nearly a ton but is not a quarry for anglers. Also in saltwater, such highly prized game species as bluefin tuna, swordfish, and certain sharks and marlin reach weights of more than a thousand pounds, with some shark and marlin specimens weighing considerably more.

Form

The typical fish, such as the yellow perch, the largemouth bass, the striped bass, and the grouper, has a compressed body that is flattened from side to side. In others, the body is depressed from top to bottom, as in flounder, rays, and other bottom-hugging types. Still others are spindle-shaped or streamlined, like mackerel, tuna, and trout; and some, such as eels, have elongated or snakelike bodies. All fish fit into one of these four categories, but each form in turn may differ, with various adaptations in certain portions of its anatomy.

These differences fit the fish for specific environments or particular ways

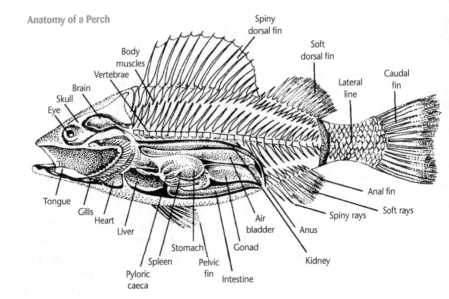

Anatomy of a Perch

of life. For example, the streamlined tuna is an open-ocean fish that moves constantly, indulges in long migrations, and pursues fast-swimming schools of smaller fish. Its bullet-shaped body is well adapted for such a life. On the other hand, the flounder's depressed body allows it to be completely undetectable as it lies flat on the sandy or muddy bottom, an adaptation that protects it from enemies, as well as allows it to grasp unsuspecting prey. Marlin, sailfish, and swordfish are large fish with long snouts (bills) used as clubs to stun prey or as swords in defense. Eels and cutlassfish have slim, snakelike bodies, enabling them to negotiate seemingly inaccessible areas to hunt for food or to escape enemies.

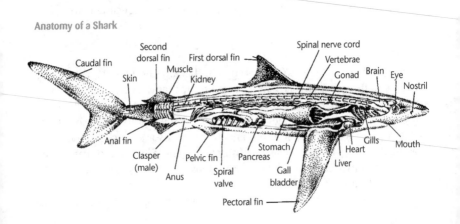

Anatomy of a Shark

Scales

A typical fish's body is covered with thin scales that overlap each other like the shingles of a roof. They are prominent outgrowths of skin, or epidermis, in which numerous glands secrete a protective coating of slime, often referred to as mucus. The slime is a barrier to the entry of parasites, fungi, and disease organisms that might infest the fish, and it seals in the fish's body fluids so that they are not diluted by the watery surroundings. The slime reduces friction so that the fish slides through the water with a minimum of resistance; it also makes the fish slippery when predators, including the human variety, try to grab hold. Some fish, such as lampreys and hagfish, give off copious amounts of slime.

As a fish grows, its scales increase in size but not in number. Lost scales may be replaced, however. The ridges and the spaces on some types of scales become records of age and growth rate. These can be read or counted like the annual rings in the trunk of a tree to determine a fish's age—the fish's growth slowing or stopping during winter when food is scarce and becoming much more rapid during the warm months when food is plentiful. Experts in reading scales can tell when a fish first spawned and each spawning period thereafter. They can determine times of migration, periods of food scarcity, illness, and similar facts about the fish's life. The number of scales in

Fish Shapes

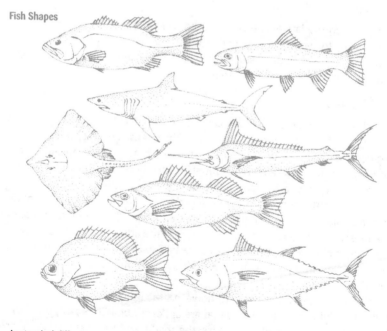

Anatomical differences among fish are most obvious in general body shape but also include body and tail fins.

Scale Types

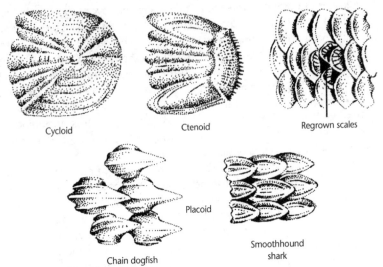

Cycloid

Ctenoid

Regrown scales

Placoid

Chain dogfish

Smoothhound shark

Cycloid scales have smooth rear margins, whereas ctenoid scales have comblike margins; placoid scales, found on sharks, are toothlike. Scales generally are layered, overlapping in rows like roof tiles.

a row along the lateral line can be used to identify closely related species, particularly the young. Growth rings also occur in the vertebrae and in other bones of the body, but to study these requires killing the fish. A few scales can be removed without harm to the fish.

Coloration

The beautiful coloration of fish can be appreciated only when observing them alive, for at death the brilliance and the intensity of color begin to fade immediately. Unquestionably, many fish equal or surpass in appearance the most spectacular colored bird or butterfly, and some of the blends and contrasts of body color are impossible to describe with justice.

The color in fish is primarily produced by skin pigments. Basic or background color is due to underlying tissues and body fluids. Iridescent colors are present in the body scales, the eyes, and the abdominal linings of some fish. The rainbowlike reflecting hues of certain kinds of fish are caused by skin pigmentation fragmenting through the irregular ridges of transparent or translucent scales.

All fish are not highly colored, however; the range extends widely from fish with bright colors to species that are uniformly drab in brown, gray, and even pitch black. In nearly all species, the shades and the acuteness of color are adapted to the particular environment a fish inhabits.

In oceanic fish, basic color may be separated into three kinds: silvery in the upper-water zone, reddish in the middle depths, and violet or black in the great depths. Those that swim primarily in the upper layers of ocean water are typically dark blue or greenish-blue on the dorsal portions, grading to silvery sides and white bellies. Fish that live on the bottom, especially those living close to rocks, reefs, and weedbeds, may be busily mottled or striped. The degree of color concentration also varies, depending on the character of the fish's surroundings. For example, a striped bass caught from a sandy area will be lighter in general coloration than one captured from deeper water or from around dark rocks.

Most types of fish change color during the spawning season. In some types of fish, the coloration intensifies perceptibly when the fish is excited by prey or by predators. Dolphin, also known as mahimahi, a blue-water angler's delight, appear to be almost completely vivid blue when seen from above in a darting school in calm waters. When a dolphin is brought aboard, the unbelievably brilliant golden yellows, blues, and greens undulate and flow magically along the dolphin's body as it thrashes madly about. These changes in shade and degree of color also take place when the dolphin is in varying stages of excitement in the water.

A striped marlin or a blue marlin following a surface-trolled bait is a wondrous spectacle of color to observe. As it eyes its quarry from side to side and

The color exhibited by most fish is adapted to their particular environments, and a wide range of colors exists, as is evident when comparing the brook trout (top), bonefish (middle), and channel catfish (bottom).

maneuvers into position to attack, the deep cobalt-blue dorsal fin and the bronze-silver sides are at their zenith. This electrifying display of color is lost almost immediately when the fish is boated.

Fins and Locomotion

Fish are propelled through the water by fins, body movement, or both. In general, the main moving force is the caudal fin, or tail, and the area immediately adjacent to it, known as the caudal peduncle. In swimming, the fins are put into action by muscles attached to the base of the fin spines and the rays. Fish with fairly rigid bodies depend mostly on fin action for propulsion. Eels, in contrast, rely on extreme, serpentlike body undulations to swim, with fin movement assisting to a minor extent. Sailfish, marlin, and other big-game fish fold their fins into grooves (lessening water resistance) and rely mainly on their large, rigid tails to go forward. Salmon and other species are well adapted for sudden turns and short, fast moves. When water is expelled suddenly over the gills in breathing, it acts like a jet stream and aids in a fast start forward.

A fish can swim even if its fins are removed, though it generally has difficulty with direction and balance. In some kinds, however, the fins are highly important in swimming. For example, the pectoral fins of a ray are broad "wings" with which the fish sweeps through the water almost as gracefully as a swallow does in the air. The sharks, which are close relatives of the rays, swim swiftly in a straight line but have great difficulty in stopping or turning because their fins have restricted movement.

Flyingfish glide above the surface of the water with their winglike pectoral fins extended. Sometimes they get additional power surges by dipping their tails into the water and vibrating them vigorously. This may enable flyingfish to remain airborne for as long as a quarter of a mile. Needlefish and halfbeaks skitter over the surface for long distances, the front halves of their bodies held stiffly out of the water while their still-submerged tails wag rapidly.

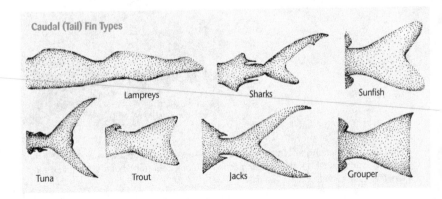

Caudal (Tail) Fin Types

Lampreys   Sharks   Sunfish

Tuna   Trout   Jacks   Grouper

Speed

Fisheries professionals are frequently asked how fast fish swim. This is a difficult question to answer precisely, because fish have a cruising speed, a maximum sustainable speed, and a top speed over relatively short distances.

Statistics for cruising (ordinary travel) speed have been taken mostly from tagged fish released at one point and recaptured at another. For example, some bluefin tuna tagged off Cat Cay, Bahamas, were recaptured in Norwegian waters. Two of these crossed the ocean in less than 3 months. Another completed the trip in the remarkable time of 52 days. These facts indicate that bluefins swim swiftly, but obviously, we do not know whether the recaptured specimens swam a direct course or indulged in detours. Also, ocean currents can be a help or a hindrance.

Maximum sustainable speed, that is, the speed that a fish can maintain for long periods, is almost impossible to judge unless measured experimentally on small fish by determining the length of time they can swim in approximately the same spot when currents of the same velocity are flowing by. Boats traveling alongside big-game fish have clocked their rate of speed.

The speed of a sailfish has been estimated to be as high as 100 yards per 3 seconds, or 68 miles per hour. All the speeds indicated by such experiments are approximate at best because many factors have to be considered, including the size of the individual, the temperature of the water, the currents, the area of the mouth where the fish was hooked, the physical condition of the particular hooked fish, and so on.

All members of the tunalike fish, such as the bluefin tuna, the bonito, and the albacore, are also extremely fast. Other species having a reputation for great speed are marlin, wahoo, dolphin, and swordfish. Generally, speeds of 40 to 50 miles per hour are attributed to these fish.

Air Bladder

The air bladder, located between the stomach and the backbone, is also known as the swim bladder, which is misleading because the air bladder has no function in the movement or locomotion of fish in any direction. The mixture of gases that it contains is not normal air, so the correct name should be "gas bladder."

The air bladder is present in most bony fish; it does not appear in lampreys, hagfish, sharks, rays, or skates. The air bladder performs several functions. It may be well supplied with blood vessels, as it is in the tarpon, and may act as a supplementary breathing organ. The tarpon has an open tube that leads from the upper side of its gullet to the air bladder. (The tarpon also has a set of gills.) Some species of fish use the air bladder as a compartment in which to store air for breathing. The fish falls back on this reserve when its usual supply of oxygen may be shut off. The air bladder plays a part in aiding equilibrium of density between the fish and the water. (It has no function of adjustment of pressure to changing levels.) In other words, the volume of water occupied by the fish should weigh about as much as the fish does. The air bladder is a compensator between them. Saltwater flatfish are species without an air bladder, and they dive to the bottom swiftly if they escape the hook near the surface of the water. (A fish does not raise or lower itself by increasing or decreasing the size of the air bladder.) It has also been definitely established that the air bladder is an efficient hearing aid in many types of fish. It is commonly known that the noises some fish make are produced by the air bladder.

Skeleton and Muscles

A fish's skeleton is composed of cartilage or bone. Basically, the skeleton provides a foundation for the body and the fins, encases and protects the brain and the spinal cord, and serves as an attachment for muscles. It contains three principal segments: skull, vertebral column, and fin skeleton.

The meat or flesh covering the fish's muscular system is quite simple. All vertebrates, including fish, have three major types of muscles: smooth (involuntary), cardiac (heart), and striated (skeletal). Functionally, there are two kinds: voluntary and involuntary.

In fish, the smooth muscles are present in the digestive tract, the air bladder, the reproductive and excretory ducts, the eyes, and other organs. The striated muscles run in irregular vertical bands, and various patterns are found in different types of fish. These muscles compose the bulk of the body and are functional in swimming by producing body undulations that propel the fish forward. The muscle segments, called myomeres, are divided into an upper and a lower half by a groove running along the midbody of the fish. The myomeres can be easily seen if the skin is carefully removed from the body or scraped away with a knife after cooking. These broad muscles are the part of the fish that we eat. Striated muscles are also attached to the base of the fin spines and rays, and they maneuver the fins in swimming.

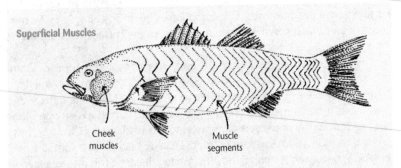

Broad striated muscles make up the bulk of the body of a fish; they run in irregular vertical bands and various patterns, and are functional in swimming.

Teeth, Food, and Digestion

A tremendous diversity exists in the form and the size of fish teeth. The character of the dentition is a clue to the fish's feeding habits and the kind of food it consumes. Of all the fish, some sharks display the most awesome arrays of teeth: profuse and well structured for grasping, tearing, and cutting. The barracuda's teeth are different from any shark's, but they also draw attention because of their ferocious appearance. They are flat, triangular, closely set, and extremely sharp. Such teeth are ideally adapted for capturing live fish, the barracuda's main diet. Small victims are usually swallowed whole; the larger ones may be cut in two and each piece swallowed separately. The bluefish, well known for its ability to chop up a school of baitfish, has teeth of a similar nature but smaller in size.

Some fish possess sharp, conical teeth (called canine, or dog, teeth). Such teeth cannot cut but do a good job of grasping and piercing. Fish fortified with canine teeth generally hold a baitfish until its struggles diminish before they swallow it.

The yellow perch, the sea bass, the catfish, and other species have multiple rows of numerous short and closely packed teeth that resemble the tips of a stiff brush. Such an arrangement meets the fish's need to grasp a variety of food off the bottom or hold prey in a sandpaperlike grip until ready to be eaten.

Some kinds of fish have sharp-edged cutting teeth called incisors located in the forward part of their mouths; some are saw-edged, others resemble human teeth, and still others are variously fused into parrotlike beaks. Some bottom-dwelling fish, such as skates, rays, and drum, have molarlike teeth that are well adapted for crunching crustaceans, mollusks, and other organisms.

Many fish have teeth in their throats. These pharyngeal teeth are sharp in some species, molariform in others, and only remnants in still others. There are fish that have teeth on the roofs of their mouths (vomerine and palatine) and on the tongue. Some fish have teeth on the very edges of their mouths (premaxillary and/or maxillary). And many planktonic feeders, such as the menhaden, have no teeth at all; instead, their long gill rakers help in retaining the microscopic organisms they take into their mouths.

Fish are a tremendously diversified group of animals whose members feed on an extensive variety of foods. Some, when mature, feed exclusively on other fish; others feed entirely on plants. The sea lamprey, a parasitic, highly unattractive eel-like fish, uses its funnel-shaped mouth, lined with radiating rows of sharp teeth, to attach itself to the body of a live fish; then, using its toothed tongue, it rasps a hole in its prey and sucks out blood and body fluids.

Fish also differ in the way they feed. Predators entrap or cut their prey by using their well-developed teeth. Grazers or browsers feed on the bottom. Fish that feed on tiny organisms sifted from the water by using their long gill rakers are known as strainers. Suckers and sturgeon have fleshy, distensible lips well suited to suck food off the bottom and thus are suckers. Some lampreys depend on the blood and the fluids of other fish to live; they are categorized as parasites.

Generally, fish that live in a temperate zone, where seasons are well defined, will eat much more during the warm months than they will during the cold months. In this zone a fish's metabolism slows down greatly during winter. The body temperature of most fish changes with the surrounding environment and is not constant, as it is in mammals and birds.

The digestive system of fish, as in all other vertebrates, dissolves food, thereby facilitating absorption or assimilation. This system, or metabolic process, is capable of removing some of the toxic properties that may be present in foods on which fish feed.

The basic plan of the digestive tract in a typical fish differs in some respects from that of other vertebrate animals. The tongue cannot move as it does in higher vertebrates, and it does not possess striated muscles. The esophagus, or gullet (between the throat and stomach), is highly distensible and usually can accept any type or size food that the fish can fit into its mouth. Although choking does happen, a fish rarely chokes to death because of food taken into its mouth.

Fish stomachs differ in shape from group to group. The predators have elongated stomachs. Those that are omnivorous generally have saclike stomachs. Sturgeon, gizzard shad, and mullet, among others, have stomachs with heavily muscled walls used for grinding food, just as the gizzard of a chicken does. Some of the bizarre deep-sea fish possess stomachs capable of huge distention, thereby enabling them to hold relatively huge prey. On the other hand, some fish have no stomachs; instead, they have accessory adaptations, such as grinding teeth, that crush the food finely so that it is easily absorbed.

Intestinal structure also differs in fish. The predators have shortened intestines; meaty foods are more easily digested than plant foods. In contrast, herbivores, or plant eaters, have long intestines, sometimes consisting of many folds. Sharks and a few other fish have intestines that incorporate a spiral or coiled valve that aids in digestion. Lampreys and hagfish have no jaws and do not have a well-defined stomach or curvature of the intestine. Lampreys need a simple digestive system because they are parasites that subsist on the blood and juices they suck from other fish. During the long migration from the sea upriver to spawn, the various species of salmon never feed. Their digestive tracts shrink amazingly, allowing the reproductive organs to fill up their abdomens.

Gills and Breathing

Like all other living things, fish need oxygen to survive. In humans, the organs responsible for this function are the lungs. In fish, the gills perform the job. However, in some scaleless fish, the exchange of gases takes place through the skin. In fish embryos, various tissues temporarily take up the job of breathing. Some fish are capable of obtaining oxygen directly from the air through several adaptations, including modifications of the mouth cavity, the gills, the intestine, and the air bladder.

Because a fish has no opening between its nostrils and mouth cavity as humans do, it has to breathe through its mouth. When the fish opens its mouth, a stream of water is drawn in. During this intake of water the gill cover is held tight, thereby closing the gill opening. Then the fish closes its mouth and drives the water over the gills and out the external openings by using special throat muscles. Gill rakers, located along the anterior margin of the gill arch, strain water that is passed over the gills. As the water passes over the gills, the exchange of gases takes place; that is, oxygen (which has been absorbed from the air by water exposed to it) is taken in through the walls of the fine blood vessels in the gill filaments, and carbon dioxide is given off. The blood, well oxygenated, then travels through the fish's body.

Different kinds of fish vary in their oxygen demands. A few fish can breathe air. Air breathers use only about 5 percent of the oxygen available to them with each breath of air.

Some fish, like lampreys, get

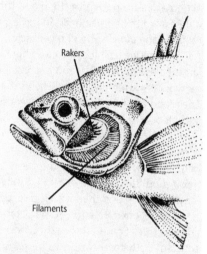

This cutaway view shows the first gill arch of a sunfish. The rakers, which strain the water, are on the left; the filaments, which transfer dissolved oxygen to the blood, are on the right.

oxygen from water that is both taken in and expelled through the gill sacs. Rays and skates usually have five paired external gill slits (rarely six or seven) located on the bottom sides of their heads. Sharks also have the same number of gill slits, but these are located laterally (on the sides). In a shark, the water used for respiration is taken in through the mouth and expelled through the gill slits. Rays and skates, however, draw in water through the spiracles located on the tops, or close to the tops, of their heads (an excellent adaptation for bottom-dwelling fish). The water flows over the gills and out the gill slits located on the undersides of their heads.

The rapidity with which a fish breathes varies with different species. A human in good health under normal circumstances breathes about 20 to 25 times a minute. Some types of fish have a breathing rate as low as 12 times a minute, yet others take as many as 150 breaths per minute. If the fish is exerting itself, or if the oxygen content of the water becomes low, the rate of breathing will be faster, and the fish pants like a runner after finishing the mile.

Blood Circulation

The circulatory system of a fish, which consists of the heart, the blood, and the blood vessels, carries to every living cell in the body the oxygen and nourishment required for living; it carries away from the cells the carbon dioxide and other excretory products.

In function, the fish's muscular heart is similar to that of other vertebrates, acting as a pump to force the blood through the system of blood vessels. It differs from the human heart in having only two, rather than four, compartments—one auricle and one ventricle.

The fish's heart is located close behind the fish's mouth. Blood vessels are largest close to the heart and become progressively smaller, terminating in a network of extremely fine capillaries that meander through the body tissues. The blood of a fish, like blood in all vertebrates, is composed of plasma (fluid) and blood cells (solid).

A fish's circulatory system is much simpler than that of a human. In humans, the blood is pumped from the heart into the lungs, where it is oxygenated; it then returns to the heart and receives a good thrust to travel throughout the body. In contrast, fish blood passes from the heart to the gills for purification and then travels directly to all other parts of the body.

Fish are often referred to as "cold-blooded" creatures, but this is not entirely true. Some are "warm-blooded," although they cannot sustain a constant body temperature as humans do. Instead, the fish's body temperature approximates that of its surrounding medium: water. Fish blood is thicker than human blood and has low pressure because it is pumped by a heart with only two chambers. Consequently, the flow of blood through a fish's body is slow. Because the blood flows slowly through the gills where it takes on oxygen, and because water contains less oxygen than air, fish

Vascular System of a Fish
(arteries white, veins black)

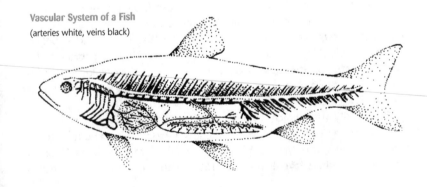

blood is not as rich in oxygen as is human blood. Also, because of the slow flow of blood through the gills, the blood cools and approaches the temperature of the water surrounding the fish.

Senses and Nerves

A fish's eyes are adapted or modified for underwater vision, but they are not very different from human eyes. Fish do not have true eyelids. Human eyelids prevent the eyes from becoming dry and also protect against dirt. A fish's eyes are always covered by water; therefore, they require no lids.

The metallic-looking ring, called the iris, encircling the dark center, or lens, of the fish's eye cannot move as it does in the human eye. The human iris can expand or contract, depending upon light conditions. Because light never attains great intensity underwater, a fish needs no such adaptation. The big difference between a human eye and the eye of a fish occurs in the lens. In humans it is fairly flat or dishlike; in fish, it is spherical or globular. Human eyes are capable of changing the curvature of the lens to focus at varying distances—flatter for long-range focusing and more curved for shorter range. Although the eye of a fish has a rigid lens and its curvature is incapable of change, it can be moved toward or away from the retina (like the focusing action of a camera).

Fish can distinguish colors. There are indications that some kinds of fish prefer one color to another and also that water conditions may make one color more easily distinguished than others.

Many kinds of fish have excellent vision at close range. Fish that live in the dusky or dimly lit regions of the sea commonly have eyes that are comparatively larger than the eyes of any other animal with backbones. Fish that live in the perpetual darkness of caves or other subterranean waters usually have no eyes, but those inhabiting the deep sea, far below the depth to which light rays can penetrate, may or may not have eyes. The reason that most deep-sea fish have well-developed eyes is the prevalence of bioluminescence. Deep-sea squid, shrimp, and other creatures, as well as fish, are equipped with light-producing organs. The light they produce is used to recognize enemies or to capture prey.

Many fish with poor vision have well-developed senses of smell, taste, and touch. Improbable as it may seem, a fish does possess nostrils. Four nostrils are located close to the top of the snout, one pair on each side. Each pair opens into a small blind sac immediately below the skin. Water, carrying odors, passes through the sacs, which are lined with the receptors of smell. Some fish, including sharks, possess an extremely acute sense of smell.

Fish have taste organs located in the skin of their snouts, lips, mouths, and throats. A fish's tongue, unlike the human tongue, is flat, rigid, and cartilaginous and moves only when the base below it moves; nevertheless, it does possess taste buds that indicate to the fish whether to accept or to reject anything taken into its mouth. There is a close relationship between the senses

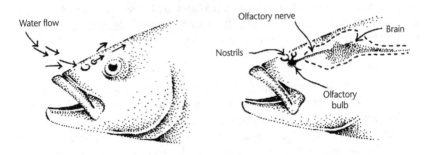

Smell receptors are located in the nostrils, and water (carrying odors) is drawn into sacs that are lined with the organs of smell. Olfactory nerves connect the nostrils and brain.

of smell and taste in fish, just as in humans. Many types of fish are first drawn to food by its odor.

Although fish obviously do not possess outer ears as humans do, they are still capable of hearing. A fish possesses only an inner ear, found in the bones of the skull. In many fish, these ear bones are connected to their air bladders. Vibrations are transmitted to the ear from the air bladder, which acts as a sounding board.

The lateral-line system, a series of sensory cells usually running the length of both sides of the fish's body, performs an important function in receiving low-frequency vibrations. Actually, it resembles a "hearing organ" of greater sensitivity than human ears. The typical lateral line is a mucus-filled tube or canal under the skin; it has contact with the outside world through pores in the skin or through scales along the line or in-between them. A nerve situated at intervals alongside the canal sends out branches to it. In some cases, the lateral line extends over the fish's tail, and in many fish it continues onto their heads and spreads into several branches along the outer bones of their skulls, where it is not outwardly visible. The fish utilizes its lateral line to determine the direction of currents of water and the presence of nearby objects, as well as to sense vibrations. The lateral line helps the fish to determine water temperature and to find its way when traveling at night or through murky waters. It also assists schooling fish in keeping together and may help a fish to escape enemies.

Many fish are noisy creatures. They make rasping, squeaking, grunting, and squealing noises. Some fish produce sounds by rubbing together special extensions of the bones of their vertebrae. Others make noises by vibrating muscles that are connected to their air bladders, which amplify the sounds. Still other fish grind their teeth, their mouth cavities serving as sound boxes to amplify the noises. Many fish make sounds when they are caught. Grunts and croakers got their names from this habit.

Since fish have a nervous system and sense organs, it would appear that they could feel pain. The fish's brain is not highly developed, however. There is no cerebral cortex (the part of the brain in higher animals that stores impressions), and so the fish has little or no memory. It is not uncommon, for example, for an angler to hook the same fish twice within a short time. Many fish are caught with lures or hooks already embedded in their jaws. Fish are essentially creatures of reflex, rather than of action produced or developed by using the brain. In all probability, physical pain in fish is not very acute, and if any impression of pain is made in the brain, it is quickly lost.

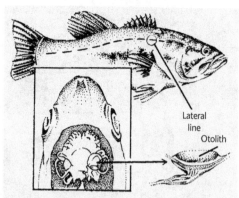

Hearing is accomplished primarily through nerves in the lateral line but also through sound waves detected by the otolith.

Reproduction

The fish, like most animals, begins life as an egg, and, as in all other vertebrates, the single-cell egg cannot develop unless it is fertilized by a sperm produced by the male. Fish sperm is most commonly referred to as milt.

Eggs may be fertilized either externally or internally. External fertilization takes place when the egg is penetrated by the sperm after the egg leaves the female's body. Most fish are reproduced by this system. Internal fertilization occurs when the male introduces the sperm into the female's body, where it makes contact with and fertilizes the egg. Some sharks are ovoviviparous; that is, the egg is fertilized internally and held within the female without attachment to her until it is ready to be extruded alive. In other species, such as some of the sharks and the sculpin, and the skate, the egg is penetrated by the sperm inside the female's body, but it does not hatch until some time after being released from the female.

Reproduction and associated activities in fish are generally referred to as spawning. The spawning season, or breeding period, is that time when the eggs of the female and the milt, or sperm, of the male are ripe. This period may last only a few days or it may extend into weeks and even months. Fish that live in tropical waters of fairly constant temperature may spawn year-round.

Age and Growth

Although birds and mammals cease to grow after becoming fully mature, fish continue to grow until they die, provided food is abundant. Growth is

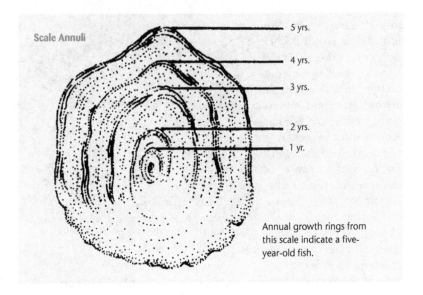

Scale Annuli

5 yrs.
4 yrs.
3 yrs.
2 yrs.
1 yr.

Annual growth rings from this scale indicate a five-year-old fish.

fastest during the first few years of life and continues at a decreasing rate. It accelerates during warm-weather months when food is abundant. During the cold months, fish do not feed much; their metabolism slows down, and growth is retarded.

The age of fish that live in temperate climates can be determined fairly accurately from various bony portions of their anatomy, because definite changes in seasons cause annual marks to appear in the bone. These year zones of growth are produced by the slowing down of the metabolism in the winter and its rapid increase in the spring. In some species the annual ridges, called annuli, are especially pronounced and easy to read in the scales and cheekbones. In fish with tiny scales, these annuli are difficult to see, even under a microscope. Spines, vertebrae, jawbones, and earbones have to be studied to determine the fish's age. In cross-section, these various bones may show annual rings that appear similar to the rings in the cross-section of a tree trunk.

In uniformly warm waters, such as the equatorial currents, fish demonstrate little, if any, seasonal fluctuation in growth, and age determination is difficult.

Migration

Migration is the mass movement of fish (or any other animals) along a route from one area to another at about the same time annually. This group travel is induced basically by factors of food and spawning. At times, mass movement may take place for other reasons, but such travel should not be confused with migration. Sudden adverse conditions, such as pollution, excessive sedimentation, or water discoloration caused by unusually severe storms, may force large groups of fish to leave the affected area.

The bluefin tuna, one of the largest of the oceanic fish, migrates about the same time each year between the coasts of southern Florida and the Bahamas, where it spawns, to waters off Nova Scotia, Prince Edward Island, and Newfoundland. On reaching these far northern waters, the bluefin will find and follow huge schools of herring, sardines, mackerel, or squid in the same localities, year after year. If the temperature rises higher than usual, or other water changes take place, the bait schools will depart from their customary haunts, and the bluefin will follow.

Inshore fish such as the shad and the striped bass may travel various distances along the coast before arriving in freshwater rivers or brackish stretches that meet the requirements for their spawning activities. Some species do not travel along a coast or migrate north and south; instead, they move offshore into deeper water in cold weather and inshore during warm weather. Others combine a north-south movement with an inshore-offshore migration.

Members of the salmon family participate in what may be termed classical migration. Salmon migrate various distances to reach their spawning sites, yet all have the same general life pattern. The eggs are hatched in shallow streams; the young spend their early lives in freshwater, grow to maturity in the ocean, and then return to the stream of their birth to spawn. The length of time spent in freshwater and saltwater habitats varies among the species and among populations of the same species.

Albacore
Thunnus alalunga

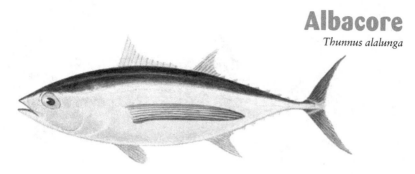

A member of the Scombridae family of tuna and mackerel, the albacore is an excellent light-tackle gamefish. It is called true albacore in some places, not to be confused with false albacore or little tunny *(see)*.

Identification. The albacore has long pectoral fins that reach to a point beyond the anal fin, as well as small finlets on both the back and the belly that extend from the anal fin to the tail. The albacore is colored dark blue, shading to greenish-blue near the tail, and is silvery white on the belly. A metallic or iridescent cast covers the entire body. The dorsal finlets are yellowish, except for the white trailing edge of the tail, and the anal finlets are silvery or dusky.

Size. The average weight for albacore is between 10 and 25 pounds. The all-tackle record is 88 pounds, 2 ounces, although commercially caught fish have weighed as much as 93 pounds. The albacore can grow to 5 feet in length.

Life history/Behavior. A schooling fish, the albacore is migratory and pelagic; that is, it lives and feeds in the open sea. It roams widely, varying in location from within a few miles of shore to far offshore, as currents and water temperatures dictate. Its availability can change widely from year to year. Albacore have been described as one of the world's fastest migrant fish, and tagging studies have tracked them across entire oceans.

Albacore spawn from July through October along the west coast of North America and in the summer season in the Southern Hemisphere of the mid-Pacific.

Food and feeding habits. The albacore diet consists of fish, squid, and crustaceans. Albacore feed in schools, which sometimes consist of other tuna-family members, and these schools are typically found around floating objects such as sargassum. Although they will feed at middle depths, they ordinarily feed close to the surface.

OTHER NAMES
longfin tuna, long-finned tunny, longfin, true albacore, albacore tuna, albie, and pigfish; French: *germon;* Hawaiian: *áhi pahala;* Japanese: *binchô, binnaga;* Portuguese: *albacora;* Spanish: *albacora, atún blanco.*

Distribution. *Albacore are found worldwide in tropical and temperate seas, including the Mediterranean, but they also make seasonal migrations into colder zones such as New England, southern Brazil, and the northern Gulf of Mexico. In the western Atlantic, albacore range from Nova Scotia to Brazil, although they rarely range north of New York and are absent from the Straits of Florida; in the Pacific Ocean, they range from Alaska to Mexico. Albacore are abundant in the Pacific but less common in the Atlantic.*

Habitat. *Albacore favor tropical, subtropical, and temperate waters, commonly in the 60° to 66°F range. These fish seldom come close to shore and prefer deep, wide-open waters.*

Alewife

Alosa pseudoharengus

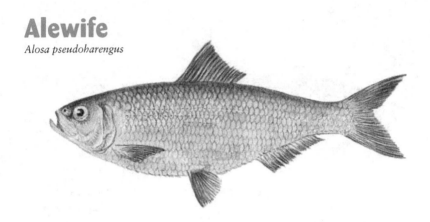

OTHER NAMES

herring, sawbelly, gray herring, grayback; French: *gapareau, gaspereau;* Spanish: *alosa, pinchagua.*

Distribution. *Sea-run alewives extend from Newfoundland and the Gulf of St. Lawrence to South Carolina. Alewives were introduced into the upper Great Lakes and into many other inland waters, although some naturally landlocked populations exist.*

Habitat. *Alewives are anadromous, inhabiting coastal waters, estuaries, and some inland waters, although some spend their entire lives in freshwater. They have been caught as far as 70 miles offshore in shelf waters.*

A small herring, the alewife is important as forage for gamefish in many inland waters and along the Atlantic coast. It is used commercially in pet food and as fish meal and fertilizer, and it has been a significant factor in the restoration of trout and salmon fisheries in the Great Lakes.

Identification. Small and silvery gray with a greenish to bluish back tinge, the alewife usually has one small dark shoulder spot and sometimes other small dusky spots. It has large eyes with well-developed adipose eyelids. The alewife can be distinguished from other herring by its lower jaw, which projects noticeably beyond the upper jaw.

Size. Alewives can grow up to a half pound in weight and to 15 inches in length; they usually average 6 to 12 inches in saltwater and 3 to 6 inches in freshwater.

Life history/Behavior. The alewife is a schooling fish and is sometimes found in massive concentrations detectable on sportfishing sonar. In late April through early June, saltwater alewives run up freshwater rivers from the sea to spawn in lakes and sluggish stretches of river. Landlocked alewives move from deeper waters to nearshore shallows in lakes or upstream in rivers, spawning when the water is between 52° and 70°F. A saltwater female deposits 60,000 to 100,000 eggs, whereas a freshwater female deposits 10,000 to 12,000 eggs. They deposit the eggs randomly, at night, and both adults leave the eggs unattended. Young alewives hatch in less than a week, and by fall they return to the sea or to deeper waters. Adult landlocked alewives cannot tolerate extreme temperatures, preferring a range of 52° to 70°F—the same temperatures they spawn in.

Food and feeding habits. Young alewives feed on minute free-floating plants and animals, diatoms, copepods, and ostracods; adults feed on plankton, as well as on insects, shrimp, small fish, diatoms, copepods, and their own eggs.

Amberjack, Greater

Seriola dumerili

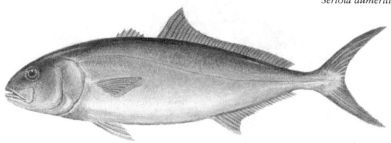

The greater amberjack is the largest of the jacks, the most important amberjack to anglers, and, like most of its brethren, a strong fighter. It is high on the list of tropical marine fish suspected of causing ciguatera poisoning, although this problem may be isolated to certain areas.

Identification. This fish is greenish-blue to almost purple or brown above the lateral line and silver below the lateral line. A dark olive-brown diagonal stripe extends from the mouth across both eyes to about the first dorsal fin. A broad amber stripe runs horizontally along the sides. The fins may also have a yellow cast.

The greater amberjack has short foredorsal fins, a bluntly pointed head, and no detached finlets. The amber stripe sometimes causes anglers to confuse the greater amberjack with the yellowtail, but it can be distinguished by the 11 to 16 developed gill rakers on the lower limb of the first branchial arch; the yellowtail has 21 to 28 gill rakers.

Size. Averaging roughly 15 pounds in weight and commonly ranging up to 40 pounds, the greater amberjack often weighs more than 50 pounds and has been reported to exceed 170 pounds. The all-tackle record is 155 pounds, 10 ounces. It can reach a length of more than 5 feet.

Life history/Behavior. The greater amberjack often occurs in schools, but it is not primarily a schooling fish and occasionally remains solitary. Migrations appear to be linked to spawning behavior, which in the Atlantic occurs from March through June. Evidence suggests that spawning may occur in offshore oceanic waters, but few studies have been conducted, although spawning fish are known to congregate over reefs and wrecks.

Food and feeding habits. Greater amberjack feed on fish, crabs, and squid.

OTHER NAMES

amberjack, jack, amberfish, jack hammer, horse-eye bonito, horse-eye jack, Allied kingfish (Australia); French: *poisson limon, sériole couronnée;* Hawaiian: *kahala;* Japanese: *kanpachi;* Spanish: *coronado, pez de limón, serviola.*

Distribution. *In North America greater amberjack occur off Hawaii, off the coasts of Florida, and in nearby Caribbean waters. Amberjack in some waters are resident fish, but others are migratory coastal pelagic fish that swim with the current edges and eddies.*

Habitat. *Greater amberjack are found mostly in offshore waters and at considerable depths, as well as around offshore reefs, wrecks, buoys, oil rigs, and the like. They can be caught anywhere in the water column, to depths of several hundred feet, but they are mostly associated with near-bottom structure in the 60- to 240-foot range.*

Amberjack, Lesser

Seriola fasciata

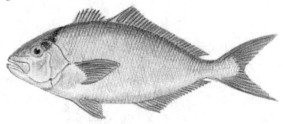

OTHER NAMES

amberjack, jack; French: *sériole babianc;* Spanish: *medregal listado.*

Distribution. *In the western Atlantic, the lesser amberjack ranges from Massachusetts to Brazil.*

Habitat. *Lesser amberjack are believed to live deeper than do other amberjack, commonly in water from 180 to 410 feet deep, and to spawn in offshore waters.*

The lesser amberjack is the smallest amberjack, seldom encountered by, and relatively unknown to, anglers.

Identification. The lesser amberjack has an olive-green or brownish back above the lateral line and is silver below the lateral line. A dark olive-brown diagonal stripe extends from the mouth across both eyes to about the first dorsal fin. It is very similar in appearance to the greater amberjack *(see: Amberjack, Greater)* but has a deeper body profile, proportionately larger eyes, and eight spines in the first dorsal fin.

Size. Reports on the size of this species vary markedly, from up to 12 inches in length to under 10 pounds.

Food and feeding habits. Lesser amberjack feed on fish and squid.

Anchovies

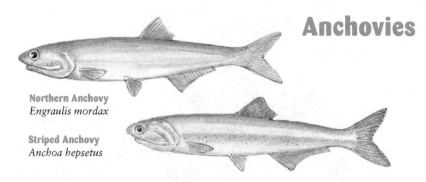

Northern Anchovy
Engraulis mordax

Striped Anchovy
Anchoa hepsetus

Similar in appearance, these anchovies differ mostly in range, although the northern anchovy can be slightly longer. The northern anchovy is one of the most important forage fish in the Pacific and is used as bait for tuna and other large gamefish. A minor percentage of northern anchovies harvested are processed for human consumption, marketed in pickled or salted forms. The striped anchovy is also an important forage fish for game species, although it is too small and fragile to be used often for bait.

Identification. Anchovies are silvery fish that look like miniature herring. They have overhanging snouts and long lower jaws that extend behind the eyes. The striped anchovy has a ribbonlike stripe along each side and some yellow about the head. Anchovy species are difficult to differentiate, but the fin rays and the pattern of pigmentation on the striped anchovy distinguish it; it has 14 to 17 dorsal fin rays, 15 to 18 pectoral fin rays, and 20 to 24 anal fin rays, as well as melanophores outlining all its dorsal scales.

Size. The northern anchovy can reach 9 inches, although 4 to 5 inches is more common; the striped anchovy can reach 6 inches, but the average length is less than 4 inches.

Life history/Behavior. Northern anchovies spawn through the year, although they do so mainly in the winter and the early spring. Spawning occurs in nearshore and offshore environs, predominantly in depths of less than 33 feet and in temperatures of 50° to 55°F. Striped anchovies spawn from April through July in harbors, estuaries, and sounds. The eggs of both species are elliptical and float near the surface, hatching within a few days after being released. The young mature in 3 to 4 years.

Food. Both anchovies feed on plankton.

OTHER NAMES
Northern Anchovy
pinhead, North Pacific anchovy, California anchovy, bay anchovy; French: *anchois du Pacifique nord, anchois de California;* Spanish: *anchoveta de California, anchoa del Pacifico.*

Striped Anchovy
broad-striped anchovy; French: *anchois rayé;* Spanish: *anchoa legitima.*

Distribution. *In the eastern Pacific, the northern anchovy is found from northern Vancouver Island south to Cabo San Lucas, Baja California. Two subspecies are recognized:* E. mordax mordax *extends from British Columbia to Baja California, while* E. mordax nanus *inhabits California's bays. In the western Atlantic, striped anchovies are found from Massachusetts south to Fort Pierce, Florida, and the northern Gulf of Mexico, but rarely in southern Florida and not in the Florida Keys.*

Habitat. *Both northern and striped anchovies form dense schools and favor shallow coastal waters, including bays and inlets. Striped anchovies are able to tolerate a wide range of salinities.*

Angelfish, Queen

Holacanthus ciliaris

OTHER NAMES

French: *demoiselle royale;*
Spanish: *isabelita patale.*

Distribution. *Queen angelfish are a common to occasional presence in Florida, the Bahamas, and the Caribbean; they are present in Bermuda and the Gulf of Mexico, and south to Brazil, as well as on coral reefs in the West Indies.*

Habitat. *Queen angelfish inhabit coral reefs in shallow water, although juveniles prefer offshore reefs, and mature fish sometimes frequent depths of 20 to 80 feet. They are often indistinguishable from the colorful sea fans, sea whips, and corals they swim among.*

The queen angelfish is not widely sought by anglers, although it is an attractive incidental catch and is most popular as an aquarium fish.

Identification. The queen angelfish has a moderately large body that is deep and compressed. It can be distinguished from its nearest relatives, butterflyfish, by its stout spines, its blunter snout, and the spines on the gill cover. It has 14 dorsal spines, and the spine at the angle of the preopercle is relatively long.

Most noteworthy about the appearance of the queen angelfish is its coloration. It is speckled yellowish-orange and blue, and the amount of blue varies with the individual and differs in intensity. It has a bright blue border on the soft dorsal and anal fins, with the tips of the fins colored orange and the last few rays of them colored bluish-black. It also has a yellowish-orange tail, as well as a dark bluish-black spot on the forehead, ringed with bright blue, which forms the queen's "crown."

The coloring of the young queen angelfish is dark blue and similar to that of young blue angelfish, but the rear edges of the dorsal and the anal fins are not yellow, as they are in the blue angelfish. There are bluish-white bars on the body of the queen angelfish, as with the blue angelfish, but these are curved on the queen angelfish, instead of straight.

Angelfish in the Caribbean are generally brighter in color than those along the coasts of North and South America.

Size. Although reported to reach a length of nearly 2 feet, queen angelfish probably do not exceed 18 inches, and they average 8 to 14 inches.

Behavior. The queen angelfish is usually found alone or in a pair but not in groups.

Food. Adults feed primarily on sponges but also consume algae and minute organisms.

Barracuda, Great

Sphyraena barracuda

An excellent gamefish, the great barracuda leads a list of marine fish that cause ciguatera when eaten, although small fish are apparently not poisonous. Not every barracuda causes ciguatera, but there is no safe or reliable way of recognizing toxic fish.

Identification. The great barracuda is long and slender, with a large, pointed head and large eyes. The dorsal fins are widely separated, and the first dorsal fin has five spines, whereas the second has 10 soft rays. In a large underslung jaw, the great barracuda has large, pointed canine teeth. It also possesses a bluish-gray or greenish-gray body coloration above the lateral line and a silvery-white belly. A few irregular black blotches are usually scattered on the sides of the body, especially toward the tail. The young have one dark stripe down each side, which mutates to become blotches as the fish grow. The great barracuda also occasionally has 18 to 22 diagonal dark bars above the lateral line. It grows much larger, in general, than its relative the Pacific barracuda.

Size. Known to reach a weight of 106 pounds and a length of 6½ feet, the great barracuda averages 5 to 20 pounds in weight; larger specimens are rare. The all-tackle world record is an 85-pounder.

Life history/Behavior. Young barracuda under 3 pounds usually inhabit shallow waters, such as harbors and coastal lagoons, until they become adults and live farther offshore, sometimes far out to sea. Smaller barracuda will occasionally school, but the large ones are typically solitary. Curiosity is a trait of all barracuda, and they will follow waders or divers as a result.

Food and feeding habits. The great barracuda eats whatever is available in its habitat; needlefish, small jacks, and mullet are among the mainstays. They are attracted by shininess or flashes and movement, feeding by sight, rather than by smell.

OTHER NAMES

'cuda, sea pike, giant sea pike; French: *barracuda, brochet de mer;* Hawaiian: *kaku, kupala;* Japanese: *onikamasu;* Portuguese: *barracuda, bicuda;* Spanish: *barracuda, picuda.*

Distribution. Great barracuda range from Massachusetts to Brazil, although not in abundance from the Carolinas northward. They are caught mainly around Florida, in the Florida Keys, in the Bahamas, and throughout the West Indies.

Habitat. Young barracuda live in inshore seagrass beds, whereas adults range from inshore channels to the open ocean. They are also found in bays, inlets, lagoons, and the shallows of mangrove islands, as well as around reefs, wrecks, piers, sandy or grassy flats, and coastal rivers where saltwater and freshwater mingle. They prefer shallow areas and appear to move inshore in the summer, and offshore in the fall and the winter.

Barracuda, Pacific

Sphyraena argentea

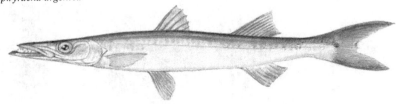

California barracuda, barry, snake, scoots, scooter; French: *bécune argentée.*

Distribution. *Pacific barracuda occur along the Pacific coast of North America from Alaska to Magdalena Bay, Baja California, although their common range is between Point Conception, California, and Magdalena Bay. The Pacific barracuda is the only barracuda found along the Pacific coast of North America.*

Habitat. *Pacific barracuda prefer warmer water. Only caught off California during the spring and the summer, they are caught in Mexican waters throughout the year, reflecting a northerly spring migration and a southerly fall migration.*

The Pacific barracuda is the best known of the four types of barracuda found in Pacific waters and is one of California's most prized resources.

Identification. The Pacific barracuda is slim-bodied, with a tapered head, a long thin snout, and large canine teeth in a lower jaw that projects beyond the upper jaw. It also has a forked tail, large eyes, and short, widely separated dorsal fins with five dorsal spines and 10 dorsal rays. The anal fins have two spines, followed usually by nine rays. Grayish-black on the back with a blue tinge, shading to silvery white on the sides and the belly, it has a yellowish tail that lacks the black blotches on the sides of the body that are characteristic of other barracuda. Large females have a charcoal-black edge on the pelvic and the anal fins, whereas the male fins are edged in yellow or olive.

Size/Age. The Pacific barracuda is shorter than the great barracuda. It reportedly can grow to 5 feet but has been recorded only to 4 feet; it rarely weighs more than 10 pounds, and although specimens of about 12 pounds have been captured, most of the fish caught by anglers are much smaller. They live for at least 11 years, and the females grow larger than the males.

Life history/Behavior. Spawning takes place off outer Baja California in the open ocean, peaking in June but extending from April through September. The eggs are pelagic, and once they hatch, the young come inshore and stay in the shallow, quiet bays and coastal waters while they grow. When small, they travel in schools, although adults are normally solitary. They are naturally curious and attracted to shiny objects.

Food and feeding habits. The Pacific barracuda feeds by sight, rather than by smell, and eats small anchovies, smelt, squid, and other small, schooling fish.

Bass, Kelp (Calico)

Paralabrax clathratus

One of a large number of sea bass found in the eastern Pacific, the kelp bass is one of the most popular sportfish in Southern California, as a mainstay of party boat trips to the northern Baja. Because it is a powerful fighter and an excellent food fish, it is highly sought by anglers. Its popularity and nonmigratory status put kelp bass populations at risk from overfishing.

Identification. A hardy fish with the characteristic elongated and compressed bass shape, the kelp bass has a notch between its spiny and its dorsal fins. The longest spines in the first dorsal fin are longer than any of the rays in the second dorsal fin. It is brown to olive green, with pale blotches on the back and lighter coloring on the belly.

Kelp bass are easily distinguishable from various sand bass by their third, fourth, and fifth dorsal spines, which are about the same length; sand bass have a third dorsal spine that is much longer than the fourth and fifth dorsal spines. Kelp bass also superficially resemble freshwater black bass, except that their dorsal spines are longer and much heavier, and their overall appearance is rougher.

Size/Age. Kelp bass grow slowly, taking 5 to 6 years to reach a length of 12 inches, when they are capable of spawning. Fish weighing 8 to 10 pounds may be 15 to 20 years old. The largest kelp bass are said to exceed 15 pounds, although the largest fish caught was only 14 pounds, 7 ounces. They can grow to 1½ feet in length.

Life history/Behavior. Spawning occurs from May through September and peaks in July. Kelp bass do not migrate and instead tend to be territorial.

Food and feeding habits. An omnivorous feeder, kelp bass favor assorted fish and small shrimplike crustaceans when young. Adults consume anchovies, small surfperch, and other small fish.

OTHER NAMES

calico bass, California kelp bass, rock bass, rock sea bass, sand bass, bull bass, kelp salmon, cabrilla; Spanish: *cabrilla alguera*.

Distribution. Primarily found along the central and southern California coast and northeastern Baja, kelp bass range from the Columbia River in Washington to Magdalena Bay in Baja California.

Habitat. Kelp bass typically linger in or near kelp beds, over reefs, and around rock jetties and breakwaters or structures in shallow water; larger fish hold in deeper water, to roughly 150 feet.

Bass, Striped

Morone saxatilis

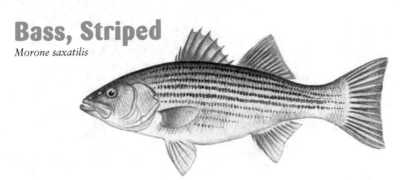

OTHER NAMES

striper, rock, rockfish, striped sea bass, striper bass, linesider, squid hound, and greenhead; French: *bar rayé;* Spanish: *lubina estriada.*

Distribution. On the Atlantic coast of the United States, the striped bass commonly occurs from the St. Lawrence River south to the St. Johns River in northern Florida. It has also ranged along the coasts of Florida, Louisiana, Alabama, and Mississippi in the Gulf of Mexico. Some fish migrate north from North Carolina, Virginia, or Maryland during the summer and return during the fall. Others living in estuarine river systems, such as the St. Lawrence, the Santee Cooper, or the Savannah, are nonmigratory.

Striped bass were introduced to San Francisco Bay in 1879 and 1882; today, along the Pacific coast, they are abundant in the bay area and extend from Washington to California; some California fish migrate north to Oregon and are occasionally found off the west coast of Vancouver Island.

An excellent sportfish that attains large sizes, the striped bass is a member of the temperate bass family (often erroneously placed with the sea bass family). It has been considered one of the most valuable and popular fish in North America since the early 1600s, originally for its commercial importance and culinary quality and in more recent times for its recreational significance.

Identification. A large fish with a large mouth, the striped bass is more streamlined than its close relative the white bass. It has a long body and a long head, a somewhat laterally compressed body form, and a protruding lower jaw. Of the two noticeably separate dorsal fins, the first one has 7 to 12 stiff spines, usually 9, which make this fin quite a bit higher than the second; the second dorsal fin has one sharp spine and 8 to 14, ordinarily 12, soft rays. The striped bass also has a forked tail and small eyes.

These fish are mostly bluish-black or dark green above, fading into silver on the sides and white on the bellies. On each side of a striped bass's body, there are seven or eight prominent black horizontal stripes that run along the scale rows, which are its distinctive markings; one of the stripes runs along the lateral line, and the rest are equally divided above and below it. The stripe highest up on the side is usually the most noticeable, although on some fish, one or more of the stripes are interrupted.

In freshwater, the striped bass has been crossed with the white bass to create a hybrid called the whiterock bass or the sunshine bass. Striped bass differ from hybrids in the regularity of their stripes, whereas the hybrid usually has interrupted stripes. The narrow body of the striped bass also distinguishes it from the white bass.

Size/Age. Growing rapidly in early life, striped bass average 5 to 10 pounds, although they often reach weights in the 30- to 50-pound range. The maximum size that a freshwater striped bass can achieve is unknown, although the largest sport-caught freshwater striper weighed 67 pounds, 1 ounce. The all-tackle record for the species—78 pounds,

8 ounces—belongs to a saltwater fish, but larger ones have been reportedly taken commercially. Striped bass normally live 10 to 12 years; however, most fish more than 11 years old and more than 39 inches long are female.

Life history/Behavior. Striped bass males are sexually mature by their second or third year, whereas females are sexually mature sometime between their eighth and ninth years; males measuring at least 7 inches and females as small as 34 inches are known to spawn. Spawning occurs in fresh or slightly brackish waters from mid-February in Florida to late June or July in Canada, and from mid-March to late July in California, when the water temperature is between 50° and 73°F; peak spawning activity is observed between 54° and 68°F. They prefer the mouths of freshwater tributary streams, where the current is strong enough to keep the eggs suspended.

When mating, each female is accompanied by several smaller males. The spawning fish swim near the surface of the water, turning on their sides and rolling and splashing; this display is sometimes called a "rock fight." The semi-buoyant eggs are released and drift with the current until they hatch 2 to 3 days later, depending on the water temperature.

Food and feeding habits. A voracious, carnivorous, and opportunistic predator, the striped bass feeds heavily on small fish, including large quantities of herring, menhaden, flounder, alewives, silversides, eels, and smelt, as well as invertebrates such as worms, squid, and crabs. Freshwater striped bass prefer shad, herring, minnows, amphipods, and mayflies. There has been controversy over the effect of freshwater stripers on other gamefish—most notably, on largemouth bass—but bass and other popular sportfish do not appear to be important components in the diet of freshwater stripers.

Habitat. *Striped bass inhabit saltwater, freshwater, and brackish water, although they are most abundant in saltwater. They are anadromous and migrate in saltwater along coastal inshore environs and tidal tributaries. They are often found around piers, jetties, surf troughs, rips, flats, and rocks. A common regional name for stripers is "rockfish," and indeed their scientific name,* saxatilis, *means "rock dweller," although they do not necessarily spend most of their lives in association with rocks. They run far upstream during spawning runs and are also found in channels of medium to large rivers at that time. The striped bass is entirely a coastal species, off the coast of the Carolinas and southward, never ranging more than a few miles offshore; along the entire Atlantic coast, it is rarely caught more than a short distance from shore except during migration.*

Striped bass were introduced into freshwater lakes and impoundments with successful results. In some freshwater populations, striped bass were not introduced but were landlocked, due to man-made barriers that blocked their return to the sea. In freshwater, stripers are commonly found in open-water environs or in the tailrace below dams. They are seldom found near shore or docks or piers, except when chasing schools of baitfish.

Batfish

Shortnose Batfish
Ogcocephalus nasutus

Distribution. Most common in the Gulf of Mexico and southern Florida, batfish inhabit waters from North Carolina to Brazil. They are also found in Jamaica. In warm Atlantic and Caribbean waters, it is most common to see the longnose batfish (Ogcocephalus vespertilio), which is often camouflaged in the sand by its warty, brownish body.

Habitat. Most batfish are found along reefs, dwelling anywhere from the water's edge out as far as 1,500 feet. Some species prefer shallower water, but most batfish remain in deeper waters between 200 and 1,000 feet. Shallow-water species frequent clear water, mostly in rocky areas or around the bases of reefs; deep-water species prefer more open muddy, or clay bottoms.

Members of the Ogcocephalidae family, batfish are mostly small fish comprising nearly 60 similar species. These peculiar-looking fish employ the energy-saving tactic of luring, instead of hunting for, their food. This method is valuable in deep-sea environments, where food is scarce and thinly distributed.

Identification. The head and the trunk of the batfish are broad and flattened, having either a disk or a triangular shape, and its body is covered with broad spines. The long pectoral and rodlike pelvic fins enable the batfish to "walk" on the sea bottom. There is a protuberance, the rostrum, on the front of the head between the eyes, which can be long or short. Under the rostrum hangs a small tentacle that acts like a lure. The mouth is small but capable of opening broadly. Batfish are usually heavily armored by bony tubercles and hairlike cirri, with the exception of the gill opening on the pectoral fin. Coloration varies among individual species; for example, pancake batfish (Halieutichthys aculeatus) are yellowish with a net design, whereas polka-dot batfish (Ogcocephalus radiatus) are yellowy white with small black dots. Most are camouflaged according to their surroundings.

Batfish can be distinguished from goosefish and frogfish by the reduced fins on their heads.

Size/Age. Batfish can be between 2 and 20 inches long, but the average length is 7 inches.

Behavior. Batfish partly hide by covering themselves in sand or mud during the day, and they swim at night.

Food and feeding habits. Mostly feeding on polychaete worms and crustaceans, batfish also eat other fish. Prey are attracted by the vibrations of the batfish's lure; if a smaller fish swims close enough, the batfish explodes from its hiding spot and engulfs the prey. Batfish reportedly produce scented secretions that entice prey with their odor. Batfish are capable of swallowing fish nearly as large as themselves by suddenly opening their mouths very wide, creating a suction effect.

Bluefish
Pomatomus saltatrix

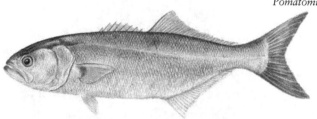

The only member of the Pomatomidae family, the bluefish is an extremely voracious and cannibalistic saltwater fish.

Identification. The body shape is fairly long, stout, and compressed, with a flat-sided belly. The mouth is large and has extremely sharp, flattened, and triangular teeth. The first dorsal fin is low and short, the second dorsal fin is long, and the anal fin has two spines and 25 to 27 soft rays. The coloring is greenish or bluish on the back and silvery on the sides; a distinguishing characteristic is a dark blotch at the base of the pectoral fins. The tail is dusky and deeply forked, and, with the exception of the whitish pelvic fins, most of the fins are dark.

Size/Age. Bluefish can grow to about 45 inches in length and more than 44 pounds in weight. They average 1½ to 2 feet and 3 pounds, although it's not uncommon for a fish to weigh around 11 pounds. The rod-and-reel record is a 31-pound, 12-ounce fish. They live for about 12 years.

Life history/Behavior. Atlantic coast bluefish spawn mainly in the spring in the South Atlantic Bight and during summer in the Middle Atlantic Bight. Bluefish migrate out to open sea to spawn, anywhere from 2 miles offshore to the continental platform. The eggs are released and drift along with plankton in surface waters, hatching about 48 hours after fertilization. Adult bluefish are commonly found in schools, especially when foraging on schools of baitfish, menhaden in particular. Along the U.S. Atlantic Coast, bluefish migrate northward in the spring and southward in the fall.

Food and feeding habits. Insatiable predators, bluefish feed on a wide variety of fish and invertebrates but target schools of menhaden, mackerel, and herring. They feed in large groups, viciously attacking schools of smaller fish.

OTHER NAMES
blue, tailor, elf, chopper, marine piranha, rock salmon, snapper blue, snapper, Hatteras blue, skipjack (Australia), shad (South Africa); French: *tassergal;* Japanese: *amikiri;* Portuguese: *anchova, enchova;* Spanish: *anjova, anchova de banco.*

Distribution. *Found world-wide in most temperate coastal regions, bluefish inhabit the western Atlantic from Nova Scotia and Canada to Bermuda and Argentina. They are rare between southern Florida and northern South America.*

Habitat. *Favoring temperate to tropical waters, bluefish range along rocky coasts and in deep, troubled waters, although they are known to be sporadic, if not cyclical, in occurrence and location. The young are often found in bays and estuaries. Adults migrate along coastal areas and are caught from the beach by surf anglers, on shoals and rips inshore, or farther offshore.*

Blue Tang

Acanthurus coeruleus

OTHER NAMES

blue tang surgeon; French: *chirurgien bayolle;* Portuguese: *acaraúna-azul;* Spanish: *navajón azul.*

Distribution. *In the western Atlantic, the blue tang is most commonly found in Bermuda and from Florida to the Gulf of Mexico and Brazil. In the eastern Atlantic, it inhabits the waters off Ascension Island.*

Habitat. *Blue tang favor inshore grassy and rocky areas and shallows above coral reefs.*

A member of the surgeonfish family that has distinctive coloration and is occasionally encountered by anglers, the blue tang is sometimes used as an aquarium fish and is also marketed fresh.

Identification. The oval, deep-bodied, and compressed blue tang is more circular than are other surgeonfish. Its coloring is almost entirely blue, ranging from powdery to deep purple, and it has many dark or light blue horizontal stripes running down the sides and blending into the background. The dorsal and the anal fins have a bright blue border, and there is a white or yellow spine on the base of the tail. Juvenile blue tang are colored bright yellow, whereas intermediate fish have blue heads and bodies and yellow tails. The yellow of the tail is the last to change to blue, and some fish are found with yellow tails. The change from juvenile to intermediate to adult coloration does not depend on size; some blue adults are smaller than yellow juveniles.

Size. Blue tang average 5 to 10 inches in length and may grow to 15 inches long.

Life history/Behavior. In the fry stage, the pelvic, the second dorsal, and the second anal spines of some fish are venomous and cause a painful sensation like a bee sting. This venomous quality is lost once they reach the juvenile stage. Blue tang form schools that may include surgeonfish and doctorfish.

Food and feeding habits. Blue tang feed entirely on algae, mostly during the day.

Bocaccio

Sebastes paucispinis

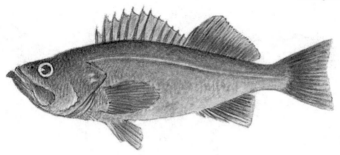

Abundant off the central and the southern coasts of California, the bocaccio is one of the most commercially important rockfish in that region. It is also a well-known gamefish in its range and a good eating fish, with soft and juicy white meat.

Identification. Although its elongate and compressed body form is less bulky than that of most fish in the scorpionfish family, the bocaccio has a large mouth. The upper jaw extends farther back than the eyes; the lower jaw extends past the upper one considerably. The first dorsal fin has spines and is deeply notched, and there are usually nine soft rays in the anal fin. Bocaccio are variably colored olive or brown on the back, reddish on the sides, and pink or white on the bellies. Young fish are generally light bronze, with speckling over the sides and the backs. As they mature, their color generally becomes darker and the speckling gradually disappears.

Size/Age. Bocaccio can grow up to 3 feet and 21 pounds and can live for 30 years.

Life history/Behavior. Bocaccio that are 1 or 2 years old travel in loose schools and move into shallow water, where they may be captured in quantity. With increasing age, they seek deeper water and move from near the surface to near the bottom. Adults are commonly found in waters of 250 to 750 feet over a somewhat irregular, hard, or rubble bottom. They are known to dwell in depths as great as 1,050 feet.

Females start maturing when they are 17 inches long. As with all rockfish, fertilization is internal, and development of the embryos takes place within the ovaries of the female until the eggs are ready to hatch.

Food. Bocaccio feed mainly on fish, including on other rockfish. Their diet consists of surfperch, mackerel, sablefish, anchovies, sardines, deep-sea lanternfish, and sanddabs, as well as squid, octopus, and crabs.

OTHER NAMES

salmon grouper, mini-grouper (juveniles), red snapper, Pacific red snapper.

Distribution. These fish inhabit waters from Punta Blanca, Baja California, to Kruzof Island and Kodiak Island, Alaska.

Habitat. Adults dwell in waters over rocky reefs but are also common in deeper water. Young bocaccio live in shallower water and form schools; they are caught more frequently than are adults, especially in rocky areas.

Bonefish
Albula vulpes

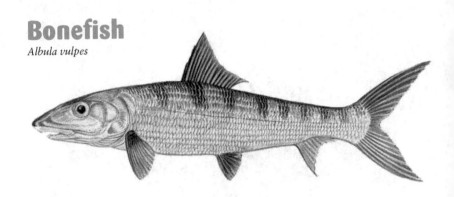

OTHER NAMES

banana fish, phantom, silver ghost, ladyfish, grubber, silver streak, tenny; French: *banane de mer, sorte de mulet;* Hawaiian: *o'io;* Japanese: *soto-iwashi;* Portuguese: *juruma;* Spanish: *macabí, zorro.*

Distribution. *Bonefish are found worldwide in tropical and subtropical waters. Around North America, they are most bountiful in the Florida Keys, the Bahamas, and the Caribbean, more so in the winter than in the summer; they are also somewhat abundant in Belize, Panama, and other Central American countries.*

Habitat. *Occurring in warm coastal areas, bonefish inhabit the shallows of intertidal waters, including around mud and sand flats, as well as in mangrove lagoons. They are also found in waters up to 30 feet deep and are able to live in oxygen-poor water because they possess lung-like bladders into which they can inhale air.*

Although the bonefish was previously thought to be the only member of the Albulidae family, there are now five recognized species. The bonefish is the only significant sportfish among them, however, and is one of the most coveted of all saltwater gamefish. In keeping with its scientific name, which means "white fox," it is indeed a wary, elusive creature, one that usually must be stalked with stealth and that bolts with startling speed when hooked or alarmed.

Although bonefish have little food value to anglers and virtually all are released, they are a subsistence food in some locations. It is generally believed that bonefish are not good table fare, but some gourmands maintain that bonefish flesh is firm and tasty and the roe a delicacy.

Identification. The bonefish has armor plates, instead of scales, on its conical head and is distinguished from the similar ladyfish by its suckerlike mouth and snout-shaped nose, which are adapted to its feeding habits. It also has a single dorsal fin and a deeply forked tail. The coloring is bright silver on the sides and the belly, with bronze or greenish-blue tints on the back; there may also be yellow or dark coloring on parts of the fin and the snout, and sometimes there are dusky markings on the sides. The young have bronze backs and nine narrow crossbands.

Size. Although the average bonefish weighs between 2 and 5 pounds, bonefish weighing up to 10 pounds are not uncommon. They can grow to 41 inches in length, averaging 1 to 2½ feet long. The all-tackle world-record catch is a 19-pound fish.

Life history/Behavior. The particulars of bonefish reproduction are not well known, although it is thought that bonefish spawn from late winter to late spring, depending on locale. With a small head and a long, transparent body, the young bonefish looks like an eel until it undergoes a leptocephalus larval stage. It grows to about 2½ inches long during this period, then experiences a metamorphosis that shrinks the young bonefish to half that size. The fins begin to appear during the shrinking, and in 10 to 12 days it attains the adult bonefish body form, only in miniature size. This growth process is similar in tarpon and ladyfish development. The young migrate out to the open sea to live on plankton, returning as juveniles to live in the shallows.

Generally, bonefish are a schooling fish; smaller specimens are seen traveling in large numbers on the flats, whereas larger ones prefer smaller schools or groups of 5 to 10 fish.

Food and feeding habits. Bonefish feed on crabs, shrimp, clams, shellfish, sea worms, sea urchins, and small fish. They prefer feeding during a rising tide, often doing so near mangroves. They root in the sand with their snouts for food and are often first detected while feeding with their bodies tilted in a head-down, tail-up manner, with all or part of their tail fins protruding from the surface. These are referred to as tailing fish. Bonefish also sometimes stir up the bottom when rooting along, which is called mudding; this can be a telltale indicator to the observant angler.

Bonito, Atlantic

Sarda sarda

common bonito, katonkel, belted bonito; French: *bonito à dos rayé, boniton, conite, pélamide;* Japanese: *hagatsuo, kigungegatsuo;* Portuguese: *cerda, sarra-jâo, serra;* Spanish: *bonito del Atlántico, cabaña cariba, cerda.*

Distribution. *In North America, the Atlantic bonito inhabits the Atlantic Ocean from Nova Scotia to Argentina in the western Atlantic. In the United States, it is most abundant from southern New England to New Jersey. The Atlantic bonito is rare in the Caribbean and the Gulf of Mexico; it is absent in the West Indies.*

Habitat. *Atlantic bonito occur in brackish water and saltwater, particularly in tropical and temperate coastal environs. Schooling and migratory, they often inhabit surface inshore waters.*

A relative of tuna, the Atlantic bonito has a reputation as a tough fighter and a tasty fish, making it highly popular with anglers.

Identification. The Atlantic bonito has a completely scaled body (some types of bonito have only partially scaled bodies), a noticeably curved lateral line, and six to eight finlets on the back and the belly between the anal fin and the tail. The caudal peduncle has a lateral keel on either side, with two smaller keels above and below the main keel. It doesn't have a swim bladder or teeth on its tongue. The back is blue or blue-green, fading to silvery on the lower sides and the belly; a characteristic feature of the Atlantic bonito is the dark lines that extend from the back to just below the lateral line. It can be distinguished from the tuna by its slimmer body, a mouth full of teeth, and dark lines on its back, rather than on its belly.

Size. The Atlantic bonito averages 2 to 10 pounds, although it may attain a weight of 20 pounds and a length of 36 inches. An 18-pound, 4-ounce specimen holds the all-tackle world record.

Life history/Behavior. In coastal waters, spawning occurs from January through July, depending on locale (June and July in the western Atlantic). Bonito reach sexual maturity at about 16 inches in length. Spawning usually takes place close to shore, in warm coastal waters.

Food and feeding habits. Living in open waters, the Atlantic bonito feeds primarily at or near the surface, in schools that are often 15 to 20 miles offshore but are found close to shore as well. Adults prey on small schooling fish and will also eat squid, mackerel, menhaden, alewives, anchovies, silversides, and shrimp; in addition, they tend to be cannibalistic. They feed during the day but are especially active at dawn and dusk.

Bonito, Pacific

Sarda chiliensis

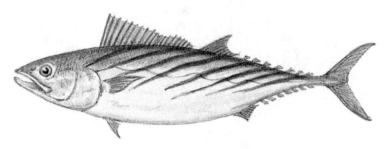

The Pacific bonito is an important gamefish, valued more for sport than for food, as is the Atlantic bonito.

Identification. Similar in size and pigmentation to the Atlantic bonito, the Pacific bonito is distinguished from most other bonito by the lack of teeth on its tongue and the possession of a straight intestine without a fold in the middle. The Pacific bonito has 17 to 19 spines on its first dorsal fin and is the only tunalike fish on the California coast that has slanted dark stripes on its back. Like other bonito, its body is cigar shaped and somewhat compressed, with a pointed and conical head and a large mouth. It is dark blue above, and its dusky sides become silvery below.

Size/Age. Pacific bonito can grow to 25 pounds and 40 inches, although they are usually much smaller. The all-tackle world record is 14 pounds, 2 ounces. Fast-growing fish, bonito will be 6 to 10 inches long by the early part of their first summer, weighing 3 pounds by that fall and 6 to 7 pounds the following spring.

Life history/Behavior. Pacific bonito form schools by size; at 2 years old, they reach sexual maturity. Spawning occurs sometime between September and February. Although spawning is usually successful each year in the southern part of their range, it may not be successful each year farther north. The free-floating eggs require about 3 days to hatch at average spring water temperatures.

Food and feeding habits. Pacific bonito prey on smaller pelagic fish, as well as on squid and shrimp, generally in surface waters. Anchovies and sardines appear to be their preferred foods.

OTHER NAMES

California bonito, eastern Pacific bonito, bonehead, Laguna tuna, striped tuna, ocean bonito; French: *bonite du Pacifique;* Japanese: *hagatsuo;* Spanish: *bonito del Pacífico.*

Distribution. *Pacific bonito occur discontinuously from Chile to the Gulf of Alaska. Their greatest area of abundance occurs in the Northern Hemisphere in warm waters between Magdalena Bay, Baja California, and Point Conception, California.*

Habitat. *Bonito live in surface to middle depths in the open sea and are migratory. Older fish usually range farther from the coast than do juveniles. Bonito may arrive off the coast in the spring as ocean waters warm, but they may not show up at all if oceanic conditions produce colder than normal temperatures.*

Bream, Sea

Archosargus rhomboidalis

Habitat. *Some sea bream are abundant in estuaries, and some are found in deeper, offshore waters. Some move up into brackish water but not into freshwater. In the estuarine environment, bream frequent seagrass beds, underwater reefs and rocks, bridge pilings that grow mussels, and oyster beds.*

Numerous members of the Sparidae family that are found in temperate and tropical waters are referred to as sea bream, or seabream. They are related to porgies, have moderate to important significance commercially (depending on abundance and geography), and are commonly caught by inshore anglers. These fish are tough, dogged fighters that are commendable on appropriate light tackle, and they rate as excellent table fare. The more commonly distributed and popular species are noted here.

The sea bream (*Archosargus rhomboidalis*) appears in the western Atlantic Ocean from the northeastern Gulf of Mexico to Argentina, including the Caribbean and the West Indies. Its bluish back is streaked with gold, the belly is silvery, and there is a black spot on each side just above the pectoral fins.

Size. Most sea bream can reach a maximum weight of between 7.5 and 10 pounds, but on average they weigh between 1 and 2 pounds. The sea bream of the western Atlantic is rarely more than a foot long.

Food. Bream are largely omnivorous and feed on crustaceans; crayfish; mollusks, including oysters and mussels; small fish; worms; and algae. Some will also eat bread, chicken gut, mullet gut, cheese, and meat, all of which are sometimes used for bait.

Bumper

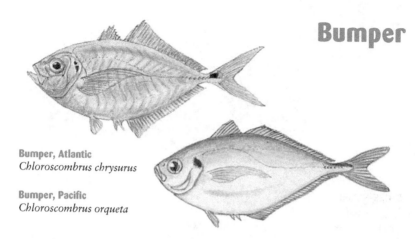

Bumper, Atlantic
Chloroscombrus chrysurus

Bumper, Pacific
Chloroscombrus orqueta

The Atlantic and the Pacific bumper are two of the smaller members of the jack family. Both species have not been greatly studied, and there is some speculation that they may be the same.

Identification. Although the bumper doesn't have a high back, it has an extended belly and a very thin body. With an overall silvery coloring, it has greenish tints on the back and yellow highlights on the sides and the belly. It also has a yellowish tail. There is a black spot on each gill cover and a black saddle on the base of the tail.

Size. Bumper rarely weigh more than half a pound and can reach a length of 10 inches in the western Atlantic or 12 inches in the eastern Atlantic.

Life history/Behavior. Small bumper have been observed in offshore waters, but they frequently range along sandy beaches. They travel in extensive schools, and juveniles are often found in association with jellyfish.

OTHER NAMES

French: *sapater;* Spanish: *casabe.*

Distribution. In the western Atlantic Ocean, Atlantic bumper are found north to Massachusetts, off Bermuda and south to Uruguay, as well as in the Caribbean Sea and the Gulf of Mexico. Bumper are said to be absent from the Bahamas and the Caribbean. The Pacific bumper ranges from Peru to California.

Habitat. Inhabiting brackish and saltwater, bumper occur over soft bottoms in shallow water. They are common in bays, lagoons, and estuaries.

Butterfish

Peprilus triacanthus

OTHER NAMES

American butterfish,
Atlantic butterfish,
dollarfish, pumpkin scad,
sheepshead; French:
stromaté fossette; Spanish:
palometa pintada.

Distribution. *Inhabiting
the western Atlantic Ocean,
butterfish occur in waters
off eastern Newfoundland
and the Gulf of St. Lawrence
in Canada, ranging down
the North American coast to
Palm Beach, Florida. They
are also found in the Gulf of
Mexico.*

Habitat. *Butterfish live
and feed in large, dense
schools along the coast in
near-surface waters less
than 180 feet deep and in
the 40° to 74°F range. They
may also inhabit brackish
waters and in the winter
may move into deeper
water. Juveniles are usually
associated with floating
weeds and jellyfish.*

The fatty and oily quality of the meat of the butterfish does not detract from its reputation as an excellent food fish. It is sold fresh, smoked, and frozen and may be prepared in many ways; the meat is white, tender, and moist and contains few bones. The fat content of the flesh varies greatly over time, at its minimum in August and its maximum in November.

Despite its culinary significance, the butterfish's importance to anglers is as a live or a dead bait for larger saltwater gamefish and as natural forage for assorted species. The shape of the butterfish resembles that of some members of the jack family.

Identification. An oval fish, the butterfish has a very thin and deep body and a blunt head. The anal and the dorsal fins are equally long. Butterfish are silvery fish, with pale blue coloring on the back and the upper sides, which often have irregular dark spots and usually possess 17 to 25 large pores directly underneath the dorsal fin.

Size/Age. The butterfish grows quickly, although it rarely exceeds more than 1 pound in weight or more than 12 inches in length. It is usually a short-lived fish, although it is thought to be capable of living longer than 4 years.

Life history/Behavior. Sexual maturity is reached when butterfish are 2 years old and close to 8 inches in length. Spawning occurs once a year from May through August in offshore waters. The eggs float freely until they hatch within 2 days; juveniles enter coves or estuaries to conceal themselves in floating weeds and among jellyfish tentacles for protection from predators.

Food and feeding habits. Feeding primarily on jellyfish, butterfish are one of very few fish that eat such low-nutrition foods. Their diet also consists of assorted small worms, crustaceans, squid, shrimp, and fish.

Capelin
Mallotus villosus

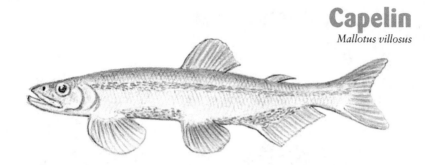

A member of the smelt family, the capelin is an important food fish for cod, pollock, salmon, seabirds, and whales. It has commercial value; females are prized for their roe, and the meat is used as animal feed and fish meal. Like other smelt in flavor and texture, it is an excellent table fish, marketed canned and frozen and prepared by frying and dry salting.

Identification. The capelin has a large mouth with a lower jaw that extends below each eye. Males have larger and deeper bodies than do females; also, the male has an anal fin with a strongly convex base, whereas the female has a straight anal fin base. Both sexes possess a single dorsal fin and extremely small scales. The body is mostly silver, and the upper back is a darker bluish-green.

Size/Age. Capelin may reach a size of 9 inches, although they are usually less than 7 inches long.

Life history/Behavior. Between March and October, capelin move inshore in large schools to spawn in shallow saltwater areas over fine gravel or on sand beaches; however, some may spawn at great depths. Spawning occurs more than once, and each female produces between 3,000 and 56,000 eggs; these are released at high tide and hatch in 2 to 3 weeks.

Food and feeding habits. Capelin feed primarily on planktonic crustaceans.

OTHER NAMES

Danish/Dutch/German/Norwegian: *lodde;* French: *capelin atlantique;* Japanese: *karafuto-shishamo.*

Distribution. *Capelin are found in the North Atlantic, especially in the Barents Sea up to Beard Island; in the White and the Norwegian Seas; off the coast of Greenland; and from Hudson Bay to the Gulf of Maine. In the North Pacific, their range extends from Korea to the Strait of Juan de Fuca between Vancouver Island, Canada, and Washington, U.S.*

Habitat. *Inhabiting saltwater, capelin are pelagic and live in the open seas.*

Catfish, Gafftopsail

Bagre marinus

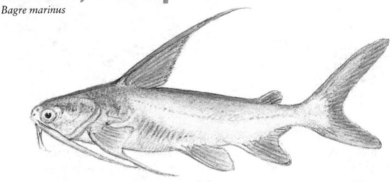

OTHER NAMES

bandera, sailboat cat, gafftopsail sea catfish, gafftop cat, tourist trout; Portuguese: *bagre-fita;* Spanish: *bagre cacumo.*

Distribution. *These fish range along the western Atlantic coast from Cape Cod to Panama and throughout the Gulf of Mexico, being abundant along Louisiana and Texas. They are absent from most of the West Indies and the Caribbean Islands but are present in western Cuba and extend to Venezuela and possibly as far south as Brazil.*

Habitat. *Gafftopsails prefer deeper channels, particularly brackish water in bays and estuaries with sandy bottoms of high organic content. They prefer water temperatures between 68° and 95°F.*

This sea catfish is a common catch by both commercial fishermen and recreational anglers in the Gulf Coast, especially between April and August. Its dark, tender, lean meat is popular as table fare and has a moderate flavor.

Identification. The gafftopsail catfish has a steel-blue dorsal fin, silvery ventral fins, and a robust body, with a depressed broad head, featuring a few flattened barbels. The dorsal and the pectoral fins have greatly elongated spines.

Size/Age. Mature gafftopsails grow to 36 inches and 10 pounds. Average small fish weigh less than a pound to 1½ pounds and are 17 inches long. The maximum age is unknown.

Life history/Behavior. Gafftopsail catfish move in large schools and migrate from bays and estuaries to shallow open waters of the Gulf of Mexico in the winter. This movement and migration in gulf coastal and estuarine waters are related to spawning activity and environmental conditions. Spawning takes place in the waters of inshore mud flats between April and July and has some unusual characteristics.

Gafftopsails reach sexual maturity at the age of 2 and are between 10 and 11 inches in length at the time. They have low fecundity, producing just 20 to 64 eggs per female; their eggs are believed to be the largest of all eggs produced by bony fish. Males carry the eggs and young in their mouths for 11 to 13 weeks until they are about 3 inches long; as many as 55 young have been reportedly carried in this manner at a time.

Food and feeding habits. Crabs, shrimp, and various small fish make up their diet, but like all catfish, gafftopsails have broad dietary interests.

Chub, Bermuda

Kyphosus sectatrix

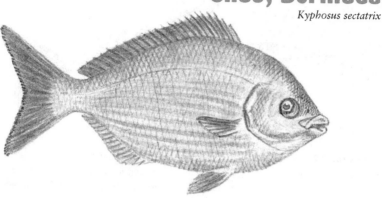

A member of the Kyphosidae family of sea chub, the Bermuda chub is a commonly encountered species, although not one that is aggressively sought by anglers. It is often caught in clear-water harbors and around reefs. Most individuals are reportedly good table fare, but their flesh spoils quickly and should be eaten soon after capture.

Identification. The Bermuda chub has an ovate profile, with a short head and a small mouth. A yellow stripe, bordered in white, runs from the edge of the mouth to the edge of the gill cover. The body is compressed and generally steel or blue-gray with muted yellowish stripes. The fins are dusky, the tail forked, and the scales are usually edged with blue. It may occasionally have white spots or blotches. A less common, very similar, but larger-growing relative is the yellow chub (*K. incisor*).

Size. Bermuda chub commonly weigh 1½ to 2 pounds and measure 10 to 12 inches in length. Reported maximum lengths and weights vary widely; the all-tackle world record is a 13-pound, 4-ounce Florida fish.

Food and feeding habits. The Bermuda chub mainly feeds on benthic algae and also on small crabs and mollusks. Because of its small mouth, it nibbles food and is regarded by anglers as an accomplished bait stealer.

OTHER NAMES

Bermuda sea chub; French: *calicagère blanche;* Spanish: *chopa blanca.*

Distribution. In the western Atlantic, the Bermuda chub occurs from Massachusetts and Bermuda south to Brazil, including the Gulf of Mexico and the Caribbean.

Habitat/Behavior. Like most other sea chub, the Bermuda chub is a schooling species that moves quickly and is often abundant in clear water around tropical reefs, harbors, and small ships.

Cobia

Rachycentron canadum

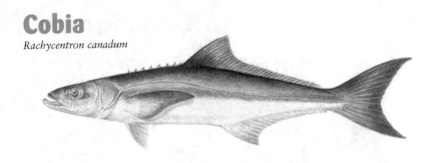

OTHER NAMES

ling, cabio, lemonfish, crab-eater, flathead, black salmon, black kingfish, sergeant fish, runner; French: *mafou;* Japanese: *sugi;* Portuguese: *bijupirá.*

Distribution. *Found worldwide in tropical and warm temperate waters, cobia inhabit the western Atlantic from Cape Cod to Argentina (being most abundant in the Gulf of Mexico).*

Habitat. *Adult cobia prefer shallow continental shelf waters, often congregating along reefs and around buoys, pilings, wrecks, anchored boats, and other stationary or floating objects. They are found in a variety of locations over mud, gravel, or sand bottoms; in coral reefs and man-made sloughs; and at depths of up to 60 feet.*

The only member of the Rachycentridae family, and with no known relatives, the cobia is in a class by itself and a popular food and sportfish for inshore anglers in areas where it is prominent.

Identification. The body of a cobia is elongated, with a broad, depressed head. The first dorsal fin consists of 8 to 10 short, depressible spines that are not connected by a membrane. Both the second dorsal fin and the anal fin each have 1 to 2 spines and 20 to 30 soft rays. The adult cobia is dark brown with a whitish underside and is marked on the sides by silver or bronze lines. A cobia's shape is comparable to that of a shark, with a powerful tail fin and the elevated anterior portion of the second dorsal fin. It can be distinguished from the similar remora (*Remora remora*) by the absence of a suction pad on the head.

Size/Age. Cobia can grow to a length of 6 feet and a weight of 90 pounds, the average size being 3 feet and 15 pounds. They generally live 9 to 10 years. The all-tackle world-record cobia weighed 135 pounds, 9 ounces.

Life history/Behavior. Adult cobia often swim alone or among small schools of other cobia or sharks. They are believed to spawn in the offshore waters of the northern Gulf of Mexico during the late spring, between April and May, and the larvae migrate shoreward. Cobia migrate from offshore to inshore environs, as well as inshore from east to west and vice versa. Little about their movements has been confirmed.

Food and feeding habits. Cobia feed mostly on crustaceans, particularly shrimp, squid, and crabs (thus the name "crab eater"), as well as on eels and various small fish found in shallow coastal waters.

Cod, Atlantic

Gadus morhua

The Atlantic cod has historically been one of the world's important natural resources, and the waters of the North Atlantic once teemed with this fish. Today, the commercial catch of cod is far below historic levels, and cod are generally in a collapsed or near-collapsed condition.

Identification. The Atlantic cod has three dark dorsal fins and two dark anal fins, none of which contain any spines. The body is heavy and tapered, with a prominent chin barbel, a large mouth, and many small teeth. Its snout is rounded on top, and the tail is almost squared. There is a characteristic pale lateral line. The coloring is highly variable on the back and the sides (ranging from brownish or sandy to gray, yellow, reddish, greenish, or any combination of these colors), gray-white on the underside, and with numerous light spots covering the body.

Size/Age. Young fish ages 2 to 5 generally constitute the bulk of the cod catch, with the average size being from 4 to 15 pounds. Larger sizes in New England are not unusual, some with a length of 30 to 40 inches. When they were more abundant, cod were caught in the 55- to 75-pound range and have been known to reach 211 pounds. The all-tackle fishing record is 98 pounds, 12 ounces. Atlantic cod can live up to 22 years.

Spawning behavior. The spawning season is during December and January off the Mid-Atlantic Bight and from February through April farther north.

Food and feeding habits. Omnivorous feeders, cod are primarily active at dawn and dusk. Their primary diet is invertebrates and assorted fish. Very young cod feed on copepods and other small crustaceans while at the surface and, after dropping to the bottom, on small worms or shrimp.

OTHER NAMES

cod, codfish, codling, scrod; French: *morue de l'Atlantique;* German: *dorsch, kabeljau;* Italian: *merluzzo bianco;* Japanese: *madara, tara;* Norwegian: *torsk;* Portuguese: *bacalhau;* Spanish: *bacalao del Atlántique.*

Distribution. Atlantic cod occur in subarctic and cool temperate waters of the North Atlantic from Greenland to North Carolina. They have generally been most abundant in the Gulf of St. Lawrence, off Newfoundland. In U.S. waters, cod are assessed as two stocks, the first being that of the Gulf of Maine, and the second being that of Georges Bank and southward.

Habitat. These fish are found primarily off the coasts along the continental shelf. They prefer cool water of 30° to 50°F and may reside in depths of up to 200 fathoms. Adults are generally found in water over 60 feet deep, whereas juveniles may be found in shallower water; both move deeper during the summer.

Cod, Pacific

Gadus macrocephalus

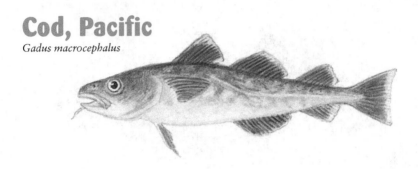

OTHER NAMES

cod, gray cod, true cod;
French: *morue du Pacifique;*
Italian: *merluzzo del
Pacifico;* Japanese: *madara;*
Portuguese: *bacalhau-do-
Pacifico;* Spanish: *bacalao
del Pacifico.*

Distribution. *The Pacific
cod inhabits waters along
the U.S. Pacific coast from
Santa Monica, California, to
northwestern Alaska. It is
common in the U.S. north-
west waters of Oregon,
Washington, and Alaska.*

Habitat. *Although
primarily a coastal bottom-
dwelling fish, the Pacific cod
can be found from shallow
waters to depths of nearly
800 feet. It prefers rocky,
pebbly ground or sandy bottoms in cold water.*

Extremely similar to Atlantic cod, and a member of the
Gadidae family, the Pacific cod is an excellent food fish and
a good sportfish. It is harvested commercially for fish sticks
and fillets and is usually sold frozen. In British Columbia, it
is the most important trawl-caught bottom fish, with millions of pounds landed there alone.

Identification. Characteristic of the cod family, the Pacific
cod has three separate and distinct dorsal fins, two anal fins,
and one large barbel under the chin. Its body is heavy and
elongated, with small scales, a large mouth, and soft rays. Its
coloring ranges from gray to brown on the back, lightening
on the sides and the belly. Numerous brown spots speckle
the sides and the back. All the fins are dusky, and the
unpaired fins are edged with white on their outer margins.

The Pacific cod can be distinguished from the Atlantic
cod, which is almost identical, by its smaller body and the
pointedness of its fins.

Size. The average size is less than 3 feet, with a weight of
15 pounds or less. The all-tackle record is 30 pounds.

Spawning behavior. The spawning season for the Pacific
cod is winter and early spring. The eggs are pelagic, or free-
floating. It generally lays great quantities of eggs; depending on the size of the fish, a female may release between 1
and 9 million eggs.

Food and feeding habits. The Pacific cod is mainly
omnivorous. The adult feeds on dominant food organisms,
especially herring, capelin, sand eels, sardines, pollock, and
other cod. Its habits are similar to those of the Atlantic cod.

Coney

Cephalopholis fulva

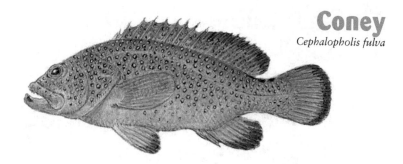

The coney is a member of the Serranidae family of grouper.

Identification. Because the coney experiences numerous color phases, it is inadvisable to try to identify this fish by color. These phases range from the common phase, in which the fish is reddish brown; to a bicolor period, in which the upper body is dark and the lower body is pale; to a bright yellow phase. The body is covered with small blue to pale spots, although the spots are uncommon in the bright-yellow phase. There are often two black spots present at the tip of the jaw and two more at the base of the tail, as well as a margin of white around the tail and the soft dorsal fin. The tail is rounded, and there are nine spines in the dorsal fin.

Size. The coney weighs about a pound, although occasionally it can weigh as much as 3 pounds. The average length is 6 to 10 inches, and the maximum length is 16 inches.

Life history/Behavior. As with many grouper, coney females transform into males, usually when they reach 20 centimeters in length. They are gregarious fish, and the males are territorial.

Food. Coney feed mainly on small fish and crustaceans.

OTHER NAMES

French: *coné ouatalibi;* Spanish: *canario, cherna cabrilla, corruncha, guativere.*

Distribution. In the western Atlantic, coney extend from Bermuda and South Carolina to southern Brazil, including the Gulf of Mexico and Atol das Rocas; they are commonly found in the Caribbean and less commonly in southern Florida and the Bahamas.

Habitat. In the Gulf of Mexico, coney occur in clear deep-water reefs, and in Bermuda and the West Indies they spend the day in caves and under ledges, preferring shallower water the rest of the time. Coney tend to drift immediately above the bottom or rest there in 10- to 60-foot depths, remaining in close proximity to protected areas.

Corbina, California

Menticirrhus undulatus

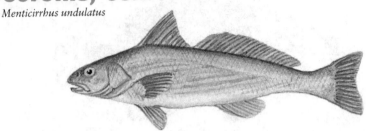

OTHER NAMES

California whiting, surf fish, sucker.

Distribution. *California corbina occur from the Gulf of California in Mexico to Point Conception, California.*

Habitat. *Preferring sandy beaches and shallow bays, the California corbina is a bottom fish, appearing along the coastal surf zone.*

The California corbina belongs to the Sciaenidae (croaker and drum) family and is a member of the whiting group. Because it lacks a swim bladder, it cannot make the croaking or drumming noises characteristic of the croaker family.

Identification. The body of the California corbina is elongated and slightly compressed, with a flattened belly. Its head is long and the mouth is small, the upper jaw scarcely reaching a point below the front of each eye. The first dorsal fin is short and high, the second long and low. Coloring is uniformly gray, with incandescent reflections and with wavy diagonal lines on the sides.

This croaker and the yellowfin croaker (*Umbrina roncador*) are the only two of the eight coastal croaker present in California waters that have a barbel on the lower jaw. The California corbina has only one weak spine at the front of the anal fin; the yellowfin croaker has two strong spines.

Size. The average corbina weighs 1 pound. The all-tackle record is 6 pounds, 8 ounces, but corbina are reported to grow to 8 pounds.

Life history/Behavior. Males mature when 2 years old, at a length of 10 inches; females mature at age 3, at 13 inches long. Spawning occurs from June through September, although it is heaviest in July and August, and takes place offshore. California corbina travel in schools or small groups, although large individuals are often solitary.

Food and feeding habits. A fussy feeder, the California corbina primarily consumes sand crabs and spits out bits of clam shells and other foreign matter; it also consumes small crustaceans and marine worms. Corbina scoop up mouthfuls of sand and separate the food by sending the sand through their gills. Adults are sometimes seen feeding in the surf, occasionally in water so shallow that their backs are exposed.

Corvina

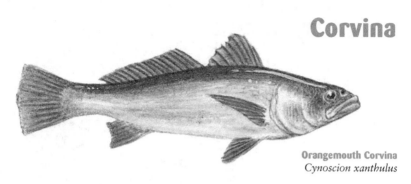

Orangemouth Corvina
Cynoscion xanthulus

Members of the Sciaenidae family (drum and croaker), corvina inhabit the Pacific Ocean and are known for the noises they make. These fish are often called corbina, as well as corvina, and both words appear in the Spanish and the Portuguese languages for common names applied to various drum and croaker.

They are typically referred to as croaker by some anglers and as weakfish by others, and they inhabit tropical and temperate seas. Almost all are inshore bottom-feeding fish, usually found over sandy bottoms, either in schools or in small groups. Corvina primarily inhabit the Gulf of California and waters south of the gulf; they are likely to inhabit the surf line and to hug the near shoreline, feeding on crustaceans, worms, and small fish. They generally have a silver sandy coloration that blends with this environment. Most, if not all, are good to eat.

Species that may be encountered include the orangemouth or yellowmouth corvina *(Cynoscion xanthulus)*, which occurs throughout the Gulf of California in Mexico and south to Acapulco, as well as in the Salton Sea in Southern California, and can grow to 36 inches; the Gulf corvina *(Cynoscion othonopterus)*, a resident of the upper Gulf of California that grows to 28 inches; the shortfin corvina *(Cynoscion parvipinnis)*, a surf fish also in the Gulf of California and south to Mazatlán that grows to 20 inches; the yellowfin corvina *(Cynoscion stolzmanni)*, ranging from the Gulf of California to Peru and growing to 35 inches; the striped corvina *(Cynoscion reticulatus)*, ranging from the Gulf of California to Panama and growing to 35 inches; and the totuava or totoaba *(Totoaba macdonaldi)*, a white seabass lookalike that was once abundant and is now endangered. It inhabits the middle and upper Gulf of California and once grew to 6 feet and 300 pounds.

Croaker, Atlantic

Micropogonias undulatus

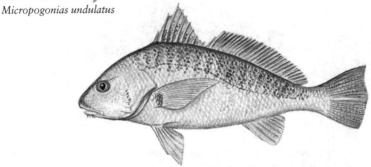

croaker, crocus, golden cracker, hardhead, king billy; Japanese: *ishimoki;* Portuguese: *corvina;* Spanish: *corbina, corvinón brasileño.*

Distribution. *The Atlantic croaker is found along the Atlantic coast from Cape Cod to the Bay of Campeche. While it is abundant off the entire coast of the Gulf of Mexico, the croaker periodically becomes most common in Louisiana and Mississippi waters.*

Habitat. *The Atlantic croaker is a bottom-dwelling, estuarine-dependent fish that becomes oceanic during spawning. It prefers mud, sand, and shell bottoms; areas around rocks; waters near jetties, piers, and bridges; and surf. Juveniles inhabit both open and vegetated shallow marsh areas. Adult croaker can occupy a wide range of salinities, from 20 to 75 parts per thousand, and temperatures of 50° to 96°F. Large fish are not found at temperatures below 50°F. Larvae and juveniles, however, are more tolerant of lower temperatures.*

The Atlantic croaker is a member of the Sciaenidae family (drum and croaker) and one of the most frequently caught estuarine and near-shore marine fish along the eastern coast of the United States. The common name "croaker" is derived from the voluntary deep croaking noises made when the fish raps a muscle against its swim bladder.

Identification. The Atlantic croaker has a small, elongated body with a short, high first dorsal fin and a long, low second dorsal fin. There are 6 to 10 tiny barbels on the chin. The middle rays of the caudal fins are longer than those above and below, creating a wedgelike appearance. Its coloring is greenish above and white below, with brownish-black spots and a silver iridescence covering the body. There are dark, wavy lines on the sides. During spawning, the Atlantic croaker takes on a bronze hue (thus the nickname "golden cracker"), and its pelvic fins turn yellow.

Size/Age. The average fish is 12 inches long and weighs 1½ pounds, although the species may grow to 20 inches. The all-tackle record weighed 5 pounds, 8 ounces. It can live up to 5 years.

Life history/Behavior. Spawning occurs at sea in the winter and the spring (the peak month is November), when the Atlantic croaker migrates to deeper, warmer water. In the southerly range, it is assumed that all croaker spawn in the open Gulf of Mexico, near the mouths of various passes that lead into shallow bays and lagoons. Adults migrate in schools or small groups to the bays in the spring and leave the marsh in the fall to enter deep gulf waters.

Food and feeding habits. Adult croaker feed on detritus, larger invertebrates, and fish. Sensory barbels allow the Atlantic croaker to find food on the bottom.

Croaker, Spotfin

Roncador stearnsii

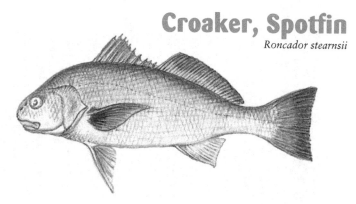

A member of the Sciaenidae (drum and croaker) family, the spotfin croaker is a small species caught by bay, surf, and pier anglers and highly valued as table fare.

Identification. The body of the spotfin croaker is elongate but heavy forward. The upper profile of the head is steep and slightly curved and abruptly rounded at the very blunt snout. The mouth is subterminal, being underneath the head. The color is silvery gray, with a bluish luster above and white below. There are dark wavy lines on the sides and a large black spot at the base of the pectoral fin.

The pectoral fin spot, the subterminal mouth, and the absence of a fleshy barbel distinguish the spotfin croaker from other California croaker. Small specimens may be confused with small white croaker, although dorsal fin counts differ. The spotfin has 11 or fewer (usually 10) dorsal fin spines; the white croaker has 12 to 15. Large male spotfins in breeding colors are known as "golden croaker."

Size. The average spotfin croaker is small to medium in size, and most weigh roughly a pound. The largest caught on rod and reel in California was 27 inches long and weighed 10½ pounds.

Life history/Behavior. Spotfin croaker travel considerably but with no definite pattern, moving extensively from bay to bay, usually in small groups but sometimes in groups numbering up to four dozen. Spawning season is from June through September, and spawning evidently takes place offshore, as no ripe fish are caught in the surf, although 1-inch juveniles do appear in the surf in the fall.

Food and feeding habits. Spotfin croaker have large pharyngeal teeth that are well suited to crushing clams, which make up a major portion of their diet; crustaceans and worms are also eaten extensively.

OTHER NAMES
spotty, spot, golden croaker.

Distribution. *Spotfin croaker range from Mazatlán, Mexico, to Point Conception, California, including the Gulf of California; in California they are most abundant south of Los Angeles.*

Habitat. *Spotfins are found along beaches and in bays over bottoms that vary from coarse sand to heavy mud and at depths varying from 4 to 50 or more feet. They prefer depressions and holes near shore.*

Croaker, White

Genyonemus lineatus

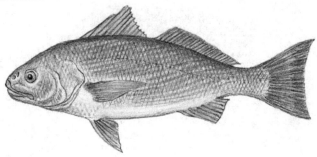

OTHER NAMES

kingfish, king-fish, king croaker, shiner, Pasadena trout, tommy croaker, little bass; Japanese: *shiroguchi.*

Distribution. *White croaker range from Magdalena Bay, Baja California, to Vancouver Island, British Columbia, but are not abundant north of San Francisco.*

Habitat. *Preferring sandy bottoms, white croaker inhabit quiet surf zones, shallow bays, and lagoons. Most of the time they are found in offshore areas at depths of 10 to 100 feet. On rare occasions, they are abundant at depths as great as 600 feet.*

A member of the Sciaenidae family, the white croaker is a small North American Pacific coast fish. The common name "croaker" is derived from the voluntary deep croaking noises made when the fish raps a muscle against the swim bladder, which acts as an amplifier. The resultant distinctive drumming noise can be heard from a far distance.

Although the flesh is edible, the white croaker is considered a nuisance, being easily hooked on most any type of live bait. Like its cousin the queenfish *(Seriphus politus; see: Queenfish),* many white croaker are caught accidentally by anglers.

Identification. The body of the white croaker is elongate and compressed. Its head is oblong and bluntly rounded, and its mouth is somewhat underneath the head. A deep notch separates the two dorsal fins. Its coloring is iridescent brown to yellowish on the back, becoming silvery below. Faint, wavy lines appear over the silvery parts. The fins are yellow to white.

The white croaker is one of five California croaker that have subterminal mouths. They can be distinguished from the California corbina *(Menticirrhus undulatus; see: Corbina, California)* and the yellowfin croaker *(Umbrina roncador; see: Croaker, Yellowfin)* by the absence of a barbel. The 12 to 15 spines in the first dorsal fin serve to distinguish white croaker from all the other croaker with subterminal mouths, as none of these has more than 11 spines in this fin.

Size/Age. The average weight is 1 pound. It is believed the white croaker can live up to 15 years, although most live far fewer years.

Food and feeding habits. White croaker consume a variety of fish, squid, shrimp, octopus, worms, small crabs, clams, and other items, living or dead.

Croaker, Yellowfin

Umbrina roncador

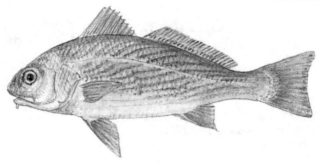

The yellowfin croaker is a member of the family Sciaenidae (drum and croaker), known for the drumlike noises it makes when it raps a muscle against its swim bladder. The resulting distinctive drumming sound is amplified by the swim bladder and can be heard at some distance.

The sciaenids are one of the most important food fish in the world because nearly all species are good to eat and are harvested commercially. Found along the Pacific coast, the yellowfin croaker is a popular catch for light-tackle surf anglers.

Identification. The body of the yellowfin croaker is elliptical-elongate; the back is somewhat arched and the head blunt. Its coloring is iridescent blue to gray, with brassy reflections on the back, diffusing to silvery white below. Dark wavy lines streak the sides. The fins are yellowish, except for the dark dorsal fins. It has a small barbel on the chin tip and two strong anal spines; the barbel and the heavy anal spines distinguish the yellowfin from other California croaker.

Size. The average weight for a yellowfin croaker is less than 1 pound. The all-tackle record is 2 pounds, 11 ounces.

Life history/Behavior. Yellowfin croaker are sexually mature at 9 inches in length. Their spawning season is in the summer, when this species is most common along sandy beaches. They move into deeper waters in the winter, traveling in schools or small groups.

Food and feeding habits. Although the yellowfin croaker primarily consumes small fish and fish fry, it also feeds on small crustaceans, worms, and mollusks.

OTHER NAMES

Catalina croaker, yellowtailed croaker, golden croaker, yellowfin drum.

Distribution. *The yellowfin croaker is found from the Gulf of California, Mexico, to Point Conception, California.*

Habitat. *These fish inhabit shallow parts of bays, channels, harbors, and other nearshore waters over sandy bottoms.*

Cutlassfish

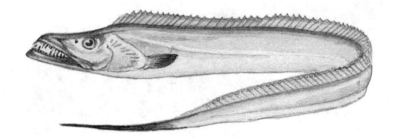

OTHER NAMES

cutlass fish, ribbonfish, Atlantic cutlassfish, Pacific cutlassfish, largehead hairtail; Japanese: *tachinouo, tachiuo, tachuo;* Portuguese: *lírio, peixe-espada;* Spanish: *espada, pez sable, sable, savola.*

Distribution. *In North America, the Atlantic cutlassfish commonly ranges from Massachusetts to Argentina and throughout the Gulf of Mexico, especially Texas. In the Pacific, cutlassfish inhabit waters from Southern California to northern Peru.*

Habitat. *Preferring muddy bottoms in shallow water, cutlassfish gather in large numbers in bays, estuaries, and shallow coastal areas.*

Cutlassfish are members of the family Trichiuridae, encompassing nearly 20 species. They are swift swimmers that generally dwell on the bottom. Used as bait for larger gamefish in the United States, cutlassfish are a valued food and a commercial species in many other countries, especially Japan, where they may be used for sashimi. They are also marketed salted/dried and frozen.

Identification. Characterized by their long, compressed bodies that taper to pointed tails, cutlassfish are also commonly known as ribbonfish. Their heads are spear-shaped, and the fish have sharp, arrowlike teeth in large mouths. Their coloring is silvery, the jaws edged with black.

Size/Age. Cutlassfish can reach up to 5 feet in length and 2 pounds in weight. The average length is 3 feet. The all-tackle record for Atlantic cutlassfish (*Trichiurus lepturus*) is a 7-pound fish caught in South Africa in 1995.

Food and feeding habits. Cutlassfish feed on anchovies, sardines, squid, and crustaceans. Adults usually feed on pelagic prey near the surface during the daytime and migrate to the bottom at night. Subadults and small juveniles do the opposite.

Dogfish, Spiny

Squalus acanthias

The spiny dogfish is the most prominent member of the Squalidae family of dogfish sharks. Some live in relatively shallow water close to shore; others inhabit great depths. They vary widely in length, and one of their chief anatomical characteristics is the lack of an anal fin.

Identification. The body of the spiny dogfish is elongate and slender. The head is pointed. The color is slate gray to brownish on top, sometimes with white spots, and fading to white below. It has spines at the beginning of both dorsal fins; these spines are mildly poisonous and provide a defense for the spiny dogfish.

Size/Age. Spiny dogfish are common at 2 to 3 feet in length; the maximum size is about 63 inches and 20 pounds. In California waters, a large fat female will be roughly 4 feet long and will weigh 15 pounds. In the northwestern Atlantic, maximum ages reported for males and females are 35 and 40 years, respectively.

Life history. Spiny dogfish tend to school by size and, for large mature individuals, by sex. Females are larger than males and produce from 3 to 14 young at a time in alternate years. The species bears live young and has a gestation period of about 18 to 22 months. Spiny dogfish are long lived and nonmigratory; heavy commercial fishing pressure in a given area will rapidly lower populations of this slow-growing, low-reproductive species.

Food and feeding habits. The spiny dogfish is voracious and feeds on practically all smaller fish, including herring, sardines, anchovies, smelt, and even small spiny dogfish and crabs. They have been known to attack schools of herring and mackerel, as well as concentrations of haddock, cod, sand lance, and other species.

OTHER NAMES

dogfish, dog shark, grayfish, Pacific grayfish, Pacific dogfish, spinarola, California dogfish, blue dog, common spiny fish, spiny dogfish, picked fish, spiky dog, spotted spiny, spurdog, white-spotted dogfish, Victorian spotted dogfish; French: *aiguillat;* Italian: *spinarolo;* Japanese: *aburatsunozame;* Portuguese: *galhudo;* Russian: *katran;* Spanish: *galludo.*

Distribution. Spiny dogfish occur in temperate and subtropical waters. In the western Atlantic, they range from Greenland to Argentina; in the eastern Pacific, they range from the Bering Sea to Chile.

Habitat. This species is common in nearshore waters along some coasts and may be found in enclosed bays and estuaries; it generally inhabits deep waters and typically favors the bottom. In temperate waters during the spring and the fall, spiny dogfish can range into coastal waters, heading more northerly in the summer. In the winter, they are distributed primarily in deeper waters along the edge of the continental shelf.

Dolphin, Common
Coryphaena hippurus

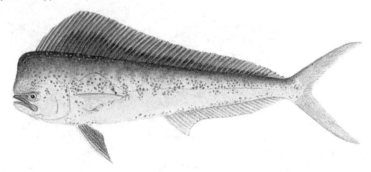

OTHER NAMES

dolphinfish, common dolphinfish, mahimahi, mahi mahi, dorado; Chinese: *fei niau fu, ngau tau yue;* French: *coryphéne commune;* Italian: *lampuga;* Japanese: *shiira, toohyaku;* Portuguese: *doirado, dourado;* Spanish: *dorado, dorado com ún, lampuga.*

Distribution. *The common dolphin is found worldwide in tropical and subtropical waters. In the western Atlantic, it occurs in areas influenced by the warm waters of the Gulf Stream and has been caught as far north as Prince Edward Island and as far south as Río de Janeiro. In the eastern Pacific, it ranges from Peru to Oregon.*

Habitat. *Common dolphin are warmwater pelagic fish, occurring in the open ocean and usually found close to the surface, although in waters of great depth. They sometimes inhabit coastal waters and occasionally areas near piers, but in the open ocean they often concentrate around floating*

The common dolphin is the larger of the two very similar species in the family Coryphaenidae, both of which are cosmopolitan in warm seas. This fish is one of the top offshore gamefish among anglers and is an excellent, hard-fighting species that puts on an acrobatic show once hooked.

Identification. The body is slender and streamlined, tapering sharply from head to tail. Large males, called bulls, have high, vertical foreheads, while the female's forehead is rounded. The anal fin has 25 to 31 soft rays and is long, stretching over half of the length of the body. The dorsal fin has 55 to 66 soft rays. Its caudal fin is deeply forked; there are no spines in any of the fins; and the mouth has bands of fine teeth.

Coloring is variable and defies an accurate, simple description. Generally, when the fish is alive in the water, the common dolphin is rich iridescent blue or blue-green dorsally; gold, bluish-gold, or silvery gold on the lower flanks; and silvery white or yellow on the belly. The sides are sprinkled with a mixture of dark and light spots, ranging from black or blue to golden. The dorsal fin is rich blue, and the anal fin is golden or silvery. The other fins are generally golden yellow, edged with blue. Dark vertical bands sometimes appear when the fish is attacking prey. The color description of the dolphin is difficult because it undergoes sudden changes in color, which occur in an instant, often when the fish is excited.

When the fish is removed from the water, however, the colors fluctuate between blue, green, and yellow; the brilliant colors that were apparent when in the water fade quickly. After death, the fish usually turns a uniform yellow or silvery gray.

Size/Age. The average size is 5 to 15 pounds, although larger catches up to 50 pounds are not uncommon. The all-tackle world record is an 87-pounder caught in Costa Rica in 1976, and it has been rumored that fish up to 100 pounds have been caught by commercial longliners. The maximum length is reportedly 82 inches.

Dolphin are fast growing and short lived. Few common dolphin live longer than 4 years, and most live just 3 years. Males grow larger than females and are capable of growing to 60 pounds in just 2 years, although this is exceptional and the result of consistently favorable warm water temperatures and abundant food.

Life history/Behavior. The common dolphin is a prolific spawner and grows rapidly, meaning that it must by nature be an eating machine. Spawning season begins primarily in the spring or early summer and lasts several months in warmer waters. Dolphin reach sexual maturity in their first year of life and produce a large volume of eggs.

Dolphin are schooling fish and are often congregated in large numbers, sometimes by the thousands. They are almost always between the surface and 100-foot depths, but they are encountered by anglers on or just under the surface and are probably the most surface-oriented of all big-game fish. This, plus the fact that they are visually oriented feeders that primarily forage in daylight, helps endear them to anglers. Offshore anglers frequently encounter packs of dolphin and are able to elicit strikes from several fish in quick order.

These fish are evidently also migratory. It is believed that dolphin in both hemispheres migrate away from the equator in the spring and the summer and toward the equator in the fall and the winter.

Food. Common dolphin are extremely fast swimmers and feed in pairs, small packs, and schools, extensively consuming whatever forage fishes are most abundant. Flyingfish and squid are prominent food in areas where these exist, and small fish and crustaceans that are around floating sargassum weed are commonly part of the diet, especially for smaller dolphin. Dolphin are very aggressive feeders, and they can move extremely fast to capture a meal.

objects, especially buoys, driftwood, and seaweed lines or clusters. The young commonly frequent warm nearshore waters in sargassum beds or other flotsam. In developing countries, commercial fishermen may place floating bundles of bamboo reeds, cork planks, and the like in the water to concentrate dolphin before seining or gillnetting commences.

Dolphin, Pompano

Coryphaena equiselis

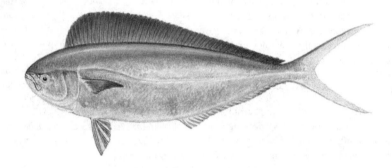

mahimahi, blue dolphin, small dolphin, dolphinfish, pompano dolphinfish; French: *coryphéne dauphin;* Japanese: *ebisu-shiira;* Portuguese: *dourado;* Spanish: *dorado.*

Distribution/Habitat.

The pompano dolphin is found worldwide in tropical seas; in the United States it is most commonly encountered in Hawaii. The pompano dolphin reportedly prefers surface temperatures above 75°F. It is considered more oceanic than the common dolphin is but may enter coastal waters.

The pompano dolphin is the smaller of the two Coryphaenidae family species and is often confused with the females and the young of its larger relative the common dolphin *(C. hippurus).* Like its relative, it is caught commercially and by anglers, and it is an excellent food fish. The pompano dolphin is usually presented in fish markets and restaurants under its Hawaiian name, mahimahi. This species, and its relative, are often referred to as "dolphinfish" to distinguish them from the so-called dolphin of the porpoise family, which is an unrelated mammal and not sought by anglers.

Identification. This species is almost identical to the common dolphin in coloring and general shape, although it has greater body depth behind the head than the common dolphin has and a squarish, rather than rounded, tooth patch on the tongue. There are fewer dorsal rays on the pompano dolphin—48 to 55, versus the common dolphin's 55 to 65.

Size. The average size is 20 to 24 inches and 4 to 5 pounds, although it reportedly grows to 50 inches.

Life history/Behavior. Little is known of the life history of the pompano dolphin, other than that it is a schooling tropical water species, prone to near-surface feeding and attracted to objects. This fish is similar to the common dolphin in most behavioral respects.

Food. The pompano dolphin's diet consists of small fish and squid.

Drum, Black

Pogonias cromis

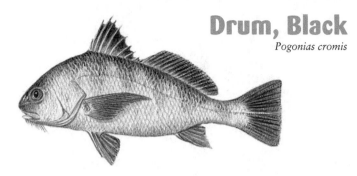

The black drum is the largest member of the Sciaenidae family (drum and croaker). The common term "drum" refers to the loud and distinctive "drumming" noise that occurs when the fish raps a muscle against the swim bladder. This voluntary noise is assumed to be associated with locating and attracting mates, and it can sometimes be heard from a good distance, even by people above the water.

Identification. The black drum has a short, deep, and stocky body, with a high, arched back and a slightly concave tail. The lower jaw sports numerous barbels, or short whiskers. There are large pavementlike teeth in the throat, and the mouth is low. The dorsal fins have 11 spines, 20 to 22 dorsal rays, and 41 to 45 scales along the lateral line, which runs all the way to the end of the tail. Coloring is silvery with a brassy sheen and blackish fins, turning to dark gray after death.

Size/Age. Average small drum weigh 5 to 10 pounds; large specimens commonly weigh 20 to 40 pounds. In Delaware Bay, fish from 40 to 70 pounds are fairly common in the spring. The all-tackle record is 113 pounds. Black drum live up to 35 years.

Life history/Behavior. Black drum adults form schools and migrate in the spring to bay and river mouths for the spawning season; in the Gulf of Mexico this is from February to May. Larval black drum remain in shallow muddy waters until they are 4 to 5 inches long; then they move near shore.

Food and feeding habits. Adult black drum feed on crustaceans and mollusks, with a preference for blue crabs, shedder crabs, shrimp, oysters, and squid. They locate food with their chin barbels and crush and grind shells with their pharyngeal teeth.

OTHER NAMES

drum, sea drum, common drum, banded drum, butterfly drum, gray drum, striped drum, oyster drum, oyster cracker; French: *grand tambour;* Japanese: *guchi, ishimochi, nibe;* Portuguese: *corvina;* Spanish: *corvinón negro, corbina, corvina negro, corvina, roncador.*

Distribution. *Black drum are found in the western Atlantic Ocean, from Massachusetts to southern Florida and across the Gulf of Mexico to northern Mexico. They rarely occur north of New Jersey.*

Habitat. *An inshore bottom fish, the black drum prefers sandy bottoms in salt or brackish waters near jetties, breakwaters, bridge and pier pilings, clam and oyster beds, channels, estuaries, bays, high marsh areas, and shorelines. Larger fish often favor shoal areas and channels.*

Black drum can survive wide ranges of salinity and temperature. The small fish inhabit brackish and freshwater habitats; the adults usually prefer estuaries in which salinity ranges from 9 to 26 parts per thousand and the temperature ranges from 53° to 91°F.

Drum, Red

Sciaenops ocellatus

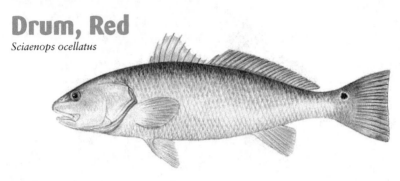

OTHER NAMES

channel bass, redfish, rat
red (schooling juveniles
less than 2 pounds), bull
red (more than 10
pounds), puppy drum
(under 18 inches), drum,
spottail bass, red bass, red
horse, school drum;
French: *tambour rouge;*
Spanish: *corvinón ocelado,
pez rojo, corvina roja,
pescado colorado.*

Distribution. *Red drum
are found in the western
Atlantic Ocean from the
Gulf of Maine to the Florida
Keys, although they are rare
north of Maryland, and all
along the Gulf Coast to
northern Mexico.*

Habitat. *An estuarine-
dependent fish that
becomes oceanic later in
life, the red drum is found in
brackish water and saltwater on sand, mud, and grass
bottoms of inlets, shallow
bays, tidal passes, bayous,
and estuaries. The red drum
also tolerates freshwater, in
which some have been
known to dwell perma-
nently. Larger red drum prefer deeper waters of lower
estuaries and tidal passes,
whereas smaller drum
remain in shallow waters*

Commonly known as a channel bass and a redfish, the red
drum is second only to the black drum *(see: Drum, Black)* in
size among members of the drum family, Sciaenidae, but
probably first in the hearts of anglers. The common term
"drum" refers to the loud and distinctive "drumming" noise
that occurs when the fish raps a muscle against the swim
bladder. The noise is voluntary and is assumed to be associated with locating and attracting mates, and it can sometimes be heard from a good distance, even by people above
the water.

Identification. The red drum is similar in appearance to
the black drum, although its maximum size is smaller and it
is more streamlined. The body is elongate, with a subterminal mouth and a blunt nose. On adults the tail is squared,
and on juveniles it is rounded. There are no chin barbels,
which also distinguishes it from the black drum. Its coloring
is coppery red to bronze on the back, and silver and white
on the sides and the belly. One black dot (also called an eye-
spot) or many are found at the base of the tail.

Size/Age. The average adult red drum is 28 inches long
and weighs roughly 15 pounds. Although red drum can
attain enormous sizes, they seldom do so. A 30-pounder is
generally rare south of the Carolinas or in the Gulf of Mexico, although fish weighing up to 60 pounds are caught in
offshore locations. Thirty- to 50-pound fish are most prominent in the mid-Atlantic, principally in North Carolina and
Virginia; these sizes are considered trophies.

Red drum can live 50 or more years. They are reported to
live to at least 40 years in the Gulf of Mexico, and the all-
tackle record, a North Carolina fish of 94 pounds, 2 ounces,
was reportedly 53 years old.

Life history/Behavior. Males are mature by 4 years of
age at 30 inches and 15 pounds, females by 5 years at 35
inches and 18 pounds. The spawning season is during the
fall, although it may begin as early as August and end as late
as November. Spawning takes place at dusk in the coastal

waters of the northern Gulf of Mexico, near passes, inlets, and bays, and is often tied to new- or full-moon phases. Right before spawning, males change color and become dark red or bright bluish-gray above the lateral line. Both males and females, hours before mating, chase and butt each other, drumming loudly. A female may release up to 4.5 million eggs, although very few survive to adulthood. Currents and winds carry the larvae into estuarine nursery areas.

Adult red drum form large schools in coastal waters, an activity presumably associated with spawning, although it occurs throughout the year. Anglers often see them at the surface or moving under schools of blue runner and little tunny. Sight casting to schools is a favored activity.

Drum are known generally to remain in the waters where they were hatched, although some populations migrate seasonally, and large reds may move offshore, as previously noted.

Food and feeding habits. As a bottom fish, this species uses its senses of sight and touch and its downturned mouth to locate forage on the bottom through vacuuming or biting the bottom. Juveniles consume copepods, amphipods, and tiny shrimp. In the summer and the fall, adults feed on crabs, shrimp, and sand dollars. Fish such as menhaden, mullet, pinfish, sea robins, lizardfish, spot, Atlantic croaker, and flounder are the primary foods consumed during the winter and the spring. In shallow water, red drum are often seen browsing head-down with their tails slightly out of the water, a behavior called "tailing."

near piers and jetties and on grassy flats.

Red drum can survive wide ranges of salinity and temperature. Smaller drum prefer lower salinity levels than do larger ones. Optimum salinity levels range from 5 to 30 parts per thousand, optimum temperatures from 40° to 90°F.

More big reds and fewer small ones exist in a fairly short stretch of the mid-Atlantic because of the rich feeding opportunities. This is said to keep the fish from migrating southward each fall, as they prefer to move offshore to warmer continental shelf waters until spring.

Eel, American Conger

Conger oceanicus

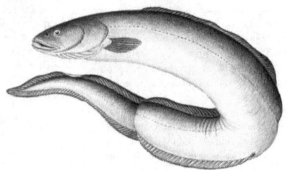

Distribution. *The American conger occurs in the western Atlantic from Cape Cod, Massachusetts, to Florida and in the northern Gulf of Mexico.*

Habitat. *This species ranges widely from shallow inshore waters, occasionally in brackish environs, to waters hundreds of feet deep. The eels usually suspend over rocky or broken bottoms or may linger around wrecks, piers, pilings, and jetties.*

Conger eels are widely distributed members of the small Congridae family of marine eels that inhabit temperate and tropical waters.

Identification. Conger are distinguished from moray eels by having pectoral fins (morays have none) and by the dark or black margin on their dorsal and anal fins. Conger eels are scaleless, and their dorsal fins originate over the tips of the pectorals. They grow much larger than American eels, with which they are sometimes confused in inshore environs.

Size/Age. The American conger is reportedly capable of growing to 7½ feet and 87 pounds, although it is most frequently encountered at 10 to 20 pounds and 5 feet in length. Females grow larger than males.

Life history. The life history of this fish is similar to that of the American eel, although the latter enter freshwater. Sexual maturity occurs between 5 and 15 years of age, and spawning congers migrate seaward, spawning in the summer in water that may be more than 1,000 feet deep.

Food. The diet of the nocturnal-feeding conger eel includes fish, shrimp, small shellfish, and crustaceans.

Eels, Moray

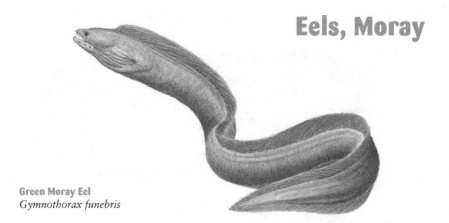

Green Moray Eel
Gymnothorax funebris

The Muraenidae family of morays is the most infamous group within the order Anguilliformes, which are jawed fish called eels. They constitute a family of more than 80 species, occurring in greatest abundance in tropical and subtropical waters.

The typical moray's body is flattened from side to side, pectoral fins are lacking, and the scaleless skin is thick and leathery. The dorsal and the anal fins are low, sometimes almost hidden by the wrinkled skin around them. The gill opening is small and round, and the teeth are large. Most morays are large, reaching a length of 5 to 6 feet. Some are as long as 10 feet.

Normally, morays are nocturnal, but they never miss an opportunity to appear from their rocky lairs when a meal is in the offing. They feed on small fish, octopus, crustaceans, and mollusks.

The green moray *(Gymnothorax funebris)*, which lives in tropical and subtropical waters of both North and South America and averages 5 to 6 feet long, is an unusual brownish-green, due to a yellow slime that covers the eel's blue body. The green moray inhabits coral reefs, sometimes going into deep water to prowl for food.

The spotted moray *(G. moringa)* occurs in the same range as the green moray. It is usually under 3 feet long and has prominent dark spots or a chainlike pattern of dark lines on its usually yellowish body.

The California moray *(G. mordax)* is similar in appearance and habits to the spotted moray. It grows to 5 feet, is found up to 65 feet deep, and may live more than 30 years. The blackedge moray *(G. nigromarginatus)*, prevalent in the subtropical Atlantic, the Caribbean, and the Gulf of Mexico, is of similar size, but the black pattern is more pronounced, with black margins on the dorsal and the anal fins.

Habitat. *Morays live primarily in coral reefs or in similar rocky areas. A moray will anchor the rear half of its body in coral and rocks, allowing the front of its body to sway with the current. In this position, with its mouth agape, it is ready to grasp any prey that comes close. This gaping stance appears menacing, but it is an adaptation suited not only to foraging but also to respiration, allowing the eel to pump water across its gills.*

Eels, Snake

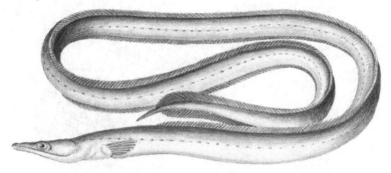

Snake Eel
Ophichtus macrorhynchus

Snake eels in the Ophichthidae family have long, cylindrical, snakelike bodies and can move backward extremely effectively. Their tails are stiff and sharp, rather than broad and flat, as with morays. The snake eel's tail is used like an awl to burrow tail-first into sand or mud. The nostrils are located in two short, stout barbels on top of the nose, which the eel uses to probe into crevices and cavities as it searches for food. Compared to morays and most other eels, snake eels are docile creatures, commonly seen crawling over the bottom like snakes.

In most snake eels, the dorsal fins extend almost the full length of their bodies, beginning just behind their heads but stopping short of the tips of their tails. Their anal fins are only about half as long as their bodies, also stopping before the tips of their tails. Pectoral fins are lacking or very small. Only a few of the profuse species reach a length exceeding 3 feet; most of them are less than a foot long. They are typically brightly colored and are generally strikingly marked with bands, spots, or both. Snake eels are found throughout the world in subtropical and tropical seas, a few ranging into temperate waters.

One of the several dozen species in the Atlantic and the Caribbean is the spotted snake eel *(Ophichtus ophis)*, averaging 2 feet in length and occasionally growing to 4 feet. Its yellowish body is covered with large brown spots. The yellow snake eel *(O. zophochir)* is a similar species that lives in the Pacific.

Another genus represented by numerous species is *Myrichthys*, which includes the sharptail eel *(M. acuminatus)*, in the Atlantic, and the tiger snake eel *(M. tigrinus)*, in the Pacific.

Eulachon
Thaleichthys pacificus

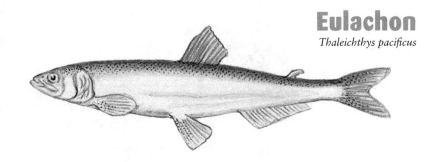

The eulachon is a member of the smelt family, Osmeridae. It is one of the largest members of this family of small Pacific coast fish and has been important to the Chinook Indians. High in oil content (15 percent of its body weight), eulachon used to be dried and fitted with wicks for use as candles.

Like other smelt, the eulachon is important as forage food for Pacific salmon, as well as for marine mammals and birds. It is also harvested or caught commercially and is a highly esteemed seafood by Native Americans from California to Alaska. Although some are hard-salted, these surf smelt are too delicate to be preserved and are generally smoked.

Identification. The eulachon is a small slender fish, with a stubby adipose fin just in front of the tail. The lower jaw projects slightly beyond the tip of the snout. Its coloring is bluish-black on the back, fading to silvery white on the belly. Smelt are so similar in appearance that it is difficult to differentiate among species. Its larger size, however, helps distinguish the eulachon from its relatives.

Size/Age. The eulachon can reach up to 12 inches. It generally lives 2 to 3 years.

Spawning behavior. Eulachon spawn between March and May, when they enter freshwater tributaries from Northern California to the Bering Sea. They mature when they reach 2 to 3 years of age and die following spawning.

Food. The eulachon feeds on planktonic crustaceans.

OTHER NAMES
candlefish, hooligan;
French: *eulachon, eulakane.*

Distribution. *This fish is common throughout cool northern Pacific waters, with a range from west of St. Matthews Island and Kuskokwim Bay in the Bering Sea, and Bowers Bank in the Aleutian Islands to Monterey Bay in California.*

Habitat. *This fish is found near shore and in coastal inlets and rivers. It spends its life at sea prior to spawning.*

Flounder, Gulf

Paralichthys albigutta

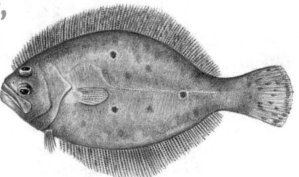

OTHER NAMES
flounder; Spanish:
lenguado tres ojos.

Distribution. *The gulf
flounder generally occurs in
the same range as the
southern flounder; it is common from Cape Lookout,
North Carolina, to Corpus
Christi, Texas, including
southern Florida and the
Bahamas.*

Habitat. *Gulf flounder
inhabit sand, coral rubble,
and seagrass areas near
shore. They often range into
tidal reefs and are occasionally found around nearshore
rocky reefs. They commonly
favor depths of up to 60
feet.*

The gulf flounder is a member of the Bothidae family of left-
eyed flounder and is an excellent table fish. It is one of the
smaller fish in a large group of important sport and commercial flounder. Because of its size, the gulf flounder is of
minor economic significance, and it is mixed in commercial
and sport catches with summer flounder and southern
flounder.

Identification. The gulf flounder has the familiar olive-
brown background of its relatives, the summer and the
southern flounder, but it has three characteristic ocellated
spots forming a triangle on its eye side. One spot is above
the lateral line, one below, and one on the middle, although
these spots can become obscure in larger fish. Numerous
white spots are scattered over the body and the fins
(*albigutta* means "white-spotted"), and the caudal fin is in
the shape of a wedge, with the tip in the middle. This
species has 53 to 63 anal rays, which is fewer than the 63 to
73 found on the southern flounder. Like other flatfish, the
gulf flounder can change color dramatically to match the
bottom.

Size/Age. The average fish is under 2 pounds and
between 6 and 10 inches long, although it is capable of
growing to 15 inches. It is believed to live for at least 3
years. The all-tackle world-record fish is a 5-pounder,
caught in Florida.

Spawning. Spawning season is in the winter offshore.

Food. The gulf flounder feeds on crustaceans and small
fish.

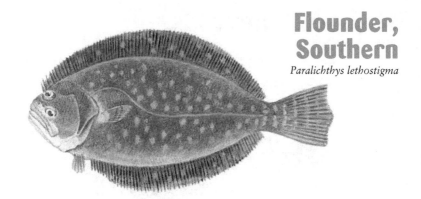

Flounder, Southern

Paralichthys lethostigma

The southern flounder is thought to be the largest Gulf of Mexico flatfish. A member of the Bothidae family of left-eyed flounder, it is a highly desired food fish, and considerable numbers are harvested by trawlers.

Identification. The southern flounder resembles the summer flounder in appearance. Its coloring is light to dark olive-brown, and it is marked with diffused dark blotches and spots, instead of distinct ocelli (spots ringed with distinct lighter areas). These spots often disappear in large fish. The underside is white, the simple fins make an even fringe around the body, and its beady eyes are located extremely close together. It can be distinguished from the summer flounder by having fewer gill rakers and by the presence of distinct spots. It is also similar to the gulf flounder, which has no distinct ocelli.

Size/Age. Mature individuals grow to 36 inches and more than 12 pounds. The average size is 12 to 24 inches and 2 to 3 pounds. The all-tackle record is 20 pounds, 9 ounces. Southern flounder can live up to 20 years in the Gulf of Mexico.

Spawning behavior. Southern flounder spawn in offshore waters. In the northern Gulf of Mexico, they move out of bays and estuaries in the fall; this occurs quickly if there is an abrupt cold snap, but it happens more slowly if there is gradual cooling. Spawning occurs afterward, in the late fall and the early winter. A female typically releases several hundred thousand eggs, which hatch and migrate into the estuaries and change from upright swimmers into left-eyed bottom dwellers.

Food and feeding habits. The southern flounder feeds partly by burying itself in the sand and waiting to ambush its prey. Small flounder consume shrimp and other small crustaceans, whereas larger flounder eat blue crabs, shrimp, and fish such as anchovies, mullet, menhaden, Atlantic croaker, and pinfish.

OTHER NAMES
flatfish, flounder, halibut, mud flounder, plie, southern fluke; Spanish: *lenguado de Floride.*

Distribution. *The southern flounder can be found from North Carolina to northern Mexico, although it is not present in southern Florida.*

Habitat. *As an estuarine-dependent bottom fish, the southern flounder commonly inhabits inshore channels, bay mouths, estuaries, and sometimes freshwater. It is tolerant of a wide range of temperatures (50° to 90°F) and is often found in waters where salinities fluctuate from 0 to 20 parts per thousand. No other flounder of the eastern United States is regularly encountered in this type of environment. Anglers regularly catch this fish inshore from bridges and jetties.*

Flounder, Starry

Platichthys stellatus

OTHER NAMES

rough jacket, great flounder, California flounder,
diamond back, emery-
wheel, emery flounder,
grindstone, sandpaper
flounder; Japanese:
numagarei.

Distribution. *The starry
flounder ranges from central
California to Alaska, and
south from the Bering Sea
to Japan and Korea. This is
one of the most numerous
fish of central Northern California backwaters, particularly in San Francisco Bay.*

Habitat. *It is usually found
near shore over mud, sand,
or gravel bottoms. Often
entering brackish or freshwater, the starry flounder is
most abundant in shallow
water but can be found in
depths of at least 900 feet.
Juveniles are often intertidal.*

The starry flounder is a smaller and less common member
of the Pacific coast Pleuronectidae family of right-eyed
flounder. Flounder and other flatfish are known for their
unique appearance, having both eyes on either the left or
the right side of the head, although the starry flounder can
be either left-eyed or right-eyed.

It is a popular sportfish because of its willingness to bite
and its strong fighting qualities. Although the starry flounder has tasty flesh, it is important mainly as a sportfish, having only moderate commercial value. Processing is difficult
due to its rough skin, and it must be deep-skinned to
remove its unappealing, dark fat layer.

Identification. The starry flounder belongs to the right-
eyed family of flatfish, but, as noted, it can also be left-eyed.
Its head is pointed, and it has a small mouth. The anal spine
is strong. The caudal fin is square or slightly rounded. Its
coloring is olive to dark brown or almost black on the upper
side and creamy white on the blind side. The unpaired fins,
its outstanding feature, are white to yellow to orange with
black bars. There are patches of rough, shiny, starlike scales
scattered over the eyed side of the body, which give rise to
its name.

Size. The average size is 12 to 14 inches, although it can
grow to 3 feet and 20 pounds. Females grow faster than
males and attain larger sizes.

Spawning behavior. Spawning occurs in the late winter
and the early spring in California waters less than 25 fathoms deep.

Food. Adult starry flounder consume a variety of items,
including crabs, clams, shrimp, and sand dollars. Large individuals also eat some fish, such as sardines, sanddabs, and
surfperch.

Flounder, Summer

Paralichthys dentatus

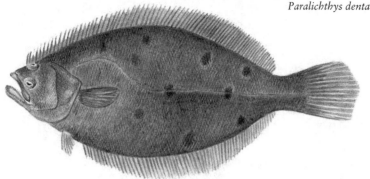

The summer flounder, most commonly called fluke, is a member of the Bothidae family of flatfish, or left-eyed flounder. Fishing for summer flounder off jetties and bridges is a mainstay of mid-Atlantic coastal sportfishing.

Identification. The body is wide and somewhat flattened, rimmed by long dorsal and anal fins. Its mouth is large and well equipped with teeth. The eyes are on the left side of the body and close together. The teeth are well developed on the right side of the jaw. Background coloring is usually gray, brown, or olive but adjusts to the environment to keep the fish camouflaged. There are also many eyespots that change color. The blind side is white and relatively featureless.

Size. The average summer flounder weighs 2 to 5 pounds, the latter being about 23 inches long. It is capable of growing to 35 inches in length but rarely does, and the all-tackle world record is a 22-pound, 7-ounce fish caught at Montauk, New York. Historical data indicate that female summer flounder may live up to 20 years, but males rarely exceed 7 years of age.

Spawning behavior. Sexual maturity is reached at age 3. Spawning takes place during the fall and the winter, while the fish are moving offshore into deeper water or when they reach their winter location. Currents carry newly hatched flounder into the estuaries and sounds, where they undergo a transformation in shape and become bottom dwellers.

Food and feeding habits. Adults are largely piscivorous and highly predatory, feeding actively in midwater, as well as on the bottom. Extremely fast swimmers, they often chase baitfish at the surface, which is not characteristic of most other flatfish. Fluke are known to eat what is available, including shrimp, crabs, menhaden, anchovies, silversides, sand launce, killifish, weakfish, hake, and other flounder.

OTHER NAMES

fluke, northern fluke, flounder; Dutch: *zomervogel;* French: *cardeau d'été.*

Distribution. *The summer flounder occurs in the western Atlantic from Maine to South Carolina and possibly to northeast Florida, and it is most abundant from Cape Cod to North Carolina.*

Habitat. *A bottom-dwelling fish, the summer flounder prefers sandy or muddy bottoms and is common in the summer months in bays, harbors, estuaries, canals, and creeks and along shorelines, as well as in the vicinity of piers and bridges or near patches of eelgrass or other vegetation. It typically prefers relatively shallow waters and depths of up to 100 feet during warmer months, then moves offshore in the winter to deeper, cooler water of 150 to 500 feet.*

Flounder, Winter

Pseudopleuronectes americanus

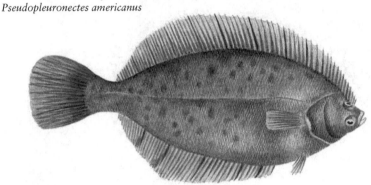

flounder, lemon sole, sole, blackback, blueback, black flounder, dab, mud dab, flatfish, Georges Bank flounder; French: *plie rouge;* Italian: *sogliola limanda;* Spanish: *mendo limon.*

Distribution. Winter flounder are common from Chesapeake Bay north to the Gulf of St. Lawrence. Stragglers occur south to Georgia and north to Labrador.

Habitat. Winter flounder are found inshore in estuaries and coastal ocean areas. In the mid-Atlantic they stay inshore from January through April. Smaller fish occur in shallower water, although larger fish will enter water only a foot deep. They range anywhere from well up into the high-tide mark to depths of at least 400 feet. Preferring sand-mud bottoms, they are also found over sand, clay, or fine gravel and on hard bottom offshore.

One of the most common and well-known flounder of shallow Atlantic coastal waters, the winter flounder belongs to the Pleuronectidae family of flatfish. It is a right-eyed flatfish, with both eyes on the right side of its body, and gets its name because it retreats to cold, deep water in the summer and reappears in shallower water close to shore in the winter; its relative the summer flounder does the opposite.

Identification. The body is oval and flat with a tiny mouth. Color varies from reddish-brown to dark brown with small black spots. The underside is whitish and occasionally brown, tinged with blue around the edges. The caudal fin is slightly rounded. The winter flounder differs from the similar yellowtail flounder in its straight lateral line, no arch over the pectoral fin, thicker body, and widely spaced eyes.

Size. Most winter flounder weigh between 1 and 1½ pounds and average less than a foot in length, although they are capable of growing to 8 pounds and 2 feet. The all-tackle world record is 7 pounds. Larger fish are sometimes called "sea flounder" to distinguish them from the smaller bay fish.

Life history/Behavior. Spawning occurs in shallow water over sandy bottoms from January through May. Winter flounder eggs stick together and sink to the bottom, where they hatch in roughly 16 days, depending on water temperature. These fish move from deep water toward shallow water during the fall and offshore again in the spring.

Food and feeding habits. When on a soft bottom, the winter flounder will lie buried up to its eyes, waiting to attack prey. Because of its small mouth, its diet includes only smaller food like marine worms, small crustaceans, and small shelled animals like clams and snails.

Flyingfish

Atlantic Flyingfish
Cypselurus heterurus

Flyingfish are members of the Exocoetidae family and are closely related to halfbeaks, balao, and needlefish. The flyingfish has normal-length jaws, unlike these other species; the fins are soft rayed and spineless; and the lateral line is extremely low, following the outline of the belly. The dorsal and anal fins are set far back on the body. The pectoral fins of flyingfish are greatly expanded, forming winglike structures. The round eggs are generally equipped with tufts of long filaments that help to anchor the eggs in seaweeds.

These fish travel in schools and are abundant in warm seas. They are an important food fish for pelagic species, especially for billfish, and may be used as rigged trolling bait for bluewater fishing. Flyingfish are readily observed in offshore environs when they suddenly burst through the water's surface and glide for a short distance before reentering the water.

About 22 species are found off the Atlantic and the Pacific coasts of North America. The largest of all North American flyingfish is the California flyingfish *(Cypselurus californicus)*, which may be 1½ feet long. It is found only off the coasts of Southern California and Baja California. It is one of the "four-winged" flyingfish, because the pelvic, as well as the pectoral, fins are large and winglike.

The common Atlantic flyingfish *(C. heterurus;* also *C. melanurus)*, found in warm waters throughout the Atlantic, is two-winged, with a black band extending through the wings. It averages less than 10 inches in length.

Other common species of warm Atlantic and Caribbean waters are the margined flyingfish *(C. cyanopterus)*, the bandwing flyingfish *(C. exsiliens)*, and the short-winged flyingfish *(Parexocoetus mesogaster)*, the latter ranging through all warm seas and noted for shorter wings than found in most species.

OTHER NAMES
French: *exocet;* Spanish: *volador.*

Gag

Mycteroperca microlepis

Distribution. *In the western Atlantic, gags are found from North Carolina (sometimes as far north as Massachusetts) to the Yucatán Peninsula, Mexico, although they are rare in Bermuda and absent from the Caribbean and the Bahamas; they are also reported along Brazil. They are the most common grouper on rocky ledges in the eastern Gulf of Mexico.*

Habitat. *Young gags inhabit estuaries and seagrass beds, whereas adults are usually found offshore around rocky ledges, undercuts, reefs, and occasionally inshore over rocky or grassy bottoms. Adults may be solitary or may occur in groups of 5 to 50 individuals.*

Gags belong to the branch of the grouper family that is characterized by a long, compressed body and 11 to 14 rays in the anal fin. Gags have white, flaky flesh that makes excellent eating, although, like other grouper, they have deeply embedded scales that are virtually impossible to remove.

Identification. Pale to dark gray or sometimes olive gray, the larger gag is darker than the smaller gag and has blotchy markings on its side and an overall indistinctly marbled appearance. The smaller gag is paler and has many dark brown or charcoal marks along its sides. The pelvic, the anal, and the caudal fins are blackish, with blue or white edges. The gag is distinguished from the black grouper by its deeply notched preopercles and is distinguished from the otherwise similar scamp by the absence of extended caudal rays.

Size/Age. The gag weighs less than 3 pounds on average but may reach a weight of 55 pounds (about 51 inches in length). It can live for at least 15 years.

Spawning behavior. Gags reach sexual maturity when 27 to 30 inches long or 5 to 6 years of age, spawning off the Carolinas in February, and from January through March in the Gulf of Mexico. The female may lay more than a million pelagic eggs.

Food. Gags feed on such fish as sardines, porgies, snapper, and grunts, as well as on crabs, shrimp, and squid; young that are less than 20 centimeters feed mainly on crustaceans found in shallow grassbeds.

Goosefish
Lophius americanus

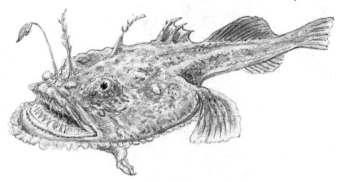

The goosefish has been described as mostly mouth with a tail attached. A member of the Lophiidae family of deep-sea anglerfish, this ugly, bottom-dwelling species of temperate waters is not a targeted gamefish but is occasionally caught by deep-water bottom anglers. More than two dozen species of anglerfish exist worldwide, with the American goosefish the largest among them.

Identification. The American goosefish is dark brown, with a mottling of dark spots and blotches. It has almost armlike pectoral fins located about midway in its greatly flattened body. Small gill openings are just behind them. The head is extremely large for its body size, and the mouth is cavernous, filled with sharp, curved teeth and opening upward. On the tip of the first spine is a flap of flesh that serves as a lure for attracting small fish within grasping range of the mouth. If the prey comes close enough, the goosefish opens its huge mouth and sucks its victim inside.

Size/Age. The growth rate is fairly rapid and similar for both sexes up to about age 4, when they are approximately 19 inches long. After this, females grow a bit more rapidly and seem to live longer, about 12 years, growing to slightly more than 39 inches. Their maximum weight is 50 pounds, and the all-tackle world record is 49 pounds, 12 ounces.

Spawning behavior. Sexual maturity occurs between ages 3 and 4. Spawning takes place from spring through early autumn, depending on latitude. Females lay a nonadhesive, buoyant mucoid egg raft, or veil, which can be as large as 39 feet long and 5 feet wide.

Food. The carnivorous and rapacious goosefish eats a wide array of fish, some nearly as large as itself, as well as assorted crustaceans and squid.

OTHER NAMES

American goosefish, anglerfish, monkfish, lotte, bellyfish, frogfish, sea devil, American angler; French: *baudroie d'Amerique;* Spanish: *rape americano.*

Distribution. *This species ranges from the Grand Banks and the northern Gulf of St. Lawrence south to Cape Hatteras, North Carolina. A similar but smaller species, the blackfin goosefish (L. gastrophysus), occurs in deeper waters from North Carolina to the Gulf of Mexico and south to Argentina.*

Habitat. *Individuals are found from inshore areas to depths exceeding 435 fathoms. Highest concentrations occur between 38 and 55 fathoms and in deeper water at about 100 fathoms. Seasonal migrations occur, apparently related to spawning and food availability.*

Graysby

Cephalopholis cruentata

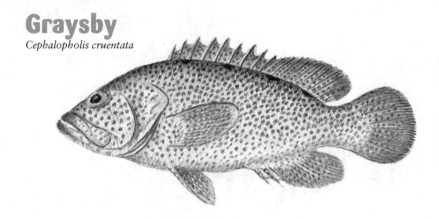

Distribution. *Graysby range from North Carolina to the northern Gulf of Mexico and south to Brazil. They are common in southern Florida, the Bahamas, and the Caribbean and are also found in Bermuda.*

Habitat. *Small ledges and caves in coral beds and reefs are the preferred haunts of graysby, where they blend with the surroundings at depths between 10 and 60 feet.*

A member of the grouper/seabass family, the graysby is a small, secretive reef fish. Graysby are commonly caught on hook and line, but their small size precludes them from being particularly sought after.

Identification. Varying from pale gray to dark brown, the graysby has many darker orangish, red-brown spots on its body, fins, and chin. There are three to five distinctive marks, like pale or dark spots, that run along the base of the dorsal fin. A white line runs between the eyes from the nape to the lower lip. The spots change color, either growing pale or darkening in contrast with the body. The tail of the graysby is more rounded than it is in similar species. There are 9 spines and 14 rays in the soft dorsal fin, compared to 15 to 17 rays in the closely related coney.

Size. The graysby generally grows to a length of 6 to 10 inches and can reach a maximum of 1 foot.

Food. Graysby are nocturnal predators, feeding mainly on fish.

Grouper, Black

Mycteroperca bonaci

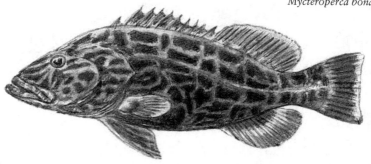

The black grouper is a fairly large and hard-fighting member of the Serranidae family. It is an excellent food fish, although the flesh is occasionally toxic and can cause ciguatera.

Identification. Depending on location, the black grouper may be olive, gray, or reddish-brown to black. It has black, almost rectangular blotches and brassy spots. It can pale or darken until its markings are hardly noticeable. It has a thin, pale border on its pectoral fins, a wide black edge and a thin white margin on its tail, and sometimes a narrow orangish edge to the pectoral fin; the tips of the tail and the soft dorsal and anal fins are bluish or black. The black grouper has a squared-off tail and a gently rounded gill cover.

Size. Regularly reaching 40 pounds, black grouper can grow to more than 100 pounds; the all-tackle world record is shared by two 114-pound fish, one from Texas and the other from Florida. The average length of the black grouper is 1½ to 3 feet; the maximum is 4 feet.

Life history/Behavior. Black grouper spawn between May and August. As in many species of grouper, the young start out predominantly female, transforming into males as they grow larger.

Food and feeding habits. Adult black grouper feed mainly on fish and sometimes squid, and juveniles feed mainly on crustaceans.

OTHER NAMES

rockfish; Portuguese: *badejo-ferro, badejo-quadrado*; Spanish: *bonaci, cuna bonaci, cuna guarei.*

Distribution. *Black grouper occur from Bermuda and Massachusetts to southern Brazil, including the southern Gulf of Mexico, and occur commonly to occasionally in the Florida Keys, the Bahamas, and Cuba and throughout the Caribbean. Adults are unknown on the northeastern coast of the United States.*

Habitat. *Black grouper are found away from shore, near rocky and coral reefs and dropoff walls in water more than 60 feet deep. Although black grouper typically drift just above the bottom, young fish may inhabit shallow water inshore, and adults occasionally frequent open water far above reefs.*

Grouper, Goliath

Epinephelus itajara

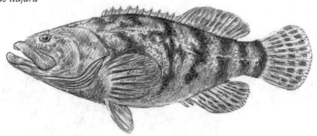

OTHER NAMES

jewfish, spotted jewfish, southern jewfish, junefish, Florida jewfish, esonue grouper; Fon (spoken in Benin): *tokokogbo;* French: *mérou géant;* Portuguese: *garoupa, mero;* Spanish: *cherna, cherne, mero, guasa, meroguasa.*

Distribution. *In the western Atlantic, goliath grouper occur from Florida to southern Brazil, including the Gulf of Mexico and the Caribbean, although they are rare in Florida, the Bahamas, and the Caribbean. In the eastern Pacific, goliath grouper occur from the central Gulf of California to Peru.*

Habitat. *Goliath grouper inhabit inshore waters and are usually found in shallow water at depths between 10 and 100 feet. They prefer rocky bottoms, reefs, ledges, dock and bridge pilings, and wrecks, where they can find refuge in caves and holes.*

The largest grouper and a member of the Serranidae family, the goliath grouper is an important gamefish and an excellent food fish.

Identification. The goliath grouper is yellowish-brown to olive green or brown. Dark brown blotches and blackish spots mottle the entire body, including the head and the fins; these markings are variable and are more prominent on the young. Irregular dark bands run vertically along the sides, although these are usually obscure. The body becomes darker with age, as the blotches and spots increase and become less noticeable in contrast to the body. The first dorsal fin is shorter than, and not separated from, the second dorsal fin. The goliath grouper is differentiated from the giant sea bass by its dorsal fin soft rays, of which it has 15 to 16; the giant sea bass has only 10.

Distinctive features also include very small eyes, a rounded tail fin, and large rounded pectoral fins. Specimens smaller than 1½ feet long bear a strong resemblance to spotted cabrilla but can be distinguished by the number of dorsal spines, of which the goliath grouper has 11 and the spotted cabrilla 10.

Size/Age. Goliath grouper can reach 8 feet in length and 700 pounds in weight. Although the average fish weighs roughly 20 pounds, weights of 100 pounds are not unusual, nor are 4- to 6-foot lengths. The all-tackle world record is a 680-pounder. They have been known to live for 30 to 50 years.

Life history/Behavior. There is some indication that the goliath grouper starts out as a female and undergoes a sex change later in life, as occurs in certain grouper. Spawning takes place over the summer months.

Food and feeding habits. A sluggish but opportunistic feeder, the goliath grouper feeds chiefly on crustaceans, especially spiny lobsters, as well as on turtles, fish, and stingrays.

Grouper, Nassau

Epinephelus striatus

The most important commercial grouper in the West Indies and a member of the Serranidae family, the Nassau grouper has been very heavily fished and is continually vulnerable to overfishing, especially during its spawning and migrating seasons.

Identification. Although its color pattern varies, the Nassau grouper usually has a light background, with a wide, dark brown stripe running from the tip of the snout through each eye to the start of the dorsal fin, as well as four to five irregular dark bars running vertically along the sides. Two distinctive features are the black dots always present around the eyes, and a large black saddle on the caudal peduncle, also always present no matter what color the fish is. The third spine of the dorsal fin is longer than the second, the pelvic fins are shorter than the pectoral fins, and the dorsal fin is notched between the spines. It has the ability to change color, from pale to almost black.

Size. The Nassau grouper is usually 1 to 2 feet in length, reaching a maximum of 4 feet and about 55 pounds, although most catches are under 10 pounds. The all-tackle world record is a 38-pound, 8-ounce Bahamian fish.

Spawning behavior. Spawning around the new moon, Nassau grouper come together in large masses of up to 30,000, making them highly vulnerable to overharvesting.

Food. Nassau grouper feed mainly on fish and crabs and, to a lesser degree, on other crustaceans and mollusks.

OTHER NAMES

hamlet; Creole: *negue;* French: *mérou rayé;* Spanish: *cherna criolla, mero gallina.*

Distribution. In the western Atlantic, Nassau grouper are found in Bermuda, Florida, the Bahamas, and the Yucatán Peninsula, and throughout the Caribbean to southern Brazil. They are absent from the Gulf of Mexico, except at Campeche Bay off the coast of Yucatán, at Tortugas, and off Key West.

Habitat. Found in depths of 20 to 100 feet, although almost always dwelling in less than 90 feet of water, Nassau grouper prefer caves and shallow to midrange coral reefs. Smaller fish are usually closer to shore and common in seagrass beds; adults are usually farther offshore on rocky reefs. Nassau grouper tend to rest on the bottom, blending with their surroundings. They are usually solitary and diurnal but occasionally form schools.

Grouper, Red

Epinephelus morio

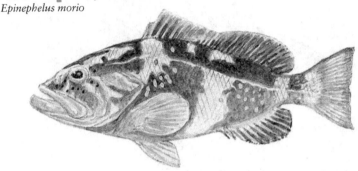

OTHER NAMES

grouper; Portuguese: *garoupa de Sao Tomé;* Spanish: *cherna americana, cherna de vivero, mero americano, mero paracamo.*

Distribution. *In the western Atlantic, red grouper range from North Carolina to southern Brazil, including the Gulf of Mexico, the Caribbean, and Bermuda; some fish stray as far as Massachusetts. They are found only occasionally in Florida and the Bahamas and rarely in the Caribbean.*

Habitat. *Red grouper are bottom-dwelling fish, occurring over rocky and muddy bottoms, at the margins of seagrass beds, and in ledges, crevices, and caverns of rocky limestone reefs; they are uncommon around coral reefs. They prefer depths of 6 to 400 feet, although they more commonly hold between 80 and 400 feet. Red grouper are usually solitary, resting on the bottom and blending with their surroundings.*

The red grouper was one of the most abundant grouper in the Caribbean and surrounding waters until spearfishing and general overfishing depleted its numbers.

Identification. Of varying coloration, the red grouper is usually dark brownish-red, especially around the mouth, and may have dark bars and blotches similar to those on the Nassau grouper, as well as a few small whitish blotches scattered in an irregular pattern. It is distinguished from the Nassau grouper by its lack of a saddle spot and its smooth, straight front dorsal fin. On the Nassau grouper the dorsal fin is notched. It has a blackish tinge to the soft dorsal, the anal, and the tail fins; pale bluish margins on the rear dorsal, the anal, and the tail fins; and small black spots around the eyes. The lining of the mouth is scarlet to orange. The second spine of the dorsal fin is longer than the others, the pectoral fins are longer than the pelvic fins, and the tail is distinctively squared off.

Size/Age. The red grouper is commonly 1 to 2 feet long and weighs up to 15 pounds, although it can reach 3½ feet and 50 pounds. The male red grouper lives longer than the female does and has been known to live for 25 years.

Spawning behavior. Like many other grouper, red grouper undergo a sex reversal; females transform into males, in this case between ages 7 and 14, or when they are 18 to 26 inches long. Spawning takes place from March through July, with a flurry of activity in April and May, in water temperatures ranging from 63° to 77°F and in depths between 80 and 300 feet.

Food and feeding habits. Red grouper feed on a wide variety of fish, invertebrates, and crustaceans, including squid, crabs, shrimp, lobsters, and octopus.

Grouper, Warsaw
Epinephelus nigritus

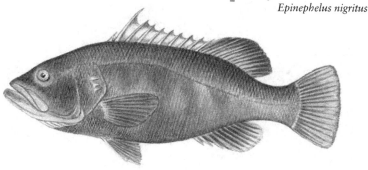

The warsaw grouper is one of the largest members of the Serranidae family of grouper and sea bass, second only to the goliath grouper in size. It has white, flaky meat that is marketed fresh. It is more widespread than the goliath grouper and caught more frequently.

Identification. The warsaw grouper has a gray-brown or dark red-brown body, occasionally irregularly spotted with several small, white blotches on the sides and the dorsal fins, although these are indiscernible in death. The young warsaw has a yellow tail and a dark saddle on the caudal peduncle. The warsaw is distinctive as the only grouper with 10 dorsal spines, the second of which is much longer than the third. It also has a squared-off tail. In contrast to the goliath grouper, the rays of the first dorsal fin on the warsaw grouper are much higher and the head is much larger.

Size/Age. The average weight of the warsaw grouper is roughly 20 pounds or less, although 100-pound fish are not uncommon. It can reach a length of 6½ feet and can weigh up to 580 pounds. The all-tackle world record is a 436-pound, 12-ounce Florida fish. The warsaw grouper grows slowly and can live as long as 25 to 30 years.

Spawning behavior. The eggs and the larvae of the warsaw grouper are thought to be pelagic, although little else is known about spawning and other behavior.

Food and feeding habits. Warsaw grouper feed on crabs, shrimp, lobsters, and fish, swallowing prey whole after ambushing it or after a short chase.

OTHER NAMES

Spanish: *mero de lo alto, mero negro.*

Distribution. *In the western Atlantic, warsaw grouper range from Massachusetts to the Gulf of Mexico and south to Río de Janeiro in Brazil, although they are rare in Cuba, Haiti, and Trinidad. They are otherwise fairly common along both coasts of Florida.*

Habitat. *Usually found over rough, rocky bottoms, deep rocky ledges, and dropoffs, warsaw grouper prefer depths of 300 to 1,000 feet. Young warsaw grouper are occasionally seen or caught near jetties and shallow-water reefs.*

Grouper, Yellowfin

Mycteroperca venenosa

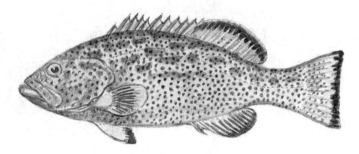

OTHER NAMES

princess rockfish, red rockfish; Spanish: *arigua, bonaci cardenal, cuna cucaracha, cuna de piedra.*

Distribution. *Found in the western Atlantic, the yellowfin grouper is most common in Bermuda, Florida, and the southern Gulf of Mexico, and it ranges to Brazil.*

Habitat. *Young yellowfin grouper prefer shallow turtlegrass beds, and adults occur on offshore rocky and coral reefs. They also hold over mud bottoms in the northern Gulf of Mexico.*

The scientific name of this member of the Serranidae family means "venomous," a reference to the yellowfin grouper's association with ciguatera poisoning. Despite this, its flesh is good to eat and is usually considered safe for commercial sale.

Identification. The yellowfin grouper has highly variable coloring, usually with a pale background and horizontal rows of darker, rectangular blotches covering the entire fish; the ends of these blotches are rounded, and they can be black, gray, brown, olive green, or red. There are also small dark spots running across the body, which grow smaller toward the belly and usually appear bright red. The outer third of the pectoral fins is bright yellow, whereas the tail has a thin, dark, irregular edge. An overall reddish cast is present in fish from deep water, and the yellowfin grouper has the ability to change color dramatically or to pale or darken.

Size. The yellowfin grouper is common to 20 pounds in weight and 3 feet in length; the all-tackle world record is a 40-pound, 12-ounce Texas fish caught in 1995.

Life history. As with other grouper, the yellowfin undergoes a sex reversal, transforming from female to male in the latter part of life.

Food. Yellowfin grouper feed mostly on coral reef species of fish and squid.

Grunion, California
Leuresthes tenuis

The California grunion is a member of the Atherinidae family of fish known as silversides. It is an important forage species for predator fish; in season, large numbers of anglers gather on the beaches to fill buckets with grunion that are undergoing a remarkable spawning ritual in the sand.

Identification. The California grunion has an elongate body and head that are more or less compressed. The mouth is small, and the scales are small, smooth, and firm. Its coloration is bluish-green above and silvery below; a bright silvery band tinged with blue and bordered above with violet extends the length of the body.

Size/Age. The maximum known size of grunion is 7½ inches. The life span is usually 3 years, with some individuals surviving 4 years.

Life history/Behavior. The most rapid growth takes place during the first year, at the end of which they are 5 inches long and capable of spawning. The spawning behavior of grunion is one of the more unusual among all marine fish. Females, accompanied by one to eight males, swim onto the beach with an incoming wave, dig themselves into the sand up to their pectoral fins, and lay their eggs. The males wrap themselves around the female and fertilize the eggs. With the next wave, the fish return to the sea. Thus, the spawning process is effected in the short period of time between waves. Most females spawn from four to eight times a year, and thousands of the fish may be along the beach at a time.

Spawning takes place from early March through September and then only for 3 or 4 nights following the full moon, during the 1 to 4 hours immediately after high tide.

Food. The feeding habits of this species are not well known; however, they subsist on small crustaceans and fish eggs.

OTHER NAMES
smelt, little smelt, grunion, lease smelt.

Distribution. *The California grunion occurs from Magdalena Bay, Baja California, to San Francisco; however, the principal range is between Point Abreojos, Baja California, and Point Conception, California. A similar species, the gulf grunion (L. sardina), is restricted to the Gulf of California.*

Habitat. *California grunion are nonmigratory and are most often found in schools a short distance from shore in water 15 to 40 feet deep.*

Grunt, Bluestriped

Haemulon sciurus

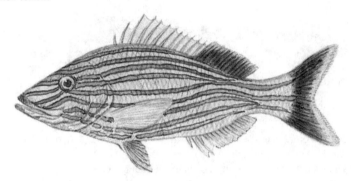

OTHER NAMES

Spanish: *ronco catire.*

Distribution. The bluestriped grunt is common from southern Florida through the Caribbean to the West Indies and southward along the Gulf of Mexico and along the coast of Central and South America to Brazil.

Habitat. The bluestriped grunt drifts along reefs, especially near the deep edges. It remains relatively close to the shore in shallow water from 12 to 50 feet deep. Juveniles are found in seagrass beds in bays, lagoons, and coastal waters.

Frequently used as an aquarium fish when young because of its magnificent coloring, the bluestriped grunt is also considered an excellent table fish and is easily caught on natural bait.

Identification. The bluestriped grunt is distinguished from all other grunts by its color pattern of continuous blue horizontal stripes over a yellow-gold body. The tail and the dorsal fins are dark and dusky with a yellow tinge. Other fins are yellow. The inside of its mouth is blood red. It has 12 dorsal spines, 16 to 17 dorsal rays, and 9 anal rays.

Size. Its average length is up to 1 foot, but it can reach as much as 18 inches in length.

Behavior. A schooling fish, the bluestriped grunt gathers in medium-size groups along reefs during the day. Scaring easily, the grunt will swim away quickly when slightly startled.

Feeding habits. Adults feed on the bottom at night over open sandy, muddy, or grassy areas, primarily foraging on crustaceans. They also consume bivalves and occasionally small fish.

Grunt, French

Haemulon flavolineatum

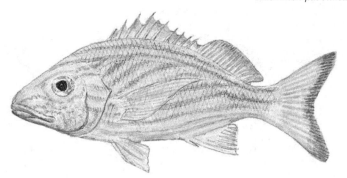

The French grunt is one of the most abundant panfish in southern Florida. These and other grunts often make up the largest biomass on reefs in continental shelf areas. Although it is too small to be of commercial value, the French grunt is an excellent panfish. It is also a common aquarium fish.

Identification. Its coloring is white to bluish or yellowish, with bright-yellow stripes. The stripes set below the lateral line are diagonal. There are yellow spots on the bottom of the head. The fins are yellow, and the inside of the mouth is blood red. It has 14 to 15 dorsal rays, 8 anal rays, and 16 to 17 pectoral rays.

Size. The average length is 6 to 10 inches, although this fish can reach 12 inches.

Behavior. The French grunt is a schooling fish, drifting in small to large groups that can number in the thousands. The schools travel in shadows during the day. Juveniles hide in grassbeds in bays, lagoons, and coastal waters.

Feeding habits. French grunts are nocturnal bottom feeders that scavenge sand flats and grassbeds near reefs for crustaceans.

OTHER NAMES
Spanish: *ronco amarillo.*

Distribution. The French grunt is abundant in Florida, the Bahamas, and the Caribbean. It also inhabits the waters of South Carolina, Bermuda, and the Gulf of Mexico, and south to Brazil.

Habitat. Preferring shallower water close to shore, the French grunt inhabits coastlines and deeper coral reefs in depths from 12 to 60 feet. Grunt populations are less prominent around islands lacking large expanses of grassbeds and sand flats.

Grunt, White

Haemulon plumieri

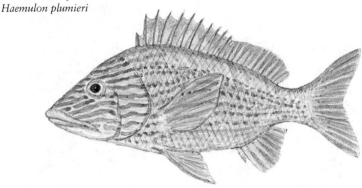

OTHER NAMES

redmouth; Spanish: *ronco margariteño.*

Distribution. *The white grunt exists in the western Atlantic, from the Chesapeake Bay throughout the Caribbean and the Gulf of Mexico south to Brazil. It was reportedly introduced unsuccessfully to Bermuda.*

Habitat. *White grunts prefer shallower water from nearshore to outer reef areas.*

The white grunt is a wide-ranging and abundant fish. This and other grunts often make up the largest biomass on reefs in continental shelf areas. The white grunt has some commercial value, as it grows to larger sizes than do most other grunts, and it is a tasty panfish that is also commonly used in aquariums.

Identification. One of the more colorful grunts, this fish has a silver-gray body, with moderate yellow body striping and numerous blue and yellow stripes on its head. The scales may be tipped with bronze and produce a checkered pattern. The inside of the mouth is red. It has 12 dorsal spines and 15 to 17 dorsal rays, 8 to 9 anal rays, and 17 pectoral rays.

Age/Size. The average length and weight are 8 to 14 inches and about a pound, although white grunts can reach 25 inches and weigh 8 pounds. They are reported to live up to 13 years.

Life history/Behavior. Like other grunts, this species is a schooling fish, often found in large groups. Schools travel in shadows during the day and are often located along the edges of reefs and at the base of coral formations. Fish are sexually mature at about 10 inches, and spawning takes place in the southeastern United States in the late spring and the summer.

Food and feeding habits. White grunts are bottom feeders that root in the sand and the bottom matter near reefs. They feed on worms, shrimp, crabs, mollusks, and small fish.

Guaguanche
Sphyraena guachancho

A member of the barracuda family, the guaguanche is a long, slender, silvery fish often mistaken for a young great barracuda. There is no concerted sportfishing effort for the species, but it is occasionally caught by anglers.

Identification. Silvery olive-brown above, the guaguanche has silvery sides with a yellow to golden stripe running along the middle of its body. Like other members of the barracuda family, it has an elongated body and large canine and shearing teeth. Its caudal fin is large, forked, and blackish, and it has widely separated dorsal fins. The pelvic fin begins below a point just in front of the first dorsal fin, which distinguishes it from the similar-looking sennet. On the young guaguanche, there are three broad bars at the rear of the body that are often interrupted in the middle of each side.

Size. The guaguanche can grow to 2 feet, although it more commonly measures 6 to 14 inches.

Food. Guaguanche feed on fish and shrimp.

OTHER NAMES
guachanche barracuda; Spanish: *picuda guaguanche;* French: *bécune guachanche.*

Distribution. *Found occasionally in Florida, the Bahamas, and the Caribbean, guaguanche occur from Massachusetts to the northern Gulf of Mexico and south to Brazil.*

Habitat. *Guaguanche inhabit shallow and generally turbid coastal waters, including sand flats, grassbeds, mud bottoms, bays, and estuaries, although they are rare around reefs. The guaguanche is a schooling species, forming schools at depths from 3 to 40 feet, and can be found near the surface at night.*

Guitarfish, Atlantic

Rhinobatos lentiginosus

OTHER NAMES

French: *poisson-guitarre tacheté;* Italian: *pesce violino;* Spanish: *guitarra.*

Distribution. *Atlantic guitarfish extend from North Carolina to the Gulf of Mexico, although they are not reported in the Bahamas or the Caribbean and are uncommon in Florida and the Yucatán. The Brazilian guitarfish (R. horkeli) and the southern guitarfish (R. percellens) are two closely related species that range from the West Indies to Brazil.*

Habitat. *Inhabiting sandy and weedy bottoms, Atlantic guitarfish are found near small reefs, usually buried in seagrass, sand, or mud at depths of 1 to 45 feet.*

A cross between a skate and a shark in appearance, the Atlantic guitarfish is a member of the Rajiformes family, along with the skate and the ray. It is occasionally encountered by anglers but is not a targeted species.

Identification. The head and the pectoral fins of the Atlantic guitarfish form a triangular disk at the front of the body. The rear of the body is thick and tapered like a shark's, and it has two large dorsal fins and a well-developed caudal fin. The Atlantic guitarfish varies in color from gray to brown, with several pale spots on its body.

Size. This species is normally 1 to 2 feet long and can attain a maximum length of 2½ feet. Females are somewhat larger than males.

Life history. Atlantic guitarfish are ovoviviparous, which means they bear live young, with up to six in a litter. At birth they are 20 centimeters long.

Food. Small mollusks and crustaceans form the diet of the guitarfish.

Haddock
Melanogrammus aeglefinus

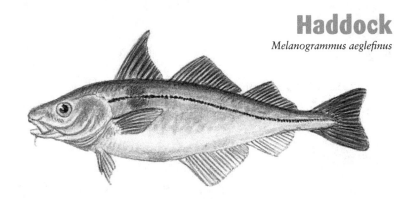

Closely related to the genus *Gadus,* the haddock is often considered a member of the Gadidae, or codfish, family. Haddock have long been important commercially and are an even more highly valued food fish than Atlantic cod, although stocks of haddock have declined rapidly since the 1960s due to overfishing.

Identification. The haddock has three dorsal fins and two anal fins; the first dorsal fin is high and pointed. The small chin barbel is sometimes hidden. Its coloring is purplish gray on the back and sides, fading to pinkish reflections and a white belly. There is a black lateral line along the side and a black shoulder blotch. The dark lateral line and the shoulder blotch can distinguish it from its close relatives in the cod family. Three dorsal fins distinguish the haddock from its relative the silver hake *(see: Hake, Silver).*

Size/Age. The average haddock is 1 to 2 feet long and weighs 1 to 5 pounds. The all-tackle record is 11 pounds, 3 ounces, but they have been reported to attain 16½ pounds. Haddock can live for 14 years.

Life history/Behavior. The spawning season is between January and June, and activity peaks during late March and early April, when large congregations form in depths of 20 to 100 fathoms. Major spawning concentrations occur on eastern Georges Bank, although some spawning also occurs to the east of Nantucket Shoals and along the Maine coast.

Haddock swim in large schools, and there is some seasonal migration to the north in the spring and south again in the fall. Adult haddock on Georges Bank appear to be relatively sedentary, but seasonal coastal movements occur in the western Gulf of Maine. There are extensive migrations in the Barents Sea and off Iceland.

Food and feeding habits. Primarily consuming crabs, snails, worms, clams, and sea urchins, the haddock seldom feeds actively on fish.

OTHER NAMES
haddie, scrod; French: *eglefin;* Italian: *asinello;* Norwegian: *kolje;* Portuguese: *arinca, bacalhau;* Spanish: *eglefino.*

Distribution. In North America the haddock is found from Newfoundland and Nova Scotia southward to southern New Jersey. It occasionally inhabits the deep water to Cape Hatteras. The highest concentrations off the U.S. coast occur on the northern and the eastern sections of Georges Bank and in the southwestern Gulf of Maine. Two stocks occur in U.S. waters: the Gulf of Maine stock and the Georges Bank stock.

Habitat. Preferring deeper water than do cod, haddock inhabit depths of 25 to 75 fathoms. Although generally a coldwater species, preferring temperatures of 36° to 50° F, they are commonly found in warm water over bottoms of sand, pebbles, or broken shells.

Hagfish

Atlantic Hagfish
Myxine glutinosa

Hagfish are one of two groups of jawless fish (the other being lampreys), which are the most primitive true vertebrates. They are members of the Petromyzontidae family. Fishlike vertebrates, jawless fish are similar to eels in form, with a cartilaginous or fibrous skeleton that has no bones. They have no paired limbs and no developed jaws or bony teeth. Their extremely slimy skin lacks scales.

The repulsive-looking hag is the most primitive of all living fish, resembling an outsize, slimy worm. The hag is exclusively marine, and only one family, Myxinidae, is known. The hag has the ability to discharge slime from its mucous sacs, which are far out of proportion to its size.

Their habit of feeding primarily on dead or disabled fish makes hagfish doubly unattractive. Commercial fishermen consider them a great nuisance because they penetrate the bodies of hooked or gillnetted fish, eating out first the intestines and then the meat, leaving nothing but skin and bones. The hagfish bores into the cavity of its victim by means of a rasplike tongue. Unlike many lampreys *(see)*, it is not a parasite. Hags' eyes are not visible externally, and they are considered blind. Food is apparently detected by scent, and large numbers of hags are often taken in deep-set eel pots baited with dead fish.

The hag can be differentiated from its close relative the lamprey, by the following characteristics: The hag has prominent barbels on its snout, no separate dorsal fin, eyes that are not visible externally, a nasal opening at the tip of the snout, and a mouth that is not funnelshaped or disklike. The largest hags are 2 feet or more in length. They range the cold, deep waters, and at least one specimen was recorded at a depth of 4,380 feet.

Hake, Pacific
Merluccius productus

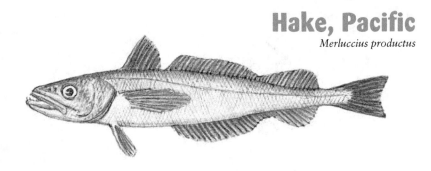

A member of the Merlucciidae family, the Pacific hake is sometimes classified as a member of the Gadidae family and thus included with codfish. It is the only representative of the hake family in the Pacific. Common in commercial and sport catches because of its abundance, the Pacific hake is not generally sought for its food value, but it is made into fish meal. Because it does not remain fresh very long, once caught, it must be immediately chilled or the flesh becomes soft and undesirable.

Many Pacific hake are caught incidentally by anglers fishing for salmon or bottom fish and are generally discarded.

Identification. The body of the Pacific hake is elongate, slender, and moderately compressed. The head is elongate and the mouth large, with strong, sharp teeth. The thin scales fall off readily. Its coloring is gray to dusky brown, with brassy overtones and black speckles on the back.

The elongated shape, the notched second dorsal and anal fin, and the coloration separate the Pacific hake from other similar fish in its family.

Size. The Pacific hake can grow to 3 feet in length. The all-tackle record is 2 pounds, 2 ounces.

Life history/Behavior. Spawning occurs in the winter or from February through April, beginning at 3 to 4 years of age, off Southern California and Baja California, Mexico. After spawning, the adults migrate northward to Oregon, Washington, and Canada and return to their spawning areas in the fall. This species is classified as demersal but is largely pelagic in oceanic and coastal areas. Adults exist in large schools in waters overlying the continental shelf, except during the spawning season, when they are several hundred miles seaward.

Food. The Pacific hake feeds on a variety of small fish, shrimp, and squid.

OTHER NAMES
Pacific whiting, whitefish, haddock, butterfish, California hake, popeye, silver hake, ocean whitefish; French: *merlu du Pacifique nord;* Spanish: *merluza del Pacífico norte.*

Distribution. *This fish occurs in the Gulf of California (isolated population) and from Magdalena Bay, Baja California, to Alaska.*

Habitat. *The Pacific hake prefers a deep, sandy environment and has been reported in depths exceeding 2,900 feet.*

Hake, Red

Urophycis chuss

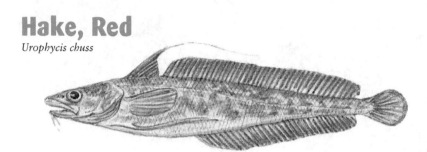

squirrel hake, ling; French: *merluche éureuil;* Spanish: *locha roja.*

Distribution. *Red hake are found from the Gulf of St. Lawrence to North Carolina but are most abundant between Georges Bank and New Jersey. Research from bottom-trawl surveys indicates that red hake have a broad geographic and depth distribution throughout the year, undergoing extensive seasonal migrations. Two stocks have been assumed, divided north and south in the central Georges Bank region.*

Habitat. *These fish generally occupy deep water over soft or sandy bottoms. Although juvenile fish may frequent shallow water along the coast, adults typically migrate to deeper water, generally between 300 and 400 feet deep, although reports indicate that they exist at depths greater than 1,650 feet.*

Red hake are somewhat of an incidental catch for deep-water anglers and have become less significant to commercial trawlers. Although not considered overexploited, red hake are now caught commercially at much lower levels than previously.

Identification. The body of the red hake is elongate with two dorsal fins—the second one long—and one long anal fin. Its coloration is variable, but the sides are usually reddish and often dark or mottled. The fins are not dark-edged, as they are in some other hake, and the pelvic fin rays are shorter than those of other hake.

Size/Age. The maximum length reached by red hake is approximately 50 centimeters, or about 19½ inches. Their maximum age is reported to be about 12 years, but few fish survive beyond 8 years of age. The all-tackle world record is 7 pounds, 15 ounces, which is their known maximum size; the common size is roughly 2 pounds.

Life history/Behavior. Red hake winter in the deep waters of the Gulf of Maine and along the outer continental shelf and slope south and southwest of Georges Bank. Spawning occurs from May through November, and significant spawning areas are located on the southwest part of Georges Bank and in southern New England south of Montauk Point, Long Island.

Food and feeding habits. Red hake feed primarily on crustaceans, but adult red hake also feed extensively on fish.

Hake, Silver

Merluccius bilinearis

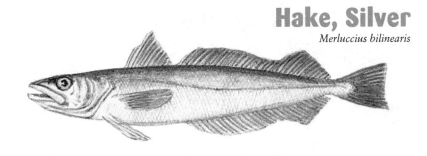

A member of the Merlucciidae family, the silver hake is primarily known as whiting. An aggressive fish and a swift swimmer, it is a good species for sportfishing.

Identification. The body of the whiting is long and slender, with a flattened head, a large mouth, and strong, sharp teeth. The second dorsal fin and the anal fin are deeply indented, giving the fin a divided appearance. The first fin is short and high. Its coloring is dark gray above, with iridescent purple hues that fade to silvery white on the belly. It has only two dorsal fins and one anal fin and lacks a chin barbel.

Size/Age. The whiting can reach 2½ feet in length and a weight of 8 pounds, although the average catch is a fish of less than 14 inches; fish exceeding 4 pounds are rare. Ages up to 15 years have been reported.

Spawning behavior. Spawning occurs in the late spring and the early summer, when whiting release their buoyant eggs at the surface, allowing them to drift with the current. Future stocks depend on the weather; if the wind blows the eggs away from inshore, very few will survive, having nothing to feed on. Peak spawning occurs earlier in the southern stock (May and June) than in the northern stock (July and August). Important spawning areas include the coastal region of the Gulf of Maine from Cape Cod to Grand Manan Island, southern and southeastern Georges Bank, and southern New England south of Martha's Vineyard.

Food and feeding habits. Whiting feed aggressively in large groups on herring, silversides, menhaden, and young mackerel, and on squid and other invertebrates. They have been known to strand themselves on shoals and in shallow waters during the height of their feeding activity after spawning.

OTHER NAMES

Atlantic hake, whiting, frostfish; French: *merlu argenté;* Spanish: *merluza norte-americana.*

Distribution. *Found from the Newfoundland banks southward to the vicinity of South Carolina, the whiting is encountered in large numbers between Cape Sable and New York. In U.S. waters, two stocks have been identified, based on morphological differences; one extends from the Gulf of Maine to northern Georges Bank, and the second occurs from southern Georges Bank to the mid-Atlantic area.*

Habitat. *Whiting primarily inhabit the cool, deep waters of the continental shelf. Adults stay in deep water offshore but make seasonal onshore-offshore migrations. They range from near the surface to over 600 feet deep. They prefer sand and pebble bottoms and temperatures between 36° and 52°F. Whiting move toward shallow water in the spring, spawn, and return to the wintering areas in the autumn.*

Halfbeaks and Balao

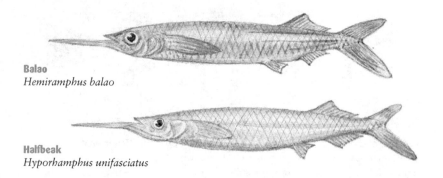

Balao
Hemiramphus balao

Halfbeak
Hyporhamphus unifasciatus

OTHER NAMES
French: *demi-bec;* Spanish:
aguja, agujeta, saltador.

Halfbeaks are closely related to flyingfish and needlefish. These sparkling, silvery fish travel in schools and are abundant in warm seas. They are important food fish for pelagic species, especially for billfish, and are used as rigged trolling bait for big-game fish encountered in blue water.

A halfbeak's body is elongated, rounded, and flattened from side to side only in the tail region. The dorsal and the anal fins are located far to the rear and directly opposite each other. In halfbeaks, only the lower jaw is long; the upper jaw is of normal length. Halfbeaks commonly leap or scoot rapidly across the surface, with only their tail vibrating in the water.

The balao *(Hemiramphus balao)* ranges from New York to the Gulf of Mexico and southward to Brazil, including the Caribbean. It averages 8 to 10 inches in length and can grow to 16 inches. The ballyhoo *(Hemiramphus brasiliensis)* is common off the Florida coast and in the Caribbean, traveling northward along the eastern coast and occasionally as far north as Massachusetts in summer. It ranges as far south as Brazil, averages 6 to 10 inches in length, and is closely related to the longfin halfbeak *(H. saltator)* of the Pacific.

The halfbeak *(Hyporhamphus unifasciatus),* which attains 12 inches, lives in the same area of the Atlantic as the ballyhoo but occurs also in the Pacific from Point Conception southward to Peru, including the Galápagos Islands. The related California halfbeak *(H. rosae)* is smaller, rarely more than 6 inches long.

Included among the Pacific halfbeaks off the coast of North America is the ribbon halfbeak *(Euleptorhamphus viridis),* which grows to as much as 18 inches and has long pectoral fins, and the smaller flying halfbeak *(E. velox),* which ranges from the Gulf of Mexico to Brazil in the western Atlantic.

Halibut, Atlantic

Hippoglossus hippoglossus

The Atlantic halibut is among the largest bony fish in the world and a member of the Pleuronectidae family of right-eyed flounder. The flounder has a unique type of maturation from larvae to adult stage, in which one eye migrates to the opposite side of the head.

The Atlantic halibut is a highly prized table fish, with white, tender flesh, but it is such a deep-dwelling fish that it is seldom deliberately pursued by anglers. It may be caught incidentally by anglers fishing for other deep-ocean dwellers. It has historically been an extremely important market species, but it has been greatly overfished by commercial interests, who primarily catch it by bottom longlining.

Identification. The body is wide and somewhat flattened, rimmed by long dorsal and anal fins. The lateral line, which has a scale count of about 160, arches strongly above the pectoral fin. The dorsal fin has 98 to 106 rays and the anal fin has 73 to 80 rays. The teeth are equally well equipped in both sides of the jaw. Its coloring is usually pearly white and featureless on the blind side. Some specimens, nicknamed "cherry-bellies," have a reddish tint on the blind side.

Size. Atlantic halibut weighing between 300 and 700 pounds have been reported, and the all-tackle rod-and-reel record is 355 pounds.

Spawning behavior. Spawning occurs from late winter through early spring in deep water. The eastern Atlantic fish spawn from March through May. A female can release up to 2 million eggs, and the fish move shallower after spawning.

Food and feeding habits. The Atlantic halibut is a voracious feeder, pursuing its prey in the open water. It forages primarily on fish, including cod and their relatives—ocean perch, herring, skates, mackerel, and other flounder. It also eats crabs, mussels, lobsters, and clams.

OTHER NAMES
common halibut, giant halibut, right-eyed flounder, chicken halibut (under 20 pounds); Dutch: *heilbot;* Finnish: *ruijanpallas;* French: *flétan de l'Atlantique;* Icelandic: *heilagfiski;* Japanese: *ohyö;* Norwegian: *kveite;* Portuguese: *alabote;* Spanish: *fletán del Atlántico, hipogloso;* Swedish: *hälleflundra, helgeflundra.*

Distribution. *The Atlantic halibut occurs in North Atlantic waters; in North America it ranges from Labrador to Virginia. This species does not occur in near-freezing polar waters, as many people believe; there, it is replaced by the Greenland halibut (Reinhardtius hippoglossoides).*

Habitat. *A deep-water species, the Atlantic halibut seldom enters water shallower than about 200 feet and is commonly found to 3,000 feet. It inhabits cold (40° to 50°F) water over sand, gravel, or clay bottoms.*

Halibut, California

Paralichthys californicus

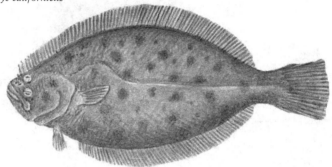

OTHER NAMES
flatty, flattie, fly swatter (small), barn door (large), alabato, Monterey halibut, chicken halibut, southern halibut, California flounder, bastard halibut, portsider; Spanish: *lenguado de California*.

Distribution. *This species occurs from Magdalena Bay, Baja California, Mexico, to the Quillayute River, British Columbia. A separate population exists in the Gulf of California in Mexico.*

Habitat. *Found mostly over sandy bottoms, California halibut appear beyond the surf line and in bays and estuaries. They range from near shore to 600 feet deep but are most commonly caught in 60 to 120 feet of water. They are not known to make extensive migrations.*

The California halibut is a large flatfish and a member of the Bothidae family, or left-eyed flounder. It is the largest and most abundant flatfish within its range, although it is greatly smaller than the more northerly Pacific halibut. It is an important commercial quarry and sportfish, one that is often deliberately sought by anglers and valued for its excellent firm, white flesh.

Identification. The body of the California halibut is oblong and compressed. The head is small and the mouth large. Although a member of the left-eyed flounder family, about 40 percent of California halibut have their eyes on the right side. The color is dark brown to black on the eyed side and white on the blind side. The gill rakers are slender and numerous, totaling about 29 on the first arch. Its numerous teeth, its very large mouth, and a high arch in the middle of the "top" side above the pectoral fin make it easily distinguishable from other flatfish.

Size. The largest California halibut recorded was 5 feet long and weighed 72 pounds. The all-tackle rod-and-reel record weighed 59 pounds, 9 ounces. Females grow larger, live longer, and are more numerous than males. In California, these fish average between 8 and 20 pounds; 20-pounders are considered large, and fish exceeding 30 pounds are trophies.

Spawning behavior. Males mature when 2 or 3 years old, but females do not mature until age 4 or 5. A 5-year-old fish may be anywhere from 11 to 17 inches long. Spawning takes place in relatively shallow water from April through July, and spawning fish feed actively.

Food and feeding habits. These halibut feed primarily on anchovies and similar small fish, often well off the bottom and during the day, although they also consume squid, crustaceans, and mollusks.

Halibut, Pacific

Hippoglossus stenolepis

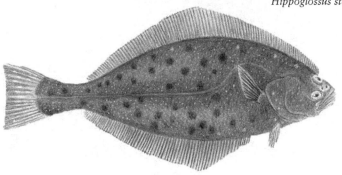

The Pacific halibut is the largest flatfish in Pacific waters and one of the world's largest bony fish. It is a member of the family Pleuronectidae, or right-eyed flounder. Since the 1980s, Pacific halibut populations have prospered, providing excellent fishing from Oregon to Alaska.

Identification. The halibut usually is dextral; that is, both eyes are on the right side of the head. Its coloration varies from olive to dark brown or black with lighter, irregular blotches. More elongate than other flatfish, the average width of the Pacific halibut's body is about one-third its length. The mouth is large, extending to the lower eye. The small, smooth scales are well buried in the skin, and the lateral line has a pronounced arch above the pectoral fin. The tail is crescent-shaped, longer at the tips than in the middle, which distinguishes it from most other flatfish.

Size. A typical sport-caught Pacific halibut is 28 to 50 inches long, weighing 10 to perhaps 60 pounds. Rod-and-reel records include several halibut in excess of 400 pounds (the all-tackle record is 459 pounds), and 500-pounders have been caught commercially. The largest specimens are females, as males seldom top 90 pounds.

Life history. Spawning occurs in the North Pacific Ocean and the Bering Sea during the winter. The eggs and the larvae float freely in the ocean current for 6 months, settling to the bottom in shallow, inshore waters, and make a counterclockwise migration through the Pacific, reaching the place where they were spawned by adulthood.

Food and feeding habits. Halibut lie on bottom waiting for tidal currents to wash food within striking range. However, they are strong swimmers and will leave the bottom to feed on pelagic fish, such as herring and sand lance. They will also inhabit virtually any place that has an abundance of crabs, squid, octopus, cod, pollack, sablefish, or other food.

OTHER NAMES
giant halibut, northern halibut, hali (Canada), barn door; Japanese: *ohyô;* Portuguese: *alabote do Pacifico;* Spanish: *fletán del Pacifico.*

Distribution. *Pacific halibut are found on the continental shelf of the North Pacific Ocean and have been recorded along the North American coast from central California to Nome, Alaska. They live on or near the bottom and have been taken as deep as 3,600 feet, although most are caught during the summer, when they are at depths of 75 to 750 feet. They generally move back into deeper water in the fall and the winter.*

Habitat. *Preferring cool water (37° to 46°F), halibut are most commonly found where the bottom is composed of cobble, gravel, and sand, especially near the edges of underwater plateaus and breaklines.*

Herring

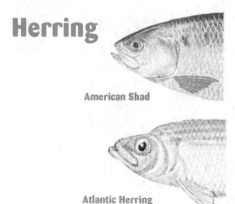

American Shad

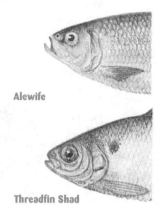

Alewife

Atlantic Herring

Threadfin Shad

Herring and their relatives are among the most important of commercial fish worldwide. They are also extremely important as forage fish for a wide variety of predatory fish, sea birds, seals, and other carnivores. In the past, some countries depended entirely on the herring (or related species) fishery for their economic survival. Wars have been waged over the rights to particularly productive herring grounds, which are found in all seas except the very cold waters of the Arctic and the Antarctic.

Most members of the herring family are strictly marine. Some are anadromous and spawn in freshwater, and a few species (those of freshwater origin) never go to sea. Herring typically travel in extensive schools; in the ocean, such schools may extend for miles, which makes harvesting possible in great quantities.

Herring are plankton feeders, screening their food through numerous gill rakers. As such, and because they are generally small, herring are seldom a deliberate quarry of recreational anglers (American and hickory shad are notable exceptions). They are primarily used as bait, either in pieces or whole, by freshwater and saltwater anglers for various game species.

Prominent species with the herring name include Atlantic herring, Pacific herring, blueback herring, and skipjack herring. At least two members of the herring family, the alewife and the blueback herring, are collectively referred to as river herring.

There is minor angling effort for some species, such as blueback and skipjack herring, when they ascend coastal rivers en masse to spawn; this fishery is generally geared more toward procuring food or bait than to pure angling sport. They may, however, be caught on light spoons and small jigs or flies. When massed, they are also taken by snagging (where legal) and in cast nets. Coastal herring are sometimes caught, snagged, or taken by a cast net, mainly for use as bait.

Herring, Atlantic

Clupea harengus

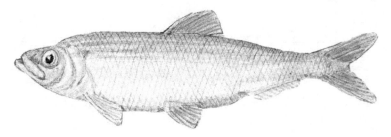

A member of the Clupeidae family of herring, the Atlantic herring is in the *Guinness Book of World Records* as the world's most numerous fish and is certainly one of the world's most valuable fish. It is used by humans in a host of ways and is extremely important as forage for predator species.

Identification. The Atlantic herring is silvery with a bluish or greenish-blue back and an elongated body. The dorsal fin begins at about the middle of the body, and there are 39 to 47 weakly developed ventral scutes. At the midline of the belly are scales that form a sharp-edged ridge. Teeth on the roof of the mouth distinguish the Atlantic herring from the similar alewife.

Size. Ordinarily less than a foot long, the Atlantic herring can grow to 18 inches. The all-tackle world record is a 1-pound, 1-ounce fish; a 3-pound, 12-ounce record stands for the skipjack herring.

Life history/Behavior. Atlantic herring usually spawn in the fall, although in any particular month of the year there is at least one group of Atlantic herring that moves into shallow coastal waters to spawn. (Blueback and skipjack herring, which are anadromous, spawn in coastal rivers in the spring.) Almost 5 inches long by the end of their first year, Atlantic herring nearly double their length in 2 years and reach maturity at age 4 or 5. Schools of herring may contain billions of individuals. In the western Atlantic, herring migrate from feeding grounds along the Maine coast during the autumn to the southern New England–mid-Atlantic region during the winter, with larger individuals tending to migrate greater distances.

Food. The Atlantic herring feeds on small planktonic copepods in its first year, graduating to mainly copepods.

OTHER NAMES

herring; Danish: *Atlantisk sild, sild;* Finnish: *silakka, silli;* French: *hareng de l'Atlantique;* German: *allec, hering;* Norwegian: *sild;* Polish: *sledz;* Spanish: *arenque del Atlántico.*

Distribution. *Atlantic herring are the most abundant pelagic fish in cool, northern Atlantic waters. In the western Atlantic Ocean, they are widely distributed in continental shelf waters from Labrador to Cape Hatteras and have been separated by biologists into Gulf of Maine and Georges Bank stocks. A related and similar species is the blueback herring (Alosa aestivalis), which ranges from Nova Scotia to Florida. The skipjack herring (A. chrysochloris) occurs in the Gulf of Mexico from Texas to the Florida Panhandle and ascends the Mississippi River and some of its tributaries.*

Habitat. *This species schools in coastal waters and has been recorded in temperatures of 34° to 64°F.*

Herring, Pacific

Clupea pallasii

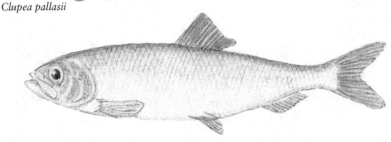

OTHER NAMES

herring, north Pacific herring; French: *hareng Pacifique;* Japanese: *nishin;* Spanish: *arenque del Pacifico.*

Distribution. *In the western Pacific Ocean, Pacific herring are found from Anadyr Bay and the eastern coasts of Kamchatka, including possibly the Aleutian Islands, southward to Japan and the west coast of Korea. In the eastern Pacific Ocean, they are found from Kent Peninsula and the Beaufort Sea southward to northern Baja California.*

Habitat. *Pacific herring inhabit coastal waters, and during the summer of their first year, the young appear in schools on the surface. In the fall, schools disappear as the young move to deep water, in depths of up to 1,558 feet, to stay there for the next 2 to 3 years.*

A member of the Clupeidae family of herring, an important food for many predatory fish, and the principal food of salmon, the Pacific herring also has many uses for human consumption. Sold fresh, dried/salted, smoked, canned, and frozen, the Pacific herring is commercially caught in the eastern Pacific for its roe; it is marketed in Asia as an extremely expensive delicacy called *kazunokokombu,* in which the roe are salted and sold on beds of kelp. Pacific herring may be used as bait by anglers but are not a sportfishing target, although they may be caught (or snagged) by coastal anglers who seek to use fresh specimens as live bait.

Identification. Similar to the Atlantic herring, the Pacific herring is silvery with a bluish or greenish-blue back and an elongated body.

Size. The Pacific herring can grow to 18 inches in length.

Life history/Behavior. Depending on latitude, mature adults migrate inshore from December through July, entering estuaries to breed. These herring do not show strong north-south migrations, with populations being localized. Like other herring, they school in great numbers.

Food and feeding habits. Pacific herring larvae feed on planktonic foods, including ostracods, small copepods, small fish larvae, euphausids, and diatoms. Juveniles feed on crustaceans, as well as on small fish, marine worms, and larval clams. Adults feed on larger crustaceans and small fish.

Hind, Red
Epinephelus guttatus

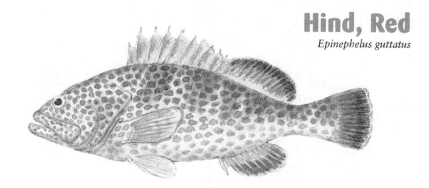

A grouper of the Serranidae family, the red hind is an important fish in the Caribbean, where large numbers are caught every year. It has excellent white, flaky meat that is usually marketed fresh.

Identification. As with all grouper, the red hind has a stout body and a large mouth. It is very similar to the rock hind in appearance, although the red hind is slightly more reddish brown in color, with dark red-brown spots above and pure red spots below over a whitish background. It differs from the rock hind in having no spots on the tail or the dorsal fin and no dark splotches on the back or the tail. The outer edges of the soft dorsal, the caudal, and the anal fins are blackish and are sometimes also edged in white. It can pale or darken to blend with surroundings.

Size/Age. The red hind can grow to 2 feet, although it is usually less than 15 inches long; most 12-inch and larger fish are males. Although it can reach 10 pounds, the red hind is rarely larger than 4 pounds in weight; the all-tackle world record is for a 6-pound, 1-ounce fish taken off Florida. The red hind can live for 17 years or longer.

Spawning behavior. Spawning takes place from March through July in 68° to 82°F waters at depths of 100 to 130 feet. At this time, mature fish of age 3 and older form large clusters over rugged bottoms. The female lays pelagic eggs in numbers between 90,000 and more than 3 million. Some fish undergo sexual inversion.

Food and feeding habits. Red hind feed on various bottom animals, such as crabs, crustaceans, fish, and octopus; they hide in holes and crevices and capture prey by ambush or after a short chase.

OTHER NAMES

strawberry grouper, speckled hind; French: *mérou couronné;* Spanish: *mero colorado, tofia.*

Distribution. *In the western Atlantic, red hind occur from North Carolina and Bermuda south to the Bahamas, the southern Gulf of Mexico, and to Brazil. They are common in the Caribbean, occasional in the Bahamas and Florida, and rare north of Florida.*

Habitat. *Red hind are one of the most common grouper in the West Indies, inhabiting shallow inshore reefs and rocky bottoms at depths of 10 to 160 feet. In Florida and the Bahamas they are usually found in quieter, deeper waters. Red hind are solitary and territorial fish, often found drifting or lying motionless along the bottom, camouflaged by their surroundings.*

Hind, Rock

Epinephelus adscensionis

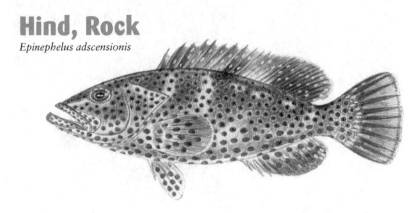

OTHER NAMES

grouper, jack, rock cod;
French: *mérou oualioua;*
Portuguese: *garoupa-
pintada;* Spanish: *mero
cabrilla.*

Distribution. *In the western Atlantic, rock hind occur
from Massachusetts to
southeastern Brazil, including Bermuda, the Bahamas,
the eastern Caribbean,
and the northern Gulf of
Mexico; they are rare north
of Florida.*

Habitat. *Solitary fish, rock
hind inhabit rocky or rough
inshore regions in shallow
waters, although they occasionally inhabit deep reefs.
They are often found drifting near the bottom.*

A grouper in the Serranidae family, the rock hind is found in
the same range as the red hind and is also good table fare.
Divers can often distinguish the two species by their behavior alone, as the rock hind is reclusive and shies away from
humans.

Identification. The rock hind has an overall tan to olive-
brown cast, with many large, reddish to dark dots covering
the entire body and the fins. Similar in appearance to the
red hind, it has one to four distinctive pale or dark splotches
along its back, appearing below the middle of the dorsal fin,
behind the dorsal fin on the caudal peduncle, and below
the spinous and the soft parts of the dorsal fin. The tail and
the anal fins have broad, whitish outer edges but lack the
additional blackish margins found on the dorsal, the caudal,
and the anal fins of the red hind. The rock hind can pale or
darken dramatically.

Size. The rock hind can reach 2 feet in length; the all-
tackle world-record fish is a 9-pounder.

Food and feeding habits. Ordinarily feeding on crabs and
fish, rock hind are said to feed on juvenile triggerfish and
young sea turtles at Ascension Island.

Jack, Almaco
Seriola rivoliana

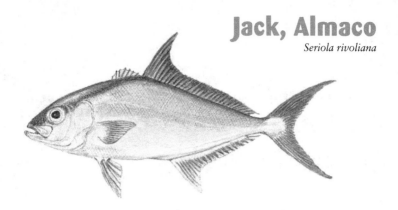

A deep-bodied amberjack and a member of the Carangidae family, the almaco jack is an excellent and widely distributed sportfish. It is a fine food fish, although it sometimes has tapeworms in the caudal peduncle area, which can be cut away, and it has been associated with ciguatera poisoning in the Caribbean.

Identification. The body and the fins can be a uniform dark brown, a dark bluish-green, or a metallic bronze or gray, with the lower sides and the belly a lighter shade, sometimes with a lavender or brassy cast. A diagonal black band usually extends from the lip through each eye to the upper back at the beginning of the dorsal fin; young fish sometimes display five or six bars. The front lobes of the dorsal and the anal fins are high and elongated and have deeply sickle-shaped outer edges. There are seven spines in the first dorsal fin. The almaco jack is similar in appearance to the greater amberjack but has a deeper, more flattened body than the greater amberjack and a more pointed head; the greater amberjack has a more elongated body, a lighter band, and a shorter front dorsal fin.

Size/Age. A large species, the almaco jack is known to grow to 3 feet in the Atlantic, although it is commonly between 1 and 2 feet long and weighs less than 20 pounds. In the Pacific, it grows to almost 5 feet and 130 pounds but usually weighs 50 to 60 pounds. In the Atlantic, the all-tackle world record is a 78-pound fish taken off Bermuda in 1990, whereas the Pacific all-tackle world record is a 132-pound fish taken off Baja California in 1964.

Spawning. Almaco jacks spawn offshore from spring through fall.

Food. An offshore predator, the almaco jack feeds mainly on fish but also on invertebrates.

OTHER NAMES

amberjack, greater amberjack, longfin yellowtail; Afrikaans: *langvin-geelstert;* Arabic: *gazala;* French: *seriole limon;* Hawaiian: *kahala;* Japanese: *songoro, hirenaga-kanpachi;* Malay/Indonesian: *chermin, aji-aji;* Portuguese: *arabaiana, xaréu limao;* Samoan: *tavai, tafala, palukata;* Spanish: *pez limon, palometa, medregal, huayaipe, fortuno, cavallas.*

Distribution. *Found around the world, almaco jacks occur in the eastern Pacific from Southern California to Peru, including the Gulf of California and the Galápagos Islands. In the western Atlantic, almaco jacks range from Cape Cod to northern Argentina.*

Habitat. *A warmwater species, almaco jacks prefer deep, open water and inhabit the outer slopes of reefs, but they rarely swim over reefs or near shore. Young fish are often associated with floating objects and sargassum. Almaco jacks often travel alone and occasionally in schools at depths of 50 to 180 feet.*

Jack, Bar

Caranx ruber

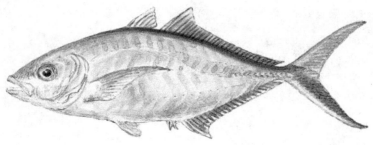

OTHER NAMES

runner, skipjack; Spanish: cojinua carbonera, cojinua negra, negrito.

Distribution. In the western Atlantic, bar jacks are found from New Jersey and Bermuda to the northern Gulf of Mexico and southern Brazil, as well as throughout the Caribbean.

Habitat. Bar jacks are common in clear, shallow, open waters at depths of up to 60 feet, often over coral reefs. Usually traveling in spawning schools, they sometimes mix with goatfish and stingrays, although they are occasionally solitary.

A member of the Carangidae family, the bar jack is small and more like a saltwater panfish, but it is a scrappy species and a good food fish.

Identification. The bar jack is silvery, with a dark bluish stripe on the back that runs from the beginning of the soft dorsal fin and onto the lower tail fin. Sometimes there is also a pale-blue stripe immediately beneath the black stripe that extends forward onto the snout. The bar jack bears a resemblance to the blue runner but has fewer and less prominent large scales along the caudal peduncle than the blue runner does. The bar jack has 26 to 30 soft rays in the dorsal fin and 31 to 35 gill rakers on the lower limb of the first arch. When feeding near bottom, it can darken almost to black.

Size. Usually 8 to 14 inches in length, the bar jack reaches a maximum of 2 feet.

Food and feeding habits. Opportunistic feeders, bar jacks feed mainly on pelagic and benthic fish, some shrimp, and other invertebrates.

Jack, Crevalle
Caranx hippos
Jack, Pacific Crevalle
Caranx caninus

These two members of the Carangidae family are almost identical in appearance and were formerly thought to be the same species.

Identification. Both species are bluish-green to greenish-gold on the back and silvery or yellowish on the belly. They are compressed, and the deep body has a high, rounded profile, as well as a large mouth. The tail and the anal fin may be yellowish, and the ends of the dorsal fin and the upper tail are occasionally black. There is a prominent black spot on the gill cover and another at the base of each pectoral fin. The soft dorsal and anal fins are almost identical in size. The two species are distinguished externally from each other only by the presence of a larger maximum number of scutes, up to 42 on the Pacific crevalle jack, as opposed to 26 to 35 on the crevalle jack.

Size. Averaging 3 to 5 pounds in weight and 1 to 2½ feet in length, the crevalle jack can regularly weigh as much as 10 pounds; the Pacific crevalle jack is usually smaller. The all-tackle world record for the crevalle jack is a 58-pound Angolan fish and for the Pacific crevalle jack is a 39-pound Costa Rican fish.

Life history/Behavior. Spawning occurs offshore from March through September. Young fish occur in moderate to large fast-moving schools, and crevalle jacks occasionally school with horse-eye jacks, although larger fish are often solitary.

Food and feeding habits. Voracious predators, they feed on shrimp, other invertebrates, and smaller fish. Crevalle jacks will often corner a school of baitfish at the surface and feed in a commotion that can be seen for great distances, or they will chase their prey onto beaches and against sea-walls. Fish of both species often grunt or croak when they are caught.

OTHER NAMES
crevalle jack
common jack, crevally, toro, trevally, horse crevalle; Spanish: *cavallo, chumbo, cocinero, jurel común*.

Pacific crevalle jack
toro, crevally, cavalla, jiguagua; Spanish: *aurel, burel, canche jurel, chumbo, cocinero, jurel toro, jurelito, sargentillo*.

Distribution. *In the western Atlantic, crevalle jacks occur from Nova Scotia south throughout the northern Gulf of Mexico. In the eastern Pacific, they occur from San Diego, California, to Peru.*

Habitat. *Both species can tolerate a wide range of salinities and often inhabit coastal areas of brackish water and may ascend rivers, frequenting shore reefs, harbors, and protected bays. Small fish are occasionally found over sandy and muddy bottoms of very shallow waters, as in estuaries and rivers. They are common in depths of up to 130 feet and often move into cooler, deeper water during the summer.*

Jack, Horse-eye

Caranx latus

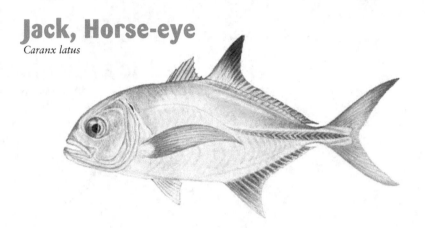

OTHER NAMES

big-eye jack, goggle-eye, horse-eye trevally; French: *carange moyole;* Portuguese: *guarajuba;* Spanish: *jurel, jurel ojo gordo, ojón, xurel.*

Distribution. *In the western Atlantic, horse-eye jacks occur from New Jersey and Bermuda throughout the northern Gulf of Mexico to Río de Janeiro in Brazil.*

Habitat. *Horse-eye jacks are most common around islands and offshore, although they can tolerate brackish waters and may ascend rivers. Adults prefer open water and may be found over reefs, whereas young are usually found along sandy shores and over muddy bottoms. Schooling in small to large groups at depths of up to 60 feet, horse-eye jacks may mix with crevalle jacks.*

Like other jack species, the horse-eye is a member of the Carangidae family and a strong-fighting fish suitable for light-tackle angling. Unlike some jacks, it is not highly esteemed as a food fish, although the quality of horse-eye jack meat can be improved by cutting off the tail and bleeding the fish directly after it is caught. This and other jacks have been implicated in cases of ciguatera poisoning.

Identification. The horse-eye jack is silvery, with yellow tail fins and usually dark edges on the dorsal and the upper tail fin. There is often a small black spot at the upper end of the gill cover, and it usually has blackish scutes. The body is compressed, and the entire chest is scaly. There are 20 to 22 soft rays in the dorsal fin and 14 to 18 gill rakers on the lower limb of the first arch. The horse-eye jack is similar in shape to the crevalle jack, although it has a less steep forehead and is either lacking the dark blotch at the base of the pectoral fins of the crevalle jack, or the blotch is more poorly defined. It can also be distinguished by its scales, which the crevalle jack lacks except for a small patch.

Size. This species is commonly found up to 30 inches and 10 pounds. The all-tackle world record is 24 pounds, 8 ounces.

Food and feeding habits. Horse-eye jacks feed on fish, shrimp, crabs, and other invertebrates.

Jack, Yellow

Caranx bartholomaei

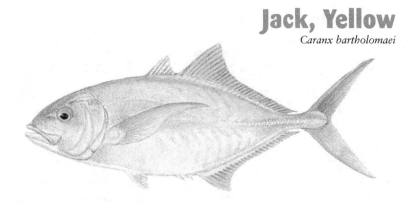

This small and spunky member of the Carangidae family is an occasional catch by anglers. Its flesh is considered fair to good eating.

Identification. Silvery with a yellow cast, the yellow jack has a bluish back and strongly yellow sides, which grow even more strikingly yellow after the fish dies. The fins are also yellowish, as is the tail. It lacks the black spot near the gill cover that the similar horse-eye jack has, and it has a less steep head. There are 25 to 28 soft rays in the dorsal fin and 18 to 21 gill rakers on the lower limb of the first arch. Young fish are more brassy in color and have many pale spots.

Size. Averaging less than 2 pounds in weight and 1 to 2 feet in length, the yellow jack can reach a maximum of 3 feet and as much as 17 pounds. The all-tackle world record weighed 19 pounds, 7 ounces.

OTHER NAMES
French: *carangue grasse;*
Spanish: *cojinua amarilla,*
cibi amarillo.

Distribution. In the western Atlantic, the yellow jack is found from Massachusetts to the Gulf of Mexico, including Bermuda, and south throughout the Caribbean and the West Indies to Maceio in Brazil.

Habitat. Common on offshore reefs, yellow jacks are usually solitary or travel in small groups in depths of up to 130 feet. Young typically roam inshore in mangrove-lined lagoons, often in association with jellyfish and floating sargassum.

Killifish

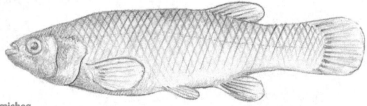

Mummichog
Fundulus heteroclitus

Habitat. *Killifish travel in schools, generally in the shallows, and are an important link in wetland and estuarine food webs. They are important prey for shorebirds, crabs, and larger fish, and many species are valued for mosquito control, as they feed on the surface and consume whatever insect larvae and small invertebrates are available. Killifish are also among the species most tolerant of high turbidity and low oxygen. Many killifish live in brackish water, as well as freshwater.*

Also called topminnows and toothed carps, these fish are members of the large Cyprinodontidae family of small fish. They are most abundant in warm climates, but a few species occur in temperate regions. The fins are soft rayed, as in cyprinid minnows, but killifish have scales on their heads and have no lateral lines. Typical family members have flattened heads, and the mouths open upward, an adaptation for feeding at the surface. Some species are used as bait, and many tropical species are kept in aquariums.

The best known of these is the mummichog *(Fundulus heteroclitus)*, a robust 3- to 5-inch species found along the Atlantic coast from Florida to Labrador. It can tolerate salinities to 35 parts per thousand. The mummichog is noted for its habit of burrowing into the silt on the bottom, sometimes to depths of 6 inches or more in winter. On the Pacific coast, the California killifish *(F. parvipinnis)* is similar in size and habits to the mummichog and occupies the same ecological niche.

Other well-known species include the banded killifish *(F. diaphanus)*, which occurs from South Carolina northward to the St. Lawrence River and westward through the Mississippi Valley, and the gold topminnow *(F. chrysotus)*, which inhabits freshwater and brackish estuaries and streams from Florida to South Carolina. Other common species of *Fundulus* include the banded topminnow *(F. cingulatus)*, the striped killifish *(F. majalis)*, and the saltmarsh topminnow *(F. jenkinsi)*.

Florida has the greatest representation of cyprinodonts in North America. Notable among these is the flagfish *(Jordanella floridae)*, a short-bodied, almost sunfishlike species attaining a maximum length of 3 inches, and the pygmy killifish *(Leptolucania ommata)*, a slender fish that rarely exceeds 1½ inches in length.

Ladyfish
Elops saurus

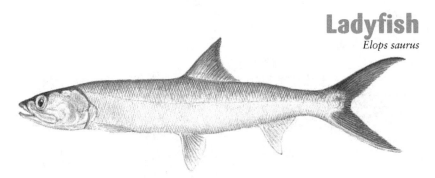

Ladyfish are members of the small Elopidae family. They occur worldwide and are related to tarpon *(see)*. They are similar in appearance to tarpon, although far smaller. Ladyfish are excellent light-tackle sportfish, commonly found in schools prowling shallow nearshore and brackish waters.

There are at least six species of ladyfish in the genus *Elops*, all of which are similar in average size, behavior, and characteristics. In the western Atlantic, the ladyfish *(E. saurus)* ranges from Cape Cod and Bermuda to the northern Gulf of Mexico and southern Brazil, although it is most common in Florida and the Caribbean. It is also known as tenpounder, as *ubarana* in Portuguese, and as *malacho* in Spanish.

In the eastern Pacific, the Pacific ladyfish *(E. affinis)* occurs from Southern California to Peru, although it is rare in northern Baja California. It is also known as *machete,* and as *chiro* and *malacho del Pacifico* in Spanish.

Identification. The ladyfish has an elongated, slender silvery body, with a blue-green back and small scales. It looks very much like a juvenile tarpon, although it can be distinguished from a tarpon by the lack of an elongated last ray on the dorsal fin. Its head is small and pointed, the mouth is terminal, and the tail is deeply forked.

Size. Some species of ladyfish may reach weights from 15 pounds to 24 pounds and a length of 3 feet; such specimens are extremely rare, and in general these fish most commonly weigh 2 to 3 pounds. The all-tackle world record is a 6-pounder.

Life history. These fish form large schools close to shore, although they are known to spawn offshore. Their ribbon-like larvae are very similar to those of bonefish and tarpon.

Food and feeding habits. Adults feed predominantly on fish and crustaceans. Ladyfish schools are often seen pursuing bait at the surface.

Habitat. Ladyfish are inshore species that prefer bays and estuaries, lagoons, mangrove areas, tidal pools, and canals. They occasionally enter freshwater and are rarely found on coral reefs.

Lingcod

Ophiodon elongatus

OTHER NAMES

cultus cod, blue cod, buffalo cod, green cod, ling; Finnish: *vihersimppu;* French: *terpuga;* Japanese: *ainame;* Portuguese: *lorcha;* Swedish: *grönfisk.*

Distribution. *The lingcod occurs in North American waters from Southern California to Alaska but is most abundant in the colder waters of the north.*

Habitat. *Lingcod inhabit colder waters in intertidal zone reefs and kelp beds that have strong tidal currents. They prefer depths from 2 to more than 70 fathoms over rock bottom.*

A Pacific marine species, the lingcod belongs to the family Hexagrammidae. Its name is misleading because it is not a true cod. A local term for lingcod is "cultus cod"; the word *cultus* is an Indian term meaning "false." The lingcod is an important and highly prized commercial and sportfish.

Identification. The lingcod has a large mouth, large pectoral fins, a smooth body, and a long, continuous dorsal fin divided by a notch into spiny and soft parts. Adults have large heads and jaws and long, pointed teeth. Juveniles have slender bodies. The lingcod's coloring is usually brown or gray, with blotches outlined in orange or blue, but is closely associated with habitat.

Size. Lingcod may grow to 50 inches or longer. Males are smaller than females, usually reaching no longer than 3 feet in length or 20 pounds in weight. Basically mature by 8 years, the male will weigh about 10 pounds and the female about 15. Commercial catches for lingcod sometimes include fish of 50 to 60 pounds. The all-tackle record is 76 pounds, 9 ounces.

Life history/Behavior. The spawning season is in the winter, from December through February, when the eggs are released in large pinkish-white masses into crevices in rocks. Egg masses can contain more than a half million eggs and are frequently found in the intertidal zone. The male protects the eggs, which hatch in 1 to 2 months. The young stay at the surface for 3 to 4 months before dropping to the bottom.

Food and feeding habits. Adults feed on herring, flounder, cod, hake, greenling, rockfish, squid, crustaceans, and small lingcod. Juveniles consume small crustaceans and fish.

Lookdown

Selene vomer

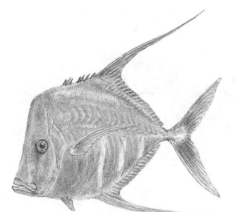

A member of the Carangidae family of jacks, the lookdown is so called because of its habit of hovering over the bottom in a partly forward-tilted position, which makes it seem to "look down." The flesh of the lookdown has an excellent flavor and is commercially marketed fresh.

Identification. Bright silver and iridescent, the lookdown has a deep and extremely compressed body that may have goldish, greenish, bluish, or purplish highlights. One of its most striking features is the unusually high forehead, as well as the low placement of the mouth on the face and the high placement of the eyes. The first rays of the second dorsal fin and the anal fin are long and streamerlike; in the dorsal fin, they may extend to the tail, whereas in the anal fin they do not extend as far. The lookdown may also have three or four pale bars across the lower body. On young fish, there are two very long, threadlike filaments that extend from the dorsal fin.

Size. Ordinarily 6 to 10 inches long and weighing less than a pound, the lookdown may reach 1 foot in length and weigh 3 pounds. The all-tackle world record is a Brazilian fish that weighed 4 pounds, 10 ounces.

Food. Lookdown feed on small crabs, shrimp, fish, and worms.

OTHER NAMES

Portuguese: *galo de penacho, peixe-galo;* Spanish: *caracaballo, joro bado, papelillo, pez luna.*

Distribution. *Endemic to the western Atlantic, lookdown are found from Maine and possibly Nova Scotia south to Uruguay, as well as in Bermuda and the Gulf of Mexico.*

Habitat. *Lookdown favor shallow coastal waters at depths of 2 to 30 feet, generally over hard or sandy bottoms around pilings and bridges and often in murky water. Occasionally occurring in small schools, lookdown hover over the bottom. Small fish may be found in estuaries.*

Lumpfish

Cyclopterus lumpus

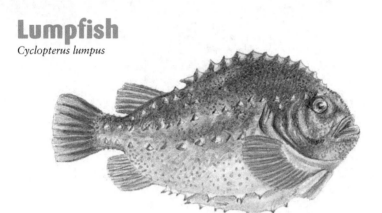

OTHER NAMES

lump, lumpsucker, nipisa, kiark-varrey; Italian: *ciclottero;* Spanish: *cicloptero.*

Distribution. *In the western Atlantic, lumpfish occur from Hudson Bay to James Bay and from Labrador to New Jersey; they are rarely found from the Chesapeake Bay south or in Bermuda.*

Habitat. *Lumpfish generally inhabit rocky bottoms of cold waters but may also occur among floating seaweed.*

One of the largest members of the Cyclopteridae family of lumpfish and snailfish, the unusual-looking lumpfish is not a quarry of anglers, but it is known as a food fish in Europe and is reportedly valued for its eggs as an inexpensive substitute for caviar.

Identification. The lumpfish is a stout-bodied, almost round fish, with a humped upper profile. It has a warty appearance, due to a ridge of prominent tubercles running along the middle of the back, as well as three other rows of tubercles on the sides, the uppermost of which extends from the tip of the snout to the base of the tail. Another distinctive feature is the way the pelvic fins are fused to form a round suction disk, which enables the lumpfish to attach itself to rocks. Of variable coloration, it is usually olive green or bluish-gray with a yellowish belly; this grows red on males during breeding. The pectoral fins are broad and fanlike, and lower rays start at the throat region. The first dorsal fin is apparent only in the young.

Size. The lumpfish can grow to 2 feet and 21 pounds, although it is usually smaller.

Life history/Behavior. Female lumpfish may lay 20,000 eggs or more, which sink to the bottom and stick. They are guarded by the male until they hatch. Lumpfish are solitary, rather than schooling, fish.

Food. The lumpfish feeds on small crustaceans and small fish.

Mackerel, Atlantic

Scomber scombrus

Like other members of the Scombridae family, the Atlantic mackerel is a fast-swimming, schooling, pelagic species that garners significant recreational and commercial interest. Sometimes it is almost completely absent, and at other times it is plentiful in swarming schools.

Identification. The Atlantic mackerel has a smooth, tapering head, a streamlined body, and brilliant coloration. An iridescent greenish-blue covers most of the upper body, turning to blue-black on the head and silvery white on the belly. The skin is satiny and has small, smooth scales. The tail is forked. A distinguishing characteristic is the series of 23 to 33 wavy, dark bands on the upper part of the body. There are two fins on the back, one spiny and one soft, followed by a number of small finlets. There are also finlets on the undersurface of the body near the tail.

Size/Age. The average size for adults is 14 to 18 inches and 1¼ to 2½ pounds. The all-tackle world record is a 2-pound, 10-ounce Norwegian fish. The maximum age is roughly 20 years.

Life history/Behavior. Atlantic mackerel native to the western Atlantic comprise two populations. The southern population appears offshore in early April, advancing toward Virginia, Maryland, and New Jersey to later spawn off New Jersey and Long Island. In late May, the northern group enters southern New England waters for a short period and mingles with the southern stock, then moves north to spawn off Nova Scotia in the Gulf of St. Lawrence in June and July.

Atlantic mackerel are moderately prolific. The eggs are released wherever the fish happen to be, leaving adverse winds to push eggs or small fry into areas where their chances of survival are slight. This behavior, combined with predation of large, as well as young, mackerel, results in a curious pattern of either superabundance or scarcity.

Food. The diet consists of fish eggs and a variety of small fish and fry.

OTHER NAMES

mackerel, common mackerel, Boston mackerel; Arabic: *scomber;* Danish: *almindelige, makrel;* Dutch: *gewone makrel;* French: *maquereau;* German: *makrele;* Italian: *lacerta, macarello;* Japanese: *hirasaba, marusaba;* Norwegian: *makrell;* Portuguese: *cavalla;* Spanish: *caballa;* Swedish: *makrill;* Turkish: *uskumru.*

Distribution. *Occurring in the North Atlantic Ocean, the Atlantic mackerel ranges from Labrador to Cape Hatteras, North Carolina, in the eastern region; and from the Baltic Sea to the Mediterranean and Black Seas in the western Atlantic.*

Habitat. *The Atlantic mackerel is pelagic, preferring cool, well-oxygenated open-ocean waters.*

Mackerel, Cero

Scomberomorus regalis

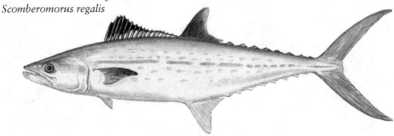

cero, spotted cero, king
mackerel, black-spotted
Spanish mackerel; French:
thazard franc; Portuguese:
cavala-branca; Spanish:
*carite, cavalla, pintada,
sierra.*

Distribution. *Found in
tropical and subtropical
waters in the western
Atlantic, cero mackerel
range from Massachusetts
to Brazil; they are common
to abundant throughout the
Florida Keys, the Bahamas,
the Antilles, and Cuba.*

Habitat. *A nearshore and
offshore resident, the cero
mackerel prefers clear
waters around coral reefs
and wrecks and is usually
solitary or travels in small
groups.*

A popular gamefish in tropical waters and a member of the
Scombridae family, the cero mackerel is a pelagic species
that also has commercial interest. It is considered excellent
table fare and is marketed fresh, smoked, and frozen. Offshore anglers may use the cero mackerel as rigged bait for
larger predatory species.

Identification. The cero mackerel is iridescent bluish-
green above and silvery below, with rows of short, yellow-
brown spots above; there are also yellow-orange streaks
and a dark stripe below, which runs the length of the body
from the pectoral fin to the base of the tail. The front of the
first dorsal fin is bluish-black and has 17 to 18 spines and 15
to 18 gill rakers on the first arch. The pectoral fins are covered with small scales. The cero mackerel differs from the
king mackerel and the Spanish mackerel in the pattern of its
spots, which are rather elongated and arranged in lines
instead of being scattered; the cero mackerel also has a lateral line that curves evenly down to the base of the tail,
which further distinguishes it.

Size. The all-tackle world-record cero mackerel weighed
17 pounds, 2 ounces. This species usually weighs less than
5 pounds.

Spawning. These fish spawn offshore in midsummer.

Food. Cero mackerel feed mainly on small schooling fish,
such as sardines, anchovies, pilchards, herring, and silversides, as well as on squid and shrimp.

Mackerel, Frigate
Auxis thazard

Frigate mackerel are an abundant member of the Scombridae family and hold an important place in the food web, especially as a forage fish for other species. They are commercially significant and marketed fresh, frozen, dried/salted, smoked, and canned.

Identification. The color of the frigate mackerel is dark greenish-blue above and silvery white below. It has 15 or more narrow, oblique, dark wavy markings on the unscaled back portion of its body. There are eight dorsal finlets and seven anal finlets. It resembles the tuna family more than it does the mackerel, with its more lunate than forked tail; as with all mackerel, however, its first and second dorsal fins are separated by a wide space.

Size. The average frigate mackerel weighs less than 2 pounds and is less than 20 inches long. The all-tackle world record is a 3-pound, 12-ounce fish.

Food. Frigate mackerel feed on small fish, squid, planktonic crustaceans, and larvae.

OTHER NAMES
bullet mackerel, frigate tuna, leadenall, mackerel tuna; Arabic: *deraiga, sadah;* French/Danish: *auxide;* Italian: *tombarello;* Japanese: *hira sóda, soda-gatsuo;* Malay/Indonesian: *aya, baculan, kayau, selasih;* Portuguese: *judeu;* Spanish: *barrileto negro, melva;* Swedish/Norwegian: *auxid;* Turkish: *gobene, tombile.*

Distribution. Frigate mackerel are cosmopolitan in warm waters, although there are few documented occurrences in the Atlantic Ocean. They are subject to periods of abundance and scarcity in particular areas.

Habitat. A schooling species, frigate mackerel inhabit both coastal and oceanic waters.

Mackerel, King

Scomberomorus cavalla

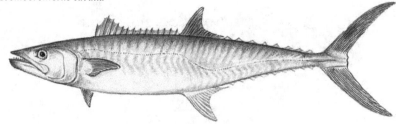

OTHER NAMES

kingfish, giant mackerel;
French: *maquereau;*
Portuguese: *cavala;*
Spanish: *carite, carite lucio,
carite sierra, rey, serrucho,
sierra.*

Distribution. *In the western Atlantic, king mackerel range from Massachusetts to Río de Janeiro, Brazil, including the Caribbean and the Gulf of Mexico, although they are only truly abundant off southern Florida. Two separate populations are suspected, one in the Gulf of Mexico and one in the Atlantic.*

Habitat. *King mackerel are primarily an open-water, migratory species, preferring warm waters that seldom fall below 68°F. They often occur around wrecks, buoys, coral reefs, ocean piers, inlets, and other areas where food is abundant. They tend to avoid highly turbid waters, and larvae are often found in warm, highly saline surface waters. A schooling species, king mackerel migrate extensively and annually along the western Atlantic coast in schools of various sizes, although the largest individuals usually remain solitary.*

The largest mackerel in the western Atlantic, the king mackerel is a prized gamefish and an important commercial species, with millions of pounds of fish landed annually. A member of the Scombridae family, the king mackerel has firm meat, most of which is sold fresh or processed into steaks. Smaller quantities are canned, salted, smoked, and frozen. It may be ciguatoxic in certain areas, however.

Identification. The streamlined body of the king mackerel is a dark gray above, growing silver on the sides and below, and there are no markings on the body, although the back may have an iridescent blue to olive tint. Most of the fins are pale or dusky, except the first dorsal fin, which is uniformly blue; the front part of this fin is never black, which distinguishes it from the Spanish mackerel and the cero mackerel. Other distinguishing features include the sharp drop of the lateral line under the second dorsal fin, as well as a relatively small number (14 to 16) of spines in the first dorsal fin and a lower gill rake count, which is 6 to 11 on the first arch. Young king mackerel may be mistaken for Spanish mackerel because of the small, round, dark to gold spots on the sides, but these fade and disappear with age.

Size/Age. Averaging less than 10 pounds in weight, the king mackerel is usually 2 to 4 feet long and weighs up to 20 pounds. It reaches a maximum length of 5½ feet and a weight of 100 pounds. Females grow larger than males. The all-tackle world record is a 93-pound fish taken off Puerto Rico in 1999. This species is believed to reach 14 years old, but those older than 7 years are rare.

Life history/Behavior. Male king mackerel become sexually mature between their second and third years and female fish between their third and fourth years. They spawn from April through November, and activity peaks in the late summer and the early fall. A large female may spawn 1 to 2.5 million eggs.

Food. King mackerel feed mainly on fish, as well as on a smaller quantity of shrimp and squid.

Mackerel, Pacific Jack

Trachurus symmetricus

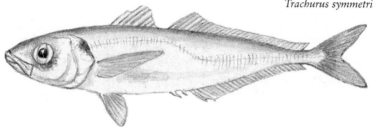

Not a true mackerel but a member of the Carangidae family of jacks, the Pacific jack mackerel is marketed fresh, smoked, canned, and frozen.

Identification. The body of the Pacific jack mackerel is somewhat compressed and elongate, with a tail that is as broad as it is deep. It is metallic blue to olive green on the back, shading to silver on the belly. Its last dorsal and anal soft rays are attached to the body or rarely separated from the fins, and the sides are covered with enlarged scales. The Pacific jack mackerel bears a resemblance to the Mexican scad, but the enlarged scales distinguish it, as do the last, attached rays of the dorsal and the anal fins. On the Mexican scad, the rays are isolated finlets.

Size/Age. The Pacific jack mackerel can weigh 4 to 5 pounds and can live 20 to 30 years.

Spawning behavior. Sexual maturity comes early for Pacific jack mackerel. Half of the females are ready to spawn at age 2, and all fish spawn by age 3. Spawning takes place from March through June over a considerable area, from 80 to more than 240 miles offshore.

Food and feeding habits. Pacific jack mackerel feed on small crustaceans and fish larvae, as well as on anchovies, lanternfish, and juvenile squid.

OTHER NAMES

horse mackerel, jack mackerel, jackfish, mackereljack, scad; Spanish: *charrito, chicharro.*

Distribution. In the eastern Pacific, Pacific jack mackerel range from southeastern Alaska to southern Baja California, extending into the Gulf of California, Mexico. They are also reported from Acapulco, Mexico, and the Galápagos Islands.

Habitat. Pacific jack mackerel are often found offshore in large schools; adults are found up to 500 miles from the coast and in depths of up to 150 feet. Young fish school near kelp and under piers, whereas larger fish often move offshore or northward.

Mackerel, Pacific Sierra

Scomberomorus sierra

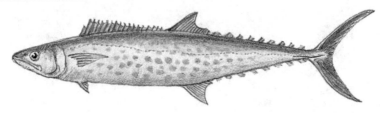

Pacific sierra; Spanish:
*macarela, serrucho, sierra,
verle.*

The Pacific sierra mackerel is an abundant fish in the Pacific along the coasts of Mexico and Central America. A member of the Scombridae family of mackerel and not to be confused with the Atlantic sierra *(Scomberomorus brasiliensis),* which occurs only in the Atlantic, the Pacific sierra mackerel is an eastern Pacific fish that is excellent to eat. It is marketed fresh and frozen. It resembles the Spanish mackerel in appearance, and the all-tackle world record is an Ecuadorian fish of 18 pounds caught in 1990.

Pacific sierra mackerel extend from La Jolla in Southern California south to the Galápagos Islands and to Paita, Peru. They have recently been reported from Antofagasta, Chile. A schooling species, Pacific sierra mackerel are found in surface coastal waters and over the bottom of the continental shelf. Thought to spawn close to the coast, they feed on small fish, especially anchovies.

Mackerel, Spanish
Scomberomorus maculatus

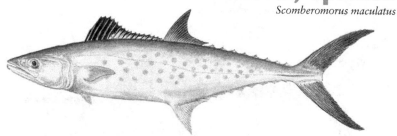

The Spanish mackerel is a popular gamefish and a good food fish of the Scombridae family.

Identification. The slender, elongated body of the Spanish mackerel is silvery with a bluish or olive-green back. There are 16 to 18 spines in the first dorsal fin, 15 to 18 soft rays in the second dorsal fin—with 8 to 9 finlets behind it, and 13 to 15 gill rakers on the first arch. The lateral line curves evenly downward to the base of the tail.

The Spanish mackerel resembles both the cero mackerel and the king mackerel, but it has bronze or yellow spots without stripes; the cero mackerel has both spots and stripes of bronze or yellow, whereas the king mackerel has neither. The Spanish mackerel lacks scales on the pectoral fins, which further distinguishes it from both the cero and the king mackerel, which have scales on them. Also, the front part of the first dorsal fin on the Spanish mackerel is black, whereas it is more blue on the king mackerel, and the second dorsal fin and the pectoral fins may be edged in black.

Size/Age. The Spanish mackerel grows to 37 inches and 11 pounds, averaging 1½ to 3 feet and 2 to 3 pounds. The all-tackle word record is a 13-pounder taken off North Carolina in 1987. Fish older than 5 years are rare, although some have been known to reach 8 years.

Spawning behavior. Spanish mackerel are able to reproduce by the second year and spawn offshore from April through September.

Food and feeding habits. Spanish mackerel feed primarily on small fish, as well as on squid and shrimp; they often force their prey into crowded clumps and practically push the fish out of the water as they feed.

OTHER NAMES
Atlantic Spanish mackerel; Portuguese: *sororoca;* Spanish: *carite, pintada, sierra, sierra pintada.*

Distribution. In the western Atlantic, there are two separate populations of Spanish mackerel: one in the Gulf of Mexico and the other along the main western Atlantic coast. The former extends from the Gulf of Mexico throughout Florida waters to the Yucatán, and the latter extends from Miami to the Chesapeake Bay and occasionally to Cape Cod. They are absent from the Bahamas and the Antilles, except around Cuba and Haiti, but are abundant around Florida.

Habitat. Occurring inshore, near shore, and offshore, Spanish mackerel prefer open water but are sometimes found over deep grassbeds and reefs, as well as in shallow-water estuaries. They form large, fast-moving schools that migrate great distances along the shore, staying in waters with temperatures above 68°F; these schools occur off North Carolina in April, off the Chesapeake Bay in May, and off New York in June, returning south in the winter.

Marlin, Blue

Makaira nigricans and Makaira mazara

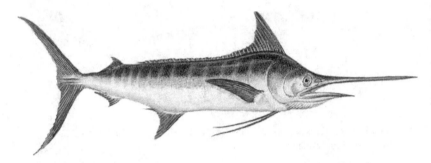

OTHER NAMES

Atlantic blue marlin, Pacific blue marlin, Cuban black marlin; French: *espadon, makaire bleu;* Japanese: *makajiki, nishikuro;* Portuguese: *agulhao preto;* Spanish: *abanco, aguja azul, castero, marlín azul.*

Distribution/Habitat.

This pelagic, migratory species occurs in tropical and warm temperate oceanic waters. In the Atlantic Ocean, it is found from 45° north to 35° south latitude and in the Pacific Ocean from 48° north to 48° south latitude. It is less abundant in the eastern portions of both oceans. In the northern Gulf of Mexico, its movements seem to be associated with the so-called Loop Current, an extension of the Caribbean Current. Seasonal concentrations occur in the southwest Atlantic (5° to 30° south latitude) from January through April, in the northwest Atlantic (10° to 35° north latitude) from June through October, and in the

A premier member of the Istiophoridae family of billfish, the blue marlin is one of the foremost big-game species worldwide. It has exceptional size and strength and is a powerful, aggressive fighter. It runs hard and long, sounds deep, and leaps high into the air in a seemingly inexhaustible display of strength. Intensively pursued commercially in many parts of its range, it is overexploited. The flesh is pale and firm and makes excellent table fare, especially when smoked. In the Orient it is often served as sashimi or in fish sausages. Blue marlin are seldom eaten in North America, and the vast majority caught by anglers are released after capture, and many of those released are tagged.

Identification. The pectoral fins of blue marlin are never rigid, even after death, and can be folded completely flat against the sides. The dorsal fin is high and pointed (rather than rounded) anteriorly, and its greatest height is less than its greatest body depth. The anal fin is relatively large and also pointed. Juveniles might not share all of these characteristics, but the peculiar lateral line system is usually visible in small specimens. In adults it is rarely visible unless the scales or the skin are removed. The lateral line of a Pacific blue marlin is a series of large loops, like a chain, along the flanks. The lateral line of all Atlantic blue marlin is a reticulated network that is more complex than the simple loops of Pacific specimens. The vent is just in front of the anal fin, as it is in all billfish except the spearfish, and the upper jaw is elongated in the form of a spear.

The back is cobalt blue and the flanks and the belly are silvery white. There may be light blue or lavender vertical stripes on the sides, but these usually fade away soon after death, and they are never as obvious as those of the striped marlin. There are no spots on the fins. Small blue marlin are similar to white marlin, but the blue has a more pointed dorsal fin at the anterior end and more pointed tips on the pectoral and the anal fins, and it lacks dorsal fin spots.

Size/Age. The blue marlin is the largest marlin existing in the Atlantic Ocean. Elsewhere, it is capable of growing to sizes that equal or exceed those of the black marlin. Japanese longline reports indicate that the blue marlin is the largest-growing member of the Istiophoridae family. It apparently grows larger on average in the Pacific Ocean, where decades ago one commercially caught specimen reportedly weighed 2,200 pounds, and an angler-caught specimen (which did not qualify for world-record status) weighed 1,800 pounds. The all-tackle world record for Atlantic blues is a 1,402-pounder caught in 1992 at Vitoria, Brazil; the all-tackle world record for Pacific blues is a 1,376-pounder caught in 1982 at Kona, Hawaii. The giants are all females, as male blue marlin rarely exceed 300 pounds. Most blue marlin encountered by anglers range between 150 and 400 pounds. Blue marlin are believed to live for more than 15 years, although fish exceeding 10 years of age are uncommon.

Life history/Behavior. The life history of the blue marlin is poorly known. The full extent of its oceanic wanderings, as well as its open-sea spawning activities, are unknown. These fish are found in the warm blue water of offshore environs, usually over considerable depths and where there are underwater structures (for example, canyons, dropoffs, ridges, seamounts) and currents that attract copious supplies of baitfish. They are usually solitary.

Food and feeding behavior. Blue marlin feed on squid and pelagic fish, including assorted tuna and mackerel, as well as on dolphin. They feed on almost anything they can catch, in fact, and they feed according to availability, rather than selectivity. Because they require large quantities of food, they are scarce when and where prey is limited.

western and central North Pacific (2° to 24° north latitude) from May through October.

Marlin, Striped

Tetrapturus audax

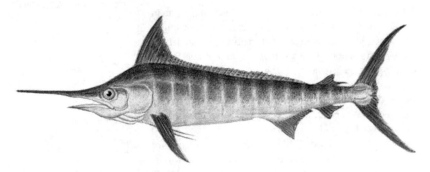

OTHER NAMES

striper, marlin, Pacific marlin, Pacific striped marlin, barred marlin, spikefish, spearfish, New Zealand marlin, red marlin (Japan); Arabic: *kheil al bahar;* French: *empéreur;* Hawaiian: *a'u, nairagi;* Japanese: *makajiki;* Portuguese: *espadim raiado;* Spanish: *agujón, marlín, marlin rayado, pez aguja.*

Distribution/Habitat.

Found in tropical and warm temperate waters of the Indian and the Pacific Oceans, the striped marlin is pelagic and seasonally migratory, moving toward the equator during the cold season and away again during the warm season. In the eastern Pacific, the striped marlin ranges as far north as Oregon but is most common south of Point Conception, California. It usually appears off California in July and remains until late October. The best California fishing locality is in a belt of water that extends from the east end of Santa Catalina Island offshore to San

Widely distributed in the Pacific Ocean, the striped marlin is the most prevalent marlin in the Istiophoridae family of billfish and a prized angling catch. It is well known for its fighting ability and has the reputation of spending more time in the air than in the water when hooked; lacking the overall size and weight of the blue marlin or the black marlin, it is more acrobatically inclined. In addition to making long runs and tail-walking, it will "greyhound" across the surface, performing up to a dozen or more long, graceful leaps. It is caught fairly close to shore in appropriate waters.

The striped marlin has red meat and is the object of extensive commercial fishing efforts, primarily by longlining. Many people throughout its Indo-Pacific range hold its flesh in high esteem, and it is rated best among billfish for sashimi and sushi preparations. Heavy fishing pressure has resulted in reduced stocks, however, as is true of all billfish.

Identification. The body of the striped marlin is elongate and compressed, and its upper jaw is extended in the form of a spear. The color is dark or steely blue above and becomes bluish-silver and white below a clearly visible and straight lateral line. Numerous iridescent blue spots grace the fins, and pale blue or lavender vertical stripes appear on the sides. These may or may not be prominent, but they are normally more prominent than those of other marlin. The stripes persist after death, which is not always true with other marlin. The most distinguishing characteristic is a high, pointed first dorsal fin, which normally equals or exceeds the greatest body depth. Even in the largest specimens, this fin is at least equal to 90 percent of the body depth. Like the dorsal fin, the anal and the pectoral fins are pointed. They are also flat and movable and can easily be folded flush against the sides, even after death.

The striped marlin has scales, fins on the belly, and a rounded spear, which set it apart from the swordfish, which

Marlin, Striped *(continued)*

has no scales or ventral fins and a flat bill; from the sailfish, which has an extremely high dorsal fin; and from a spearfish, which has neither the long spear on the upper jaw nor the body weight of the larger marlin.

Size. The largest striped marlin on record is a 494-pound fish caught in New Zealand in 1986; in the United States the largest known is a 339-pound California fish. They are common from under 100 pounds to roughly 200 pounds.

Life history/Behavior. The life history of this species is poorly known. Striped marlin are found in the warm blue water of offshore environs, usually above the thermocline. They are mostly solitary but may form schools by size during the spawning season. They are usually present where there is plenty of forage.

Food and feeding habits. The striped marlin is highly predatory, feeding extensively on pilchards, anchovies, mackerel, sauries, flyingfish, squid, and whatever is abundant. The spear of the marlin is sometimes used for defense and as an aid in capturing food. Wooden boats frequently have been rammed by billfish, and in one instance the spear penetrated $18\frac{1}{2}$ inches of hardwood, $14\frac{1}{2}$ inches of which was oak. When it uses its bill in capturing food, the striped marlin sometimes stuns its prey by slashing sideways with the spear, rather than impaling its victim, as some believe.

Clemente Island and southward in the direction of the Los Coronados Islands. The waters around the Baja Peninsula, Mexico, are especially known for striped marlin, which are particularly abundant off Cabo San Lucas.

Marlin, White

Tetrapturus albidus

OTHER NAMES

spikefish, Atlantic white marlin; French: *espadon*; Italian: *marlin bianco*; Japanese: *nishimaka; nishi-makajiki*; Portuguese: *agulhão branco, espadim branco*; Spanish: *aguja blanca, aguja de costa, blanca, cabezona, marlin blanco, picudo blanco*.

Distribution. *The white marlin occurs throughout the Atlantic Ocean from latitudes 45° north to 45° south in the west, including the Gulf of Mexico and the Caribbean Sea, and from 45° north to 35° south in the east. In North America, it is prominent in offshore waters off Maryland, North Carolina, and Florida.*

The smallest of the four marlin in the Istiophoridae family of billfish, the white marlin is a top-rated light-tackle gamefish and the most frequently encountered marlin along the East Coast of the United States, where it is almost exclusively released (often tagged) after capture.

Identification. The body of the white marlin is elongate and compressed, and its upper jaw extends in the form of a spear. It is generally lighter in color and tends to show more green than do other marlin, although it may at times appear to be almost chocolate brown along the back; the flanks are silvery and taper to a white underbelly. Several light blue or lavender vertical bars may show on the flanks. Its most characteristic feature is the rounded, rather than pointed, tips of the pectoral fins, the first dorsal fin, and the first anal fin. The first dorsal fin is convex, and the flat, movable pectoral fins can easily be folded flush against the sides of the body.

Size. Fish to 8 feet in length are common throughout their range, although white marlin can attain a length of 10 feet. The all-tackle world-record fish weighed 181 pounds, 12 ounces, and was caught in Brazil in 1979.

Life history/Behavior. Although this pelagic and migratory species usually favors deep-blue tropical and warm temperate (exceeding 81°F) waters, it frequently comes in close to shore where waters aren't much deeper than 8 fathoms. It is normally found above the thermocline, and its occurrence varies seasonally. It is present in higher latitudes in both the Northern and the Southern Hemispheres during the respective warm seasons. It is usually solitary but sometimes travels in small groups, the latter tendency reflecting feeding opportunities. Spawning occurs in the spring, with both sexes reaching maturity at around 51 inches in length.

Food and feeding behavior. White marlin feed on assorted pelagic fish and squid, including sardines and herring.

Menhaden, Atlantic

Brevoortia tyrannus

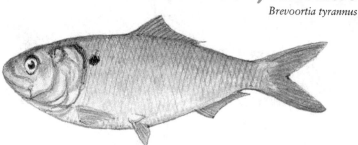

A member of the herring family, the Atlantic menhaden is a hugely important commercial species; greater numbers of this fish are taken each year by commercial fishermen than of any other fish in the United States. Excessive fishing, however, has caused population declines.

Identification. The Atlantic menhaden has a deep and compressed body, a big bony head, and a large mouth, with a lower jaw that fits into a notch in the upper jaw. It also has adipose eyelids, which make it appear sleepy. It has a dark blue back, silvery sides with an occasional reddish or brassy tint, pale yellow fins edged in black, a dark patch on the shoulder, and two or three scattered rows of smaller spots.

Size. The Atlantic menhaden can reach a length of 1½ feet.

Life history/Behavior. Atlantic menhaden form large and very compact schools, consisting of both young and adult fish; this makes them vulnerable to commercial fishermen, some of whom use spotter planes to locate the schools and direct commercial vessels to the fish, which are then encircled.

Menhaden have distinct seasonal migrations—northward in April and May and southward in the early fall. Spawning occurs year-round, although not in the same locations at the same time. For example, because high water temperatures are detrimental to breeding, the peak spawning season off the southern coast of the United States is October through March. Egg estimates for each female run in the tens of thousands to hundreds of thousands. They are free floating and hatch at sea. Once hatched, the offspring are carried into estuaries and bays, which serve as sheltered nursery areas in which young Atlantic menhaden spend their first year. The fish mature between their first and third years.

Food and feeding habits. Using long filaments on their gills, Atlantic menhaden filter zooplankton and other small plants and animals out of the water.

OTHER NAMES
pogy, bunker, bughead, bugfish, fatback, menhaden, mossbunker; Danish, Finnish, Norwegian, Polish, Swedish: *menhaden;* French: *menhaden tyran;* Spanish: *lacha tirana.*

Distribution. *This species occurs in the western Atlantic Ocean from Nova Scotia to the Indian River in southern Florida. In the northern regions, it is primarily known as bunker.*

Habitat. *Atlantic menhaden inhabit inland tidal areas of brackish water and coastal saltwater. They migrate in and out of bays and inlets and are found inshore in summer. Some populations move into deeper water in the winter.*

Milkfish

Chanos chanos

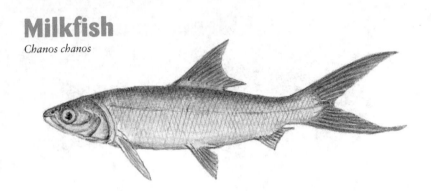

Distribution. *In the eastern Pacific, milkfish occur from San Pedro, California, to the Galápagos Islands.*

Habitat. *Adults travel in schools along continental shelves and around islands where there are well-developed reefs and where temperatures exceed 68°F. Milkfish flourish in water as hot as 90°F.*

The milkfish is very important in the Indo-Pacific, where it is used widely for food, but is mostly ignored in North America. However, its tarponlike appearance has caused anglers to misidentify it and spend much time futilely trying to catch it on artificial lures and flies.

Identification. Looking somewhat like a large mullet or a tarpon, the milkfish has a streamlined and compressed body, large eyes, and a silvery metallic coloring. It also has a small, toothless mouth; a single spineless dorsal fin; and a large forked tail fin.

Size/Age. The milkfish can reach 5 feet in length and a weight of 50 pounds and can live for 15 years. The all-tackle world record is a 24-pound, 8-ounce Hawaiian fish.

Life history/Behavior. Milkfish spawn in shallow, brackish water, and a single fish may produce 9 million eggs. These float on the surface until they hatch, and the new larvae enter inshore waters 2 to 3 weeks after hatching. Older larvae settle in coastal wetlands during the juvenile stage, occasionally entering freshwater lakes, and older juveniles and young adults return to the sea to mature sexually.

Food and feeding habits. Milkfish larvae feed on zooplankton, whereas juveniles and adults eat bacteria, soft algae, small benthic invertebrates, and sometimes pelagic fish eggs and larvae.

Mojarra

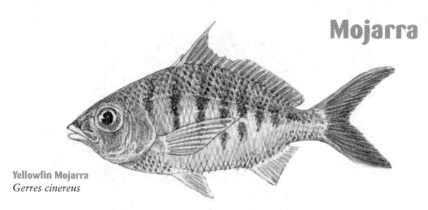

Yellowfin Mojarra
Gerres cinereus

Mojarra are members of the Gerridae family of tropical and subtropical saltwater fish. Roughly 40 species are in this family, some of which also occur in brackish water and a few rarely in freshwater. They are small and silvery and have protractile mouths. The upper jaw of the mojarra fits into a defined slot when the mouth is not extended, or "pursed." When feeding, the mouth is protruded and directed downward. The dorsal and the anal fins have a sheath of scales along the base, and the gill membranes are not united to the isthmus. The first, or spiny, dorsal fin is high in front, sloping into the second, or soft-rayed, dorsal. The tail is deeply forked.

Most mojarra are less than 10 inches long. They are important for predator species and are used as bait by some anglers. Some species are observed in schools on sandy, shallow flats.

The spotfin mojarra *(Eucinostomus argenteus)* is abundant in the western Atlantic off the coast from New Jersey to Brazil. It occurs in the eastern Pacific along the coast from Southern California to Peru. The yellowfin mojarra *(Gerres cinereus)* is common in Florida and the Caribbean.

Mullet

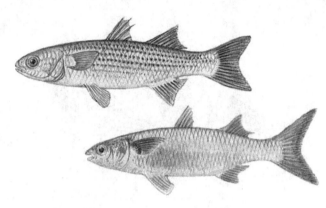

Striped Mullet
Mugil cephalus

White Mullet
Mugil curema

Distribution. *The striped mullet is cosmopolitan in all warm seas worldwide and is the only member of the mullet family found off the Pacific coast of the United States. The fantail mullet occurs in the western Atlantic in Bermuda and from Florida and the northern Gulf of Mexico to Brazil. The white mullet is found in the western Atlantic in Bermuda and from Massachusetts south to Brazil, including the Gulf of Mexico, and in the eastern Pacific from the Gulf of California, Mexico, to Iquique, Chile.*

Mullet are members of the Mugilidae family, a group of roughly 70 species whose members range worldwide. All are good food fish, and the roe is considered a delicacy. Mullet are important forage for many predator species.

Identification. The striped mullet *(Mugil cephalus)* is bluish-gray or green along the back, shading to silver on the sides and white below. Also known as the black mullet, or fatback, it has indistinct horizontal black bars, or stripes, on its sides; the fins are lightly scaled at the base and unscaled above; the nose is blunt and the mouth small; and the second dorsal fin originates behind that of the anal fin. It is similar to the smaller fantail mullet *(M. gyrans)* and the white mullet *(M. curema)*, both of which have a black blotch at the base of their pectoral fins, which is lacking in the striped mullet.

Size. The striped mullet may reach a length of 3 feet and weigh as much as 12 pounds, although the largest specimens have come from aquariums. Roe specimens in the wild are common to 3 pounds, but most striped mullet weigh closer to a pound. The fantail mullet is small and usually weighs less than a pound. The white mullet is similar in size to the fantail.

Life history/Behavior. Mullet are schooling fish found inshore in coastal environs. Many species have the unusual habit of leaping from the water with no apparent cause. Adult striped mullet migrate offshore in large schools to spawn. Fantail mullet spawn in near-shore or inshore waters during the spring and the summer. White mullet spawn offshore, and the young migrate into estuaries and along beaches.

Food and feeding habits. Mullet feed on algae, detritus, and other tiny marine forms; they pick up mud from the bottom and strain plant and animal material from it through their sievelike gill rakers and pharyngeal teeth.

Needlefish

Atlantic Needlefish
Strongylura marina

There are 32 species in the Belonidae family of needlefish, many of which are also known as longtoms or sea gar. They are often observed by coastal anglers, and some are caught frequently. Needlefish commonly skip (or leap) across the surface when hooked, when alarmed, and when attracted to lights at night.

The most distinguishing features of the needlefish are its elongated upper and lower jaws, which have numerous needlelike teeth. The upper jaw is shorter than the lower jaw; however, in two species the lower jaw is shorter. It has a slender, elongate body that is silver on the flanks and bluish or dark green along the back and also features small scales and a wide mouth.

One of the most widely dispersed species is the houndfish *(Tylosurus crocodilus crocodilus),* which is found nearly worldwide in tropical and warm temperate waters. It is common in the western Atlantic, ranging from New Jersey southward through the Caribbean to Brazil.

The houndfish averages 2 feet or less in length but occasionally attains a length of 4 to 5 feet. It is also known as hound needlefish, crocodile needlefish, and crocodile longtom, and the all-tackle world record is 7½ pounds (the record for the Mexican houndfish is 21 pounds, 12 ounces). Compared to other, generally smaller members of the family, the houndfish has a relatively short, stout beak. It is found singly or in small groups, readily strikes artificial lures, and is exciting to take on rod and reel.

The Atlantic needlefish *(Strongylura marina)* is a smaller species that inhabits coastal areas and mangrove-lined lagoons and also enters freshwater. It occurs in the western Atlantic and ranges from the Gulf of Maine to Brazil. It is absent from the Bahamas and Antilles. It grows to 31 inches and can weigh slightly more than 3 pounds.

Habitat. Most needlefish live in tropical seas, a few inhabit cooler waters of temperate regions, and some stray occasionally into freshwater.

Opaleye
Girella nigricans

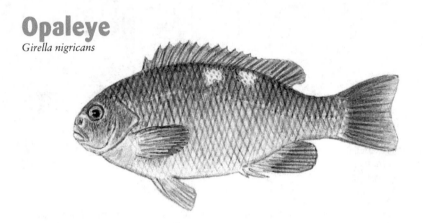

OTHER NAMES

green perch, black perch,
blue-eyed perch, bluefish,
Jack Benny, button-back;
Japanese: *mejina;* Spanish:
chopa verde.

Distribution. *Opaleye
occur from San Francisco,
California, to Cabo San
Lucas, Baja California.*

Habitat. *This species
inhabits rocky shorelines
and kelp beds. Concentra-
tions of adults are found off
California in 65 or so feet of
water.*

A member of the nibblers in the Kyphosidae family of sea
chub, the opaleye is a tough species to catch and a determined fighter on rod and reel.

Identification. The body of the opaleye is oval and compressed, the snout is thick and has an evenly rounded profile, and the mouth is small. Its coloring is dark olive green,
and most individuals have one or two white spots on each
side of the back under the middle of the dorsal fin. Bright-
blue eyes and a heavy perchlike body distinguish it from
related species.

Size. They are reported to attain a maximum length of
25½ inches and weight of 13½ pounds.

Life history/Behavior. Opaleye form dense schools in
shallow water when spawning, which occurs from April
through June. Eggs and larvae are free floating and may be
found miles from shore. Juveniles form schools of up to two
dozen individuals. At about 1 inch in length, they enter tide
pools, gradually moving deeper as they grow. Opaleye
mature and spawn when they are roughly 8 or 9 inches
long and between 2 and 3 years old.

Food and feeding habits. Opaleye primarily eat marine
algae, with or without encrustations of organisms. Other
food sources include feather boa kelp, giant kelp, sea let-
tuce, coralline algae, small tube-dwelling worms, and red
crabs.

Palometa

Trachinotus goodei

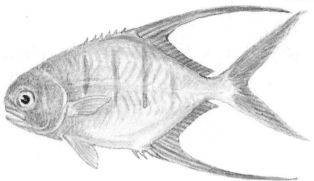

This small species is a member of the Carangidae family of jacks and pompano.

Identification. A bright silvery fish with a deep body, the palometa may be grayish-green and blue above and yellowish on the breast. It has dark, elongated dorsal and anal fins that are bordered in a bluish shade and a black-edged tail. It also has four narrow bars that vary from black to white and are located high on the sides. Traces of a fifth bar appear near the tail.

It is similar to the Florida pompano, but the front lobes of the dorsal and the anal fins are blackish and very elongate (the tips reach back to the middle of the caudal fin).

Size. The palometa rarely reaches 1 pound in weight and is usually 7 to 14 inches long; 18 inches is its maximum length. The all-tackle world record weighed 1 pound, 4 ounces.

Spawning behavior. This species is thought to spawn offshore in the spring, the summer, and the fall.

Food. Palometa feed on crustaceans, marine worms, mollusks, and small fish.

OTHER NAMES

gafftopsail pompano, joefish, longfin pompano, sand mackerel; French: *carangue quatre;* Portuguese: *galhudo;* Spanish: *palometa, pampano.*

Distribution. In the western Atlantic, palometa extend from Massachusetts to Argentina, as well as throughout the Caribbean Sea, the Gulf of Mexico, and Bermuda. They are common in the eastern and the southern Caribbean, occasional in the Bahamas and Florida, and uncommon to rare in the northwest Caribbean.

Habitat. Inhabiting waters up to 35 feet deep, palometa generally form large schools in clearwater areas of the surf zone, along sandy beaches and bays, occasionally around reefs, and in rocky areas.

Perch, Silver

Bairdiella chrysoura

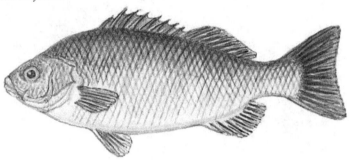

OTHER NAMES

sand perch.

Distribution. *Silver perch occur from New York southward along the Atlantic coast and also in the Gulf of Mexico.*

Habitat. *The silver perch is an inshore fish, most common in bays, seagrass beds, tidal creeks, small rivers, and quiet lagoons near estuaries. It is sometimes found in brackish marshes and also occasionally in freshwater.*

The silver perch is a member of the Sciaenidae family (drum and croaker). It is one of the most common and abundant Atlantic drum, harvested by commercial netters but seldom prominent in the angler's catch. This small panfishlike species is good to eat, but it is more likely to be used by anglers as live bait for larger predators.

The closely related bairdiella, or gulf croaker (*Bairdiella icistius*), is one of a number of marine species introduced successfully to the Salton Sea from the Gulf of California. It grows to 12 inches there and is an important forage fish.

Identification. The body of the silver perch is high and compressed. As with others in the drum family, its dorsal fins are separated by a deep notch. There are five to six pores on the chin and no barbels. Its mouth is terminal and has finely serrated teeth. Its coloring is silvery, with yellowish fins and a whitish belly. It commonly has no spots.

The silver perch can be distinguished from the unrelated white perch by the dark stripes that line the sides. It can also be distinguished from the sand seatrout by its lack of prominent canine teeth and by its chin pores.

Size/Age. The average fish is less than 12 inches long and ½ pound or less; it never weighs more than a pound. The silver perch can live up to 6 years.

Life history/Behavior. The silver perch migrates offshore in the winter and returns inshore to breed in the spring. Spawning occurs inshore between May and September in shallow, saline areas. Silver perch reach maturity by their second or third year, when 6 inches long.

Food. Adults consume crustaceans, worms, and small fish.

Perch, White

Morone americana

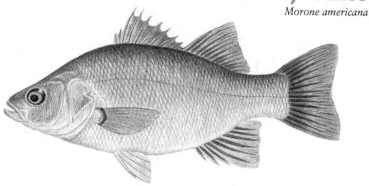

The white perch is not a true perch but a member of the temperate bass family and a relative of the white bass and the striped bass. It is abundant in some places, rare in others, similar enough to other species to be misidentified, and underappreciated as table fare.

Identification. The white perch has a deep, thin body that slopes up steeply from each eye to the beginning of the dorsal fin and that is deepest under the first dorsal fin. A large, older specimen can be nearly humpbacked at that spot. Colors can be olive, gray-green, silvery gray, dark brown, or black on the back, becoming a lighter silvery green on the sides and silvery white on the belly. The pelvic and the anal fins (both on the belly) are sometimes rosy colored, and the pelvic fins sit forward on the body, below the pectoral fins.

Size/Age. The average white perch caught by anglers weighs about three-quarters of a pound and is 9 inches long. The normal life span is 5 to 7 years, but white perch may live up to 17 years. The largest white perch recorded is a 4-pound, 12-ounce specimen.

Life history/Behavior. White perch spawn in the spring, usually when the water temperature is between 57° and 75°F, and in shallow water. They are a schooling species that stays in loose open-water schools through adulthood. They do not orient to cover and structure.

Food and feeding habits. White perch are generally more active in low light and nocturnally, moving to surface (or inshore) waters at night, retreating to deeper water during the day. They eat many kinds of small fish, such as smelt, killifish, and other white perch, and reportedly consume crabs, shrimp, and small alewives and herring.

OTHER NAMES

silver bass, silver perch, sea perch, bass, narrow-mouthed bass, bass perch, gray perch, bluenose perch, humpy; French: *bar blanc d'Amerique.*

Distribution. *White perch are found along the Atlantic coast from the southern Gulf of St. Lawrence to South Carolina and inland along the upper St. Lawrence River to the lower Great Lakes.*

Habitat. *The adaptable white perch is at home in saltwater, brackish water, and freshwater. In marine environs, it is primarily found in brackish water, estuaries, and coastal rivers and streams, and some of the latter have sea-run populations. Some white perch remain resident in brackish bays and estuaries, whereas others roam widely in search of food. They are considered demersal and tend to stay deep in their home waters, on or close to the bottom.*

Permit

Trachinotus falcatus

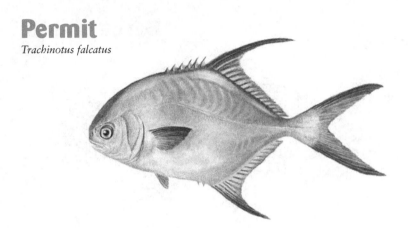

OTHER NAMES

French: *carangue plume;*
Portuguese: *sernambiguara;*
Spanish: *palometa, pam-
pano, pampano erizero,
pámpano palometa.*

Distribution. *Permit occur
in the western Atlantic,
ranging from Massachusetts
to southeastern Brazil,
including the Bahamas and
much of the West Indies.
They are most common in
Florida, the Bahamas, and
the Caribbean.*

Habitat. *Permit inhabit
shallow, warm waters in
depths of up to 100 feet,
and young fish prefer
clearer and shallower waters
than do adults. Able to
adapt to a wide range of
salinity, they occur in channels or holes over sandy
flats and around reefs and
sometimes over mud bot-
toms. They are primarily a
schooling fish when
younger, traveling in groups
of 10 or more, although
they are occasionally seen in
great numbers, and they
tend to become solitary
with age.*

An important gamefish and a particularly prized member of
the Carangidae family of jacks and pompano, the permit is
a tough fighter and a handful on light tackle.

Identification. In overall appearance, the permit is a bril-
liantly silver fish with dark fins and a dark or iridescent blue to
greenish or grayish back. The belly is often yellowish, and
sometimes the pelvic fins and the front lobe of the anal fin
have an orange tint. Many individuals have a dark, circular
black area on the sides behind the base of the pectoral fins,
and some have a dusky midbody blotch. The body is laterally
compressed, and the fish has a high back profile; young fish
appear roundish, adults more oblong. Small permit have
teeth on the tongue. The permit has 16 to 19 soft anal rays,
and the second dorsal fin has one spine and 17 to 21 soft
rays, compared with 22 to 27 in the similar Florida pompano.
It is further distinguished by its deeper body and a generally
larger body size. Also, the second and the third ribs in the
permit are prominent in fish weighing more than 10 pounds,
and these ribs can be felt through the sides of the fish to help
in differentiating it from the Florida pompano.

Size. Permit commonly weigh up to 25 pounds and are 1
to 3 feet long, but they can exceed 50 pounds and reach 45
inches in length. The all-tackle world record is a 56-pound,
2-ounce Florida fish caught in 1997.

Food and feeding habits. Over sandy bottoms, permit
feed mainly on mollusks, and over reefs they feed mostly on
crustaceans such as crabs, shrimp, and sea urchins. Like
bonefish, they feed by rooting in the sand on shallow flats.

Pigfish

Orthopristis chrysoptera

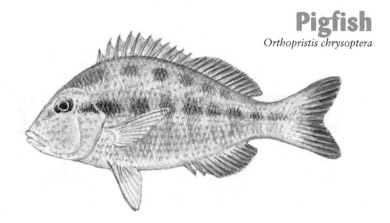

Anglers catch this species in large numbers on hook and line and also in nets in warm temperate waters. It is used mainly as bait for larger predators.

Identification. The pigfish has long anal fins, matching the soft dorsal fin in shape and in size. The head is sloped and pointed, the snout almost piglike, and the lips thin. A background color of bluish-gray is marked with brassy spots in indistinct lines that are horizontal below the lateral line but extend obliquely upward and backward above the lateral line. These oblique markings are also found on the cheeks. The fins are yellow-bronze, with dusky margins.

Age/Size. The maximum length and weight are 18 inches and 2 pounds, but pigfish are commonly 7 to 9 inches long and weigh no more than a half pound. Pigfish normally live for 3 years.

Life history/Behavior. These schooling fish are mostly nocturnal. Spawning occurs inshore in the spring and the early summer, prior to when the fish move into estuaries.

Food. Pigfish are bottom feeders that forage on crustaceans, worms, and small fish.

OTHER NAMES

Spanish: *corocoro burro.*

Distribution. The pigfish exists in the western Atlantic, from Massachusetts and Bermuda to the Gulf of Mexico. They are most abundant from the Chesapeake Bay south and do not inhabit tropical waters.

Habitat. Pigfish are found in coastal waters over sand and mud bottoms.

Pilotfish

Naucrates ductor

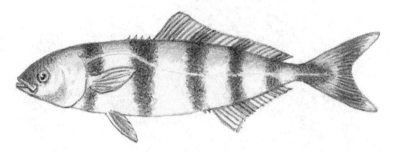

Pilotfish are a unique and circumtropical species widely found in the Atlantic, the Pacific, and the Indian Oceans. They are renowned for accompanying large sharks on their oceanic wanderings, as well as whales, rays, schools of various other fish, and ships. A pilotfish is said to have followed a sailing ship for 80 days.

This species has no angling value but is often observed by offshore anglers. It feeds on scraps of the host's leftovers, as well as on parasites, small fish, and invertebrates. Minor commercial interest exists for this species, which is of the jack family and looks somewhat like an amberjack.

The pilotfish has five to seven dark vertical bars on its elongated body and a low spinous first dorsal fin with four spines. It can grow to a maximum of 27 inches.

Pinfish
Lagodon rhomboides

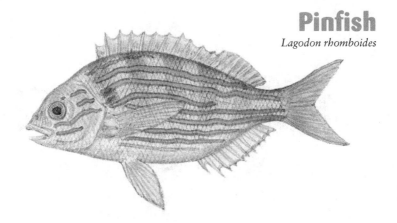

This abundant, small member of the Sparidae family is important as forage for predatory species of fish and is widely used by anglers as bait. There was once a fairly good commercial fishery for pinfish, but it is now a minor one; the flesh is oily and has a strong flavor.

Identification. The pinfish has a compressed panfishlike body, with a head that is high through the area just in front of the dorsal fin. It has a small mouth and incisorlike teeth with deeply notched edges. Its coloration is silvery overall, with yellow and blue horizontal stripes. A round black spot at the upper rear margin of each gill cover is distinctive. The name of the species comes from the needle-sharp spines on the first dorsal fin. All fins are yellowish.

A similar small porgy, the spottail pinfish *(Diplodus holbrooki)*, averages less than 10 inches in length, but occasional larger individuals do exist. It is identified by the large black band across the base of the caudal peduncle and by the black margin on the gill covers. Otherwise, the body is silvery, with only faint black bars. The spottail pinfish is common over rocky bottoms and around docks and piers. In the Caribbean it is replaced by the almost identical silver porgy *(D. argenteus).*

Size. Pinfish are capable of growing to 15 inches, but they rarely reach 10 inches in length and are common at about 7 inches. They live at least 7 years and probably longer.

Food and feeding habits. Pinfish consume crustaceans, mollusks, worms, and occasionally small fish associated with grassy habitats. They nibble at most foods, a habit that makes them a nuisance for anglers fishing with bait for other bottom-dwelling species.

OTHER NAMES
bream, saltwater bream, sailor's choice, Canadian bream; Spanish: *sargo salema.*

Distribution. *The pinfish occurs in the western Atlantic, from Massachusetts to the northern Gulf of Mexico, including Bermuda, to the Yucatán Peninsula in Mexico. The spottail pinfish is found in the Gulf of Mexico and in Florida.*

Habitat/Spawning behavior. *Pinfish are coastal and inshore species that travel in schools, sometimes in great numbers, over vegetated and sometimes rocky bottoms and around docks and pilings; they also frequent mangrove areas and may enter brackish water or freshwater. Pinfish move out of coastal waters in the winter, and spawning occurs in the winter in offshore waters.*

Pollock

Pollachius virens

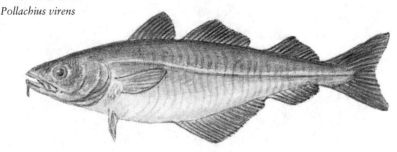

OTHER NAMES

coalfish, Boston bluefish, green cod, blisterback, saithe, coley.

Distribution. *In North America, pollock range from Greenland and Labrador south to Virginia.*

Habitat. *Generally a deep or midwater fish, the pollock prefers rocky bottoms in waters shallower than those cod or haddock prefer. They occur in depths of up to 100 fathoms, although they are found as shallow as 4 fathoms.*

A member of the Gadidae family, the pollock is the most active of the various codfish and has been popular with anglers. It is an important commercial species, taken primarily by trawls and gillnets, and not to be confused with another cod family member, the Alaska, or walleye, pollock *(Theragra calcogramma)*. A similar species sought by anglers is the European pollack *(Pollachius pollachius)*.

Identification. The pollock is olive green to greenish-brown on top and yellowish-gray on the sides and the belly, with silvery overtones. It can be distinguished from other members of the cod family, such as the Atlantic cod, the haddock, and the tomcod, by three features: The lower jaw of the pollock projects beyond the upper jaw, the tail is forked, and the lateral line is quite straight, not arching above the pectoral fins. A young pollock has codlike barbels on the chin, but these are small and usually disappear with age. The European pollack is distinguished from the pollock by its lateral line, which is decurved over the pectoral fins.

Size/Age. Pollock can grow to 3½ feet, although most adults are much smaller. The average fish weighs between 4 and 15 pounds. The all-tackle record is 50 pounds. A slow-growing fish, the pollock reaches about 30 inches at age 9. They have been reported to live as long as 31 years, but few pollock live longer than 12 years.

Life history/Behavior. The spawning season for pollock is in the late autumn and the early winter. Their eggs are free-floating and drift on the surface, and for the first 3 months, larvae are present on or near the surface. Juveniles travel in large, tightly packed schools near the surface.

Food. Pollock feed in large schools on small herring, small cod, and their relatives, and on sand eels and various tiny crustaceans.

Pompano, African
Alectis ciliaris

The African pompano is the largest and most widespread member of the Carangidae family of jacks and pompano, surrounded by a great deal of confusion because until recently, adults and young were classified as entirely different species. A strong fighter and an excellent light-tackle gamefish, it is a superb food fish and is marketed fresh or salted/dried.

Identification. The most striking characteristic of the African pompano is the four to six elongated, threadlike filaments that extend from the front part of the second dorsal and the anal fins. These filaments tend to disappear or erode as the fish grows.

The body shape of the African pompano changes as it grows; starting out short and deep, it becomes more elongated by the time the fish is 14 inches long, and the forehead becomes steeper and blunter. In both young and adult fish, their bodies are strongly compressed, and the rear halves of their body are triangular. The lateral line arches smoothly but steeply above the pectoral fins and has 24 to 38 relatively weak scutes in the straight portion and 120 to 140 scales. Shiny and silvery on the whole, a larger fish may be light bluish-green on the back; on all fish, there may be dark blotches on the operculums on the top part of the caudal peduncles, as well as on the front part of the second dorsal and the anal fins. A young African pompano has five to six ventral bars.

Size. This species is known to attain a length of 42 inches and can grow to 60 pounds; the all-tackle world record is a 50-pound, 8-ounce Florida fish. Twenty- to 30-pounders are common in South Florida.

Food. African pompano feed on sedentary or slow-moving crustaceans, on small crabs, and occasionally on small fish.

OTHER NAMES

Cuban jack, Atlantic threadfin, pennantfish, threadfin mirrorfish, trevally; Afrikaans: *draadvin-spie lvis;* Arabic: *bambo, tailar;* French: *aile ronde, carangue, cordonnier;* Hawaiian: *papio, ulua;* Malay/Indonesian: *cermin, ebek, rambai landeh;* Portuguese: *xaréu africano;* Spanish: *caballa, chicuaca, elechudo, jurel de pluma, paja blanco, palometa, pampano, sol, zapatero.*

Distribution. *African pompano occur in the western Atlantic from Massachusetts and Bermuda to Brazil, as well as throughout the Caribbean Sea and the Gulf of Mexico. In the eastern Pacific, they range from Mexico to Peru.*

Habitat. *Inhabiting waters up to 300 feet deep, African pompano often prefer to be near the bottom over rocky reefs and around wrecks. They may form small, somewhat polarized, schools, although they are usually solitary in the adult stage.*

Pompano, Florida

Trachinotus carolinus

OTHER NAMES

Portuguese: *pampo, pampo-verdadeiro;* Spanish: *palometa, pampano, pampano-amarillo.*

Distribution. *Florida pompano range from Massachusetts to Brazil and throughout the Gulf of Mexico. They are most prominent from the Chesapeake Bay to Florida and west to Texas and are abundant in the warm waters of Florida and the Caribbean.*

Habitat. *Inhabiting inshore and nearshore waters, adult Florida pompano occur along sandy beaches, including oyster bars, grassbeds, and inlets, and often in the turbid water of brackish bays and estuaries. They usually prefer shallow water but may occur in water as deep as 130 feet. Florida pompano generally form small to large schools that travel close to the shore and migrate northward and southward along the Atlantic coast, staying in waters with temperatures between 82° and 89°F.*

A member of the Carangidae family of jacks and pompanos, the Florida pompano is an excellent gamefish for its size and is an exciting catch on light tackle. It is also considered a gourmet food fish because of its delicately flavored and finely textured meat.

Identification. Mostly silvery when alive, the Florida pompano is one of the few fish that is more striking in color after death. It then has greenish-gray or dark blue shading on the back and a golden cast to the belly and the fins. Deep- or dark-water fish tend to also have gold on the throats and on the pelvic and the anal fins; young fish tend to have yellowish bellies, anal fins, and tails. The Florida pompano has a deep, flattened body; a short, blunt snout with a small mouth; and a deeply forked tail. Unlike most jacks, it has no scutes on the caudal peduncle. The first and spinous dorsal fin is very low and usually hard to see, whereas the second dorsal fin has one spine and 22 to 27 soft dorsal rays. The anal fin, which begins slightly farther back on the body than the second dorsal fin, has three spines and 20 to 23 soft anal rays. The Florida pompano is similar to the permit, although the permit is deeper-bodied and tends to be a much larger fish, growing to 40 pounds.

Size/Age. The Florida pompano has an estimated life span of 3 to 4 years. It rarely grows larger than 6 pounds and 25 inches long, and usually weighs less than 3 pounds. The all-tackle world record is an 8-pound, 1-ounce Florida fish.

Spawning behavior. Reaching sexual maturity at the end of their first year, Florida pompano spawn offshore between March and September, with a peak of activity from April through June.

Food. Florida pompano feed on mollusks, crustaceans, and other invertebrates and small fish.

Porgies

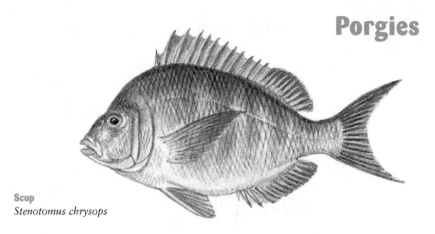

Scup
Stenotomus chrysops

The Sparidae family of porgies comprise roughly 112 species, and as a group they have worldwide distribution in the tropical and temperate waters of the Atlantic, the Pacific, and the Indian Oceans, although a few range into cooler waters.

Porgies are similar to grunts, but their bodies are even more flattened from side to side, or compressed, and high through the area just in front of the dorsal fins. As in some grunts, a porgy's eyes are located high on the head and just behind the posterior margin of the mouth. The second, or soft, dorsal fin and the anal fin are both large and are about the same shape.

Porgies are medium-size to small. Some live close to shore, others in offshore waters. They are prevalent around reefs, but some are found only over sandy bottoms; others inhabit rocky bottoms. Most species can change their colors from solid to blotched or barred and from dark to light, effecting a better camouflage. They are omnivorous and typically travel in schools. Included in the group are a number of species that are harvested for food. Many also provide good, generally light-tackle, sport for anglers. They are relatively easy to catch and, for their size, put up a strong fight.

In the United States, porgies, like grunts, are predominantly an Atlantic species off the coast. The scup *(Stenotomus chrysops)* averages less than 10 inches in length but is one of the most prominent members of this family. It is valued by both anglers and commercial fishermen along the northeastern and mid-Atlantic U.S. coast. The jolthead porgy *(Calamus bajonado)* is one of a large group of porgies found in warm waters of the Caribbean and off southern Florida, occasionally drifting with the Gulf Stream as far north as Bermuda. Distinctively shaped, it is the largest member of its genus.

Porgy, Jolthead

Calamus bajonado

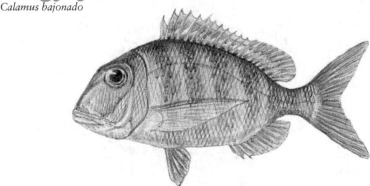

OTHER NAMES

porgy; Spanish: *pluma bajonado.*

Distribution. *The jolthead porgy occurs in the western Atlantic, from Rhode Island to the northern Gulf of Mexico, including Bermuda, and south to Brazil. It is most abundant in the West Indies.*

Habitat. *The jolthead occurs in coastal environs over vegetated sand bottoms and more frequently on coral bottoms between 20 and 150 feet deep. Large adults are usually solitary.*

A member of the Sparidae family, which includes about 112 species, the jolthead is an excellent food fish with some commercial value and a species that bottom-probing anglers often encounter along the eastern United States; it has been associated with ciguatera, however. The common name presumably comes from the fish's habit of using its head to bump or jolt clams or other mollusks loose from their attachments.

Identification. The high, rounded forehead gives the body a distinctive profile, typical of the genus. It eyes are large and are located high on the head. Yellowish-brown, with an almost metallic luster, it may be blotched with dusky splotches or nearly solid in color, depending on the bottom over which it is swimming. Some individuals are grayish. Over each eye is a blue streak, and sometimes there are faint blue lengthwise stripes on the body. The caudal fin is lunate (crescent-shaped).

Size. Among the largest of the porgies, this species is typically 20 inches long, but it can attain a length of 26 inches and a weight of 23 pounds. The all-tackle world record is a 23-pound, 4-ounce specimen.

Food and feeding behavior. The diet of jolthead porgies is sea urchins, crabs, and mollusks. Small schools are often seen feeding near shore.

Queenfish (Croaker)

Seriphus politus

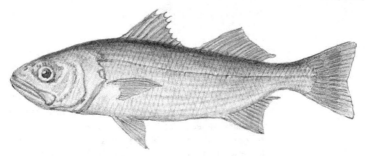

The queenfish is a small croaker and a member of the Sciaenidae family (drum and croaker). Essentially a panfish-size bottom scrounger, it is not an esteemed sport or food fish, but it is commonly caught from Pacific coast piers and may be desirable as whole or cut bait for other species.

Identification. The queenfish has an elongated, moderately compressed body. The upper profile is depressed over the eyes, and it has a large mouth. Its coloring is bluish above and becomes silvery below. The fins are yellowish. This species is distinguished from other croaker by its large mouth; by the base of its second dorsal and anal fins, which are roughly equal; and by the wide space between its two dorsal fins. There is no chin barbel on the lower jaw.

Size. The maximum length of the queenfish is 12 inches, but most fish are considerably smaller.

Spawning behavior. Spawning occurs along the coast in the summer. The eggs are free floating, and newly hatched juveniles appear in the late summer and the fall; they gradually move shoreward from depths of 20 to 30 feet into the surf zone.

Food. Queenfish feed on small, free-swimming crustaceans, crabs, and fish.

OTHER NAMES

herring, herring croaker, kingfish, shiner, queen croaker; Spanish: *corvina reina.*

Distribution. *The queenfish is found along the Pacific coast, from Yaquina Bay, Oregon, to Uncle Sam Bank in Baja California, Mexico. It is common in Southern California but rare north of Monterey.*

Habitat. *Queenfish commonly inhabit shallow water over sandy bottoms in the summer. They mostly occur in water from 4 to 25 feet deep but have been known to dwell as deep as 180 feet. They often gather in tightly packed schools, sometimes with white croaker, in shallow sandy areas near pilings and piers, and they migrate to deeper water at night.*

Rays and Skates

The various families that belong to the order of fish known as Rajiformes are generally referred to as rays and skates and include such groupings as sawfish, guitarfish, electric rays, stingrays, eagle rays, manta rays, and skates. Among the dominant distinguishing features of this order are gill openings wholly on the ventral surface and forward edges of the pectoral fins connected with the sides of the head and situated forward, past the five pairs of gill openings; eyeballs not free from the upper edges of the orbits, as they are in sharks; and no anal fin.

Most Rajiformes are easily recognized by their form. Their bodies are flattened dorso-ventrally, and the pectoral fins extend widely and seem to be part of their bodies. The tail sections are more or less defined from their bodies, their eyes and spiracles are on the top side, and their mouths and the entire lengths of the gill openings are situated on the bottom side.

Most Rajiformes live on the bottom or close to it and are comparatively sluggish. Some lie buried in the sand or mud most of the time and are poor swimmers. Skates are capable of swift propulsion when necessary, although they usually swim slowly and close to the bottom. Sawfish also spend a good part of the time along the bottom but rise to pursue fish. Eagle rays are quite active and often swim close to the surface, although they feed on the bottom. Mantas spend most of their lives swimming near the surface or not too far beneath it.

Rays and skates subsist on a variety of animal food, including all available invertebrates that inhabit sandy or muddy bottoms. Eagle rays, as a group, prefer hard-shelled mollusks, while sawfish occasionally leave their bottom foraging to crash into a school of closely packed fish. Electric rays are strictly fish eaters, sometimes taking surprisingly

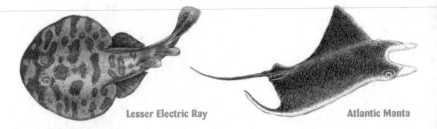

Lesser Electric Ray   **Atlantic Manta**

large prey in comparison to their size. Mantas feed on tiny plankton, small crustaceans, and small fish.

Members of this clan range in size from only a few inches to giant mantas with a breadth of about 23 feet. The spectacularly armed sawfish reach a length of more than 20 feet.

The smalltooth sawfish *(Pristis pectinata)* is commonly 15 feet long and sometimes reaches a length of 20 feet. It can weigh as much as 800 pounds. This species occurs throughout warm Atlantic waters from North Carolina to Brazil.

One of the most common stingrays along the Atlantic coast of North America is the bluntnose stingray *(Dasyatis say),* which measures about 3 feet across its pectorals. It ranges from New Jersey to Argentina and is widespread in the West Indies. The Atlantic stingray *(D. sabina)* measures only slightly more than a foot across its wings, which are very rounded. This yellowish-brown stingray occurs from Chesapeake Bay to southern Florida and the Gulf of Mexico. More common than the Atlantic stingray and ranging from New Jersey to Argentina is the southern stingray *(D. americana),* which averages about 3 feet wide. On the underside of its tail, just behind the spine, are finlike folds; above them, the tail is keeled.

The little skate *(R. erinacea)* is the most common skate species along the Atlantic coast of North America, ranging from Nova Scotia to North Carolina. It is about 1½ feet long and weighs only about a pound. The big skate *(R. binoculata),* reaches a length of 8 feet and occurs from the Bering Sea and the Aleutians to Baja California, Mexico. The more abundant California skate *(R. inornata)* averages about 2 feet in length and has four to five rows of prickly spines on its tail; it occurs from British Columbia to central Baja California. The barndoor skate *(R. laevis)* is one of the most aggressive of all skates and grows to a length of about 5 feet. It is common from Newfoundland to Cape Hatteras.

Smalltooth Sawfish

Southern Stingray

Atlantic Stingray

Skate Egg Case

Common Skate

Remoras

Sharksucker
Echeneis naucrates

Members of the Echeneidae family, remoras and sharksuckers are slim fish that have a flat sucking disk on the top of their heads. They attach themselves usually to sharks or other fish—including marlin, grouper, and rays—but sometimes to the bottoms of boats or other objects. These hitchhikers take effortless rides with their hosts, feeding on parasitic copepods found on the hosts' bodies and gill chambers.

Developed from the first dorsal fin, the sucking disk consists of a series of ridges and spaces that create a vacuum between the remora and the surface to which it attaches. By sliding backward, the remora can increase the suction, or it can release itself by swimming forward.

The sharksucker *(Echeneis naucrates),* which averages 1½ feet in length but may be as much as 38 inches long and can weigh up to 2 pounds, is the largest member of the family. Worldwide in distribution in warm seas, it is gray with a broad, white-edged black band down each side, tapering to the tail. It prefers sharks and rays as hosts and often enters shallow beach and coastal areas; it has been known on rare occasions to attach itself to bathers or divers.

Also cosmopolitan is the remora *(Remora remora),* which is common to 12 inches long and may attain a length of 34 inches. It is black or dark brown and is also found worldwide. It, too, prefers sharks as hosts. Some other species show distinct host preferences. The whalesucker *(R. australis),* for example, generally fastens itself to a whale; the spearfish remora *(R. brachyptera)* commonly attaches to billfish such as marlin.

Although often observed by anglers, remoras have no angling merits.

Rockfish

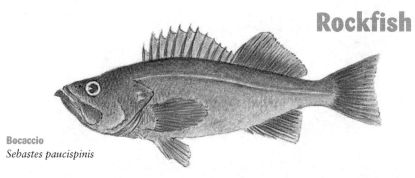

Bocaccio
Sebastes paucispinis

A diverse and important group of marine fish, rockfish are members of the Scorpaenidae family, which includes 310 species generically characterized as scorpionfish. Rockfish may be referred to as rock cod, sea bass, snapper, and ocean perch because of their resemblance to these species or to the quality of their fillets, but the latter species are not related to rockfish.

Identification. Adult rockfish range in size from 5 to 41 inches, but most species grow to between 20 and 24 inches in length. The rockfish is characterized by bony plates or spines on the head and the body, a large mouth, and pelvic fins attached forward near the pectoral fins. The spines are venomous, and although not extremely toxic, they can still cause pain and infection. Some species are brightly colored. Rockfish appear somewhat perchlike or basslike and are often called sea bass.

Food. Adult rockfish feed on a variety of food items. Adults feed on sand lance, herring, and small rockfish, as well as crustaceans.

Common species. The most common species encountered in Alaska include the black *(Sebastes melanops),* the copper *(S. caurinus),* the dusky *(S. ciliatus),* the quillback *(S. maliger),* and the yelloweye *(S. ruberrimus).*

Common species in Washington include the black, the copper, the quillback, and the yelloweye.

Common species in Oregon include the black, the blue *(S. mystinus),* the bocaccio *(S. paucispinis),* the China *(S. nebulosis),* the copper, the Pacific ocean perch *(S. alutus),* and the yelloweye.

Common species in California include the black, the blue, the bocaccio, the canary *(S. pinniger),* the chilipepper *(S. goodei),* the copper, the cowcod *(S. levis),* the greenspotted *(S. chlorostictus),* the olive *(S. serranoides),* the starry *(S. constellatus),* the vermilion *(S. miniatus),* the widow *(S. entomelas),* and the yellowtail *(S. flavidus).*

Distribution. There are roughly 68 species of rockfish in the genus Sebastes *and two in the genus* Sebastolobus *that are found along the coasts of North America. Nearly all occur in Pacific waters.*

Habitat. Rockfish can generally be separated into those that live in the shallower nearshore waters of the continental shelf and those that live in deeper waters on the edge of the continental shelf. The former comprise species that are always found in rocky bottom areas (called shelf demersal by biologists) and those that spend much of their time up in the water column and off the bottom (shelf pelagic).

Rockfish, Black

Sebastes melanops

A member of the Scorpaenidae family, the black rockfish is widely distributed in the eastern Pacific. It is an excellent food fish.

Identification. The body of the black rockfish is oval or egg shaped and compressed. The head has a steep upper profile that is almost straight; the mouth is large and the lower jaw projects slightly. The eyes are moderately large. The color is brown to black on the back, paler on the sides, and dirty white below. There are black spots on the dorsal fin. This species is easily confused with the blue rockfish; however, the anal fin of the black rockfish is rounded, whereas the anal fin of the blue rockfish is slanted or straight. The black rockfish has spots on the dorsal fin, and the blue rockfish does not.

Size. This species can attain a length of 25 inches and a weight of 11 pounds. The largest recorded weighed 10½ pounds.

Life history/Behavior. Like all members of its family, the black rockfish is ovoviviparous, with egg fertilization and development taking place in the body of the mother. When embryonic development is complete, the female releases the eggs; the exposure to seawater activates the embryo, and it escapes from the egg case. The young hatch in the spring and form large schools off the bottom in estuaries and tide pools in the summer. Adults may be abundant in the summer in shallow water near kelp-lined shores, but they occupy deeper water in the fall and the winter. They may school over rocky reefs from the bottom to the surface and are caught at varied depths, from near the surface to 1,200 feet.

Food. The diet of black rockfish includes squid, crabs' eggs, and fish. They are occasionally observed feeding on sand lance on the surface. Salmon anglers sometimes catch this fish on trolled herring.

Rockfish, Copper

Sebastes caurinus

The copper rockfish is a member of the Scorpaenidae family and is a widely distributed, hardy species. It often appears in aquarium displays.

Identification. The body of the copper rockfish is moderately deep and compressed. The head is large, with a slightly curved upper profile; the mouth is large, and the lower jaw projects slightly. Its coloring is copper brown to orange tinged with pink. The back two-thirds of the sides along the lateral line are light, the belly is white, and there are usually two dark bands radiating backward from each eye.

Size. This species can attain a length of 22 to 23 inches and a weight of 10 pounds.

Life history. Copper rockfish are ovoviviparous, like all species in the genus *Sebastes*.

Food and feeding habits. The diet of copper rockfish includes snails, worms, squid, octopus, crabs, shrimp, and fish.

OTHER NAMES

never die, whitebelly, chucklehead, rock cod, bass.

Distribution. The copper rockfish occurs from the San Benitos Islands, Baja California, to the Kenai Peninsula, Alaska.

Habitat. This fish is commonly found in shallow rocky and sandy areas and is generally caught at depths of less than 180 feet; however, some have been taken as deep as 600 feet.

Rockfish, Yelloweye

Sebastes ruberrimus

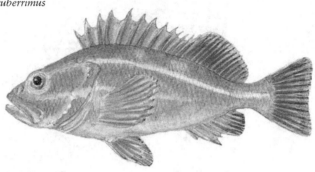

red snapper, rasphead rockfish, turkey-red rock-fish.

Distribution. *This species occurs from the Gulf of Alaska to Baja California, Mexico.*

Habitat. *Rocky reefs and boulder fields, from 10 to 300 fathoms, are the usual haunts of yelloweye rock-fish. They are abundant during the summer in shallow water along kelp-lined shores and are found in deeper water at other times.*

Also a member of the Scorpaenidae family, the yelloweye rockfish is known to many anglers as "red snapper," although it bears only a slight resemblance to a true snapper. It is one of many red to yellow species in the eastern Pacific, however, and resembles several others, making identification difficult. The large size and the excellent flesh of this species make it a favorite among anglers.

Identification. The yelloweye rockfish is orange-red to orange-yellow in body coloration; it has bright-yellow irises and black pupils and a raspy ridge above the eyes. The fins may be black at the margins. An adult usually has a light (perhaps white) band on the lateral line. A juvenile has two light bands, one on the lateral line and one shorter line below the lateral line. A large rockfish, the yelloweye is a heavy-boned, spiny fish through the head and "shoulders."

Size/Age. The yelloweye rockfish can attain a length of 36 inches and can weigh up to 33 pounds. The all-tackle world record is an Alaskan fish that weighed 39 pounds, 4 ounces.

Life history. Yelloweye rockfish are ovoviviparous, like all species in the genus *Sebastes.*

Food. The diet of yelloweye rockfish includes assorted fish, crustaceans, squid, and shrimp.

Roosterfish

Nematistius pectoralis

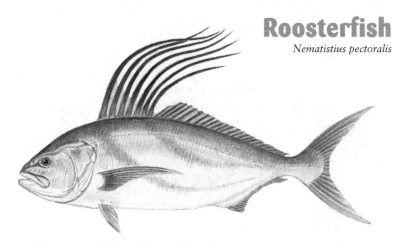

The roosterfish is a superb light-tackle gamefish and a member of the Carangidae family of jacks, so named for the comb of long dorsal fin spines that extends far above the body of the fish. It has been exploited at a local level because of its excellent quality as a food fish and is marketed fresh.

Identification. A striking, iridescent fish, the roosterfish is characterized by seven long, threadlike dorsal fin spines, which are found even on young fish. This comb stands erect when the roosterfish is excited, as when threatened, but ordinarily, the fin remains lowered in a sheath along the back. There are also two dark, curved stripes on the body and a dark spot at the base of the pectoral fin.

Size. Roosterfish can grow to 4 feet in length and exceed 100 pounds. The all-tackle world record is a 114-pound fish taken off Baja California in 1960.

Food and feeding habits. Roosterfish consume assorted small fish, with large roosters (50 pounds and over) being capable of capturing even bonito up to 2 pounds in size. When found along beaches, they may be in schools and may feed competitively, with various members of a school simultaneously chasing bait, or lures, for considerable distances.

OTHER NAMES

Spanish: *papagallo, gallo, pez de gallo, reje pluma.*

Distribution. Endemic to the eastern Pacific, roosterfish occur from San Clemente in Southern California to Peru, including the Galápagos Islands; they are rare north of Baja California, Mexico.

Habitat. Roosterfish inhabit shallow inshore areas, such as sandy shores along beaches. They are often found around rock outcroppings and rocky islands. Young fish are often found in tidal pools.

Runner, Blue

Caranx crysos

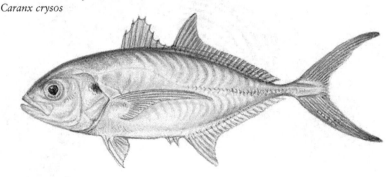

OTHER NAMES

hardtail, hard-tailed jack, runner; French: *carangue coubali;* Greek: *kokali;* Italian: *carangidi, carangido mediterraneo;* Portuguese: *carangídeos, xaralete;* Spanish: *atún, cojinua, cojinúa negra, cojinuda.*

Distribution. *In the western Atlantic, blue runners occur from Nova Scotia to Brazil, including the Caribbean and the Gulf of Mexico.*

Habitat. *Blue runners inhabit offshore waters in large schools. They are occasionally found over reefs, sometimes in pairs or solitary. Young fish frequently linger around sargassum and other floating objects.*

The blue runner is a small, spunky member of the Carangidae family that is valued as bait for big-game fishing. It is an excellent food fish and is marketed fresh, frozen, and salted.

Identification. The body of the blue runner is bluish-green to brassy, silvery, or light olive above. There is a black, somewhat elongated spot near the upper end of the gill cover, and there may be faint bluish bars on the body. A characteristic feature is the blackish shading on the tips of the tail fins. The blue runner is easily distinguished from the crevalle jack because it lacks the dark blotch found on the pectoral fins of that fish.

Size. This species usually weighs less than 1 pound and is typically 1 foot long; the all-tackle world record is an 11-pound, 2-ounce fish taken off Alabama.

Life history. Sexually mature when they reach 9 to 10 inches in length, blue runners spawn offshore from January through August.

Food. Blue runners feed primarily on fish, shrimp, squid, and other invertebrates.

Runner, Rainbow

Elagatis bipinnulata

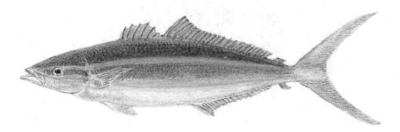

A member of the Carangidae family of jacks, the rainbow runner does not look like other jacks because it is a much slimmer, more streamlined fish. It is also an excellent food fish, with firm, white flesh, marketed fresh and salted/dried. In Japan, the rainbow runner is cooked with a special sauce or eaten raw and is considered a delicacy.

Identification. The rainbow runner is blue-green above and white or silver below, with a yellow or pink cast. On both sides, there is a broad, dark-blue, horizontal stripe from the snout to the base of the tail; a narrow, pale-blue stripe immediately below it that runs through each eye; a pale to brilliant-yellow stripe below that; and then another narrow pale-blue stripe. The tail is yellow and the other fins are a greenish- or olive yellow. The rainbow runner has a slender body that is more elongated than those of most other jacks. The first dorsal fin has six spines and the second has one spine and 25 to 27 connected soft rays. Behind this is a 2-rayed finlet. The anal fin has a single detached spine with 16 to 18 soft rays, followed by a 2-rayed finlet. The rainbow runner is similar to the cobia in shape but can be distinguished by its coloring, as well as by the finlets that follow the dorsal and the anal fins.

Size. The rainbow runner is typically 2 to 3 feet long, although it can reach 4 feet and 22 pounds. The all-tackle world record is a 37-pound, 9-ounce Mexican fish.

Food. Rainbow runners feed on invertebrates, small fish, and squid.

OTHER NAMES

runner, rainbow yellowtail, skipjack, shoemaker, Hawaiian salmon, prodigal son; Creole: *carangue saumon, dauphin vert, sorcier;* French: *carangue arc-en-ciel, comère saumon;* Hawaiian: *kamanu;* Japanese: *taumburi;* Spanish: *cola amarilla, corredores, macarela, pez rata, salmon, sardinata.*

Distribution. *Found worldwide in marine waters, the rainbow runner occurs in the western Atlantic, from Massachusetts throughout the northern Gulf of Mexico to northeastern Brazil. In the eastern Pacific, it occurs from the mouth of the Gulf of California, Mexico, to Ecuador, including the Galápagos Islands.*

Habitat. *Rainbow runners form either small polarized groups or large schools that usually remain at or near the surface, although they can inhabit depths of up to 120 feet. They occur over reefs and in deep, clear lagoons, preferring areas with a current.*

Sailfish

Istiophorus platypterus

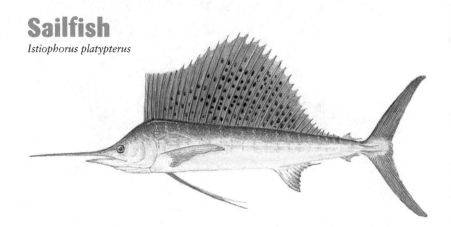

OTHER NAMES

spindlebeak, bayonetfish;
French: *voilier, espadon
vela;* Hawaiian: *a'u lepe;*
Italian: *pesce vela, pesce
ventaglio;* Japanese:
bashôkajiki; Portuguese:
veleiro, algulhão; Spanish:
*pez vela, aguja voladora,
aguja de faralá, aguja de
abanico.*

Distribution/Habitat.

*Sailfish occur worldwide in
tropical and temperate
waters of the Atlantic, the
Indian, and the Pacific
Oceans. They are pelagic
and migratory in warm offshore waters, although they
may migrate into warm
nearshore areas in parts of
their range. In the eastern
Pacific, sailfish range from
Baja California, Mexico, to
Peru, and in the western
Atlantic from Massachusetts
to Brazil. They are most
common in warm waters
along the edges of the Gulf
Stream.*

With its characteristic large dorsal fin and superlative aerial ability, the sailfish is arguably the most striking member of the Istiophoridae family of billfish. Although present taxonomy suggests that the Atlantic and the Pacific sailfish are the same species, some experts are not yet convinced. It has long been believed that Indo-Pacific specimens of sailfish attain a much greater size than do their Atlantic counterparts (and this is reflected in record catches), but a recent study of size data from the Japanese longline fishery provided evidence that eastern Atlantic specimens (identified by some ichthyologists as *I. albicans*) can attain much larger sizes than previously recorded.

The speedy sailfish is among the most exciting light-tackle big-game fish to catch. Light conventional gear, as well as spinning, baitcasting, and fly outfits, are all suitable for pursuing sailfish. The smaller specimens found in the Atlantic are especially good fun and are relatively easy for even inexperienced anglers to enjoy. Sailfish are rarely kept by western Atlantic anglers (and many are tagged when released) but are commonly kept in other places, especially off Mexico and Central America. They do have commercial significance in many parts of their range and are heavily exploited.

Identification. The sailfish is dark blue on top, brown-blue laterally, and silvery white on the belly; the upper jaw is elongated in the form of a spear. This species' outstanding feature is the long, high first dorsal fin, which has 37 to 49 total elements; it is slate or cobalt blue with many black spots. The second dorsal fin is very small, with six to eight rays. The single, prominent lateral line is curved over the pectoral fin and otherwise straight along the median line of the flanks. The bill is longer than that of the spearfish, usually a little more than twice the length of the elongated lower jaw. The vent is just forward of the first anal fin. The sides often have pale, bluish-gray vertical bars or rows or spots.

Sailfish (continued)

Although sailfish look like similar-size white marlin and blue marlin, they are readily distinguished by their large sail-like dorsal fin.

Size/Age. Sportfishing records for sailfish have long been maintained by the International Game Fish Association (IGFA), according to their Atlantic and Indo-Pacific distribution; the all-tackle world record for Atlantic fish is a 141-pounder caught off Angola in 1994; its counterpart in the Pacific is a 221-pounder caught off Ecuador in 1947. Fish from 20 to 50 or 60 pounds are commonly caught off the eastern United States, and fish from 50 to 100 pounds are common in many places in the Pacific. They can exceed 10 feet in length.

Life history/Behavior. Like other pelagic species that spawn in the open sea, the sailfish produces large numbers of eggs, perhaps 4 to 5 million. These are fertilized in the open water, where they float with plankton until hatching. Sailfish grow rapidly and reportedly can attain 4 to 5 feet in length in their first year. They reportedly swim at speeds approaching 68 mph, making them the swiftest short-distance gamefish. Sailfish may form schools or small groups of from 3 to 30 individuals and sometimes travel in loose aggregations spread over a wide area. They appear to feed mostly in midwater along the edges of reefs or current eddies.

Food and feeding habits. Sailfish eat squid, octopus, mackerel, tuna, jacks, herring, ballyhoo, needlefish, flying-fish, mullet, and other small fish. They feed on the surface or at mid-depths.

Salmon, Atlantic

Salmo salar

Distribution. *The anadromous Atlantic salmon is native to the North Atlantic Ocean and coastal rivers. Native anadromous Atlantic salmon have been extirpated from most of their more southerly range, victims of industrial growth, dams, pollution, and other factors. Self-supporting runs of anadromous Atlantics exist in Canada, especially Quebec, but also in Newfoundland, New Brunswick, and Nova Scotia.*

Habitat. *Anadromous Atlantic salmon spend most of their lives in the ocean, ascending coastal rivers to spawn. They are found in freshwater only during their spawning runs.*

The only salmon in the Salmonidae family that occurs in the Atlantic Ocean and its tributaries, the Atlantic salmon has been coveted for its excellent flesh since recorded history.

Identification. Compared to the size of its body, a mature Atlantic salmon has a small head. Its body is long and slim, and in adults the caudal or tail fin is nearly square. Individuals that return to spawn prematurely (called grilse) are mostly males and have slightly forked tails. At sea, the Atlantic salmon is dark blue on top of its head and back; its sides are a shiny silver, and the belly is white. The fins are dark, and there are numerous black marks in the shape of an X or a Y on its head and along its body above the lateral line. When the fish enters freshwater to spawn, it gradually loses its metallic shine and becomes dull brown or yellowish.

Size/Age. The Atlantic salmon can live for 8 years and is the second largest of all salmon. Unofficial historical reports talk of specimens weighing as much as 100 pounds. The all-tackle world record, a specimen weighing 79 pounds, 2 ounces, was taken in Norway in 1928. Most specimens today weigh 20 pounds or less, and fish exceeding 30 pounds are rare.

Spawning behavior. Spawning usually occurs in gravel bottoms at the head of riffles or the tail of a pool in the evening or at night. Unlike Pacific salmon, the adults do not die after spawning. Exhausted and thin, they often return to sea immediately before winter or remain in the stream until spring. Some survive to spawn a second time.

Food. In the ocean, salmon grow rapidly, feeding on crustaceans and other fish such as smelt, alewives, herring, capelin, mackerel, and cod. They do not feed during their upstream spawning migration.

Salmon, Chinook
Oncorhynchus tshawytscha

The chinook salmon is one of the most important sportfish and commercial fish in the world, especially, and historically, to the Pacific coast of North America, where this and other salmonids have long had great cultural and food significance. It is the largest member of the Salmonidae family and both the largest and the least-abundant member of the Pacific salmon genus *Oncorhynchus*.

Pacific stocks of chinook, as well as of other Pacific salmonids, however, have suffered greatly throughout large portions of their range due to dams, other habitat alterations, pollution, and excessive commercial fishing. Some chinook runs in the Pacific Northwest are threatened or endangered.

Identification. The body of the chinook salmon is elongate and somewhat compressed. The head is conical. For most of its life, the chinook's color is bluish to dark gray above, becoming silvery on the sides and the belly. There are black spots on the back, the upper sides, the top of the head, and all the fins, including both the top and the bottom half of the tail fin. Coloration changes during upstream migration; spawning chinook salmon range from red to copper to olive brown to almost black, depending on location and degree of maturation, and they undergo a radical metamorphosis. Males are more deeply colored than the females and are distinguished by their "ridgeback" condition and by their hooked nose or upper jaw, known as a kype. The young have 6 to 12 long, wide, well-developed parr marks, which are bisected by the lateral line, and no spots on the dorsal fin.

One distinguishing feature of the chinook is its black mouth and gums. The very similar-looking coho salmon has a black mouth but white gums.

Size. This species is the largest of all Pacific salmon; individual fish commonly exceed 30 pounds in Alaska and British Columbia and 20 pounds elsewhere. A 126-pound chinook salmon taken in a fish trap near Petersburg,

OTHER NAMES

king salmon, spring salmon, tyee, quinnat, tule, blackmouth, Sacramento River salmon, Columbia River salmon; French: *saumon chinook, saumon royal;* Japanese: *masunosuke.*

Distribution/Habitat. *In North America, chinook salmon occur naturally from San Luis Obispo County in Southern California to the Chukchi Sea area of Alaska; the greatest concentrations are along the British Columbia coast and Alaska. In Alaska, where the chinook is the state fish, it is abundant from the southeastern panhandle to the Yukon River. Major populations return to the Yukon, the Kuskokwim, the Nushagak, the Susitna, the Kenai, the Copper, the Alsek, the Taku, and the Stikine Rivers. Important runs also occur in many smaller streams. The chinook is rare in the Arctic Ocean. Most sea-run chinook are encountered by anglers along the coasts and in spawning rivers. Scientists estimate that there are in excess of a*

Salmon, Chinook *(continued)*

thousand spawning popula-
tions of chinook salmon on
the North American coast.

Scientific understanding
of the distribution of chi-
nook in the ocean is still
sketchy. It has been specu-
lated that most North
American chinook do not
wander more than 620
miles from their natal river,
and that fish from western
Alaska streams roam farther
than others from North
America. Large numbers are
found relatively close to
their respective shores and
also in distant offshore
waters, and their depth
preferences vary.

Alaska, in 1949 is the largest known specimen. The all-tackle world-sportfishing record is a 97-pound, 4-ounce fish caught in Alaska's Kenai River in 1986.

Life history/Behavior. Like all species of Pacific salmon, chinook are anadromous. They hatch in freshwater rivers, spend part of their lives in the ocean, and then spawn in freshwater. Sea-run chinook salmon may become sexually mature from their second through seventh year; as a result, fish in any spawning run may vary greatly in size.

Chinook salmon often make extensive freshwater spawning migrations to reach their home streams on some of the larger coastal river systems. Yukon River spawners bound for the extreme headwaters in Yukon Territory, Canada, will travel more than 2,000 river miles during a 60-day period. The period of migration into spawning rivers and streams varies greatly. Alaskan streams normally receive a single run of chinook salmon from May through July.

Chinook salmon do not feed during their freshwater spawning migration, so their condition deteriorates gradually during the spawning run. During that time, they use stored body materials for energy and for the development of reproductive products. Each female deposits from 3,000 to 14,000 eggs (usually in the lower range) in several gravel nests, or redds, which she excavates in relatively deep, moving water. The eggs usually hatch in the late winter or the early spring, depending on the time of spawning and the water temperature. The newly hatched fish, called alevins, live in the gravel for several weeks until they gradually absorb the food in the attached yolk sac. These juveniles, called fry, wiggle up through the gravel by early spring. Most juvenile chinook salmon remain in their natal water until the following spring, when they migrate to the ocean in their second year of life. These seaward migrants are called smolts.

Food and feeding habits. Chinook salmon in the ocean eat a variety of organisms, including herring, pilchards, sand lance, squid, and crustaceans. Salmon grow rapidly in the ocean and often double their weight during a single summer season. Thus, they quickly develop large, stocky bodies.

Salmon, Chum

Oncorhynchus keta

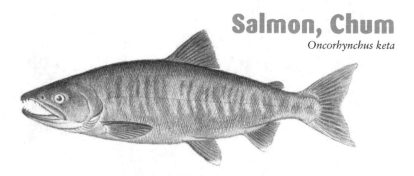

The late spawning run of the chum salmon severely affects its popularity as a sportfish. The frequently used name "dog salmon" reportedly originates with its prevalent use as dog food among aboriginals.

Identification. In the ocean, the slender, somewhat compressed, chum salmon is metallic greenish-blue on the back and silvery on the sides and has a fine black speckling on the upper sides and the back but no distinct black spots. Spawning males turn dark olive or grayish; blood-red coloring and vertical bars of green and purple reach up the sides, giving the fish its "calico" appearance. It develops the typical hooked snout of Pacific salmon, and the tips of the anal and the pelvic fins are often white.

The chum salmon is difficult to distinguish from similar-size sockeye salmon. The chum has fewer but larger gill rakers than other salmon have. The sockeye also lacks white marks on the fins and is generally smaller than the chum.

Size/Age. The average weight of chum salmon is 10 to 15 pounds. Females are usually smaller than males. These fish can reach 40 inches in length and can live to 7 years. The all-tackle world record is a 35-pounder from British Columbia.

Life history/Behavior. The chum salmon is an anadromous fish and inhabits both ocean environments and coastal streams. Spawning takes place from ages 2 to 7, most commonly at age 4, and at a weight of 5 to 10 pounds. They are sometimes called "autumn salmon" or "fall salmon" because they are among the last salmon in the season to take their spawning run, entering river mouths after mid-June but reaching spawning grounds as late as November or December.

Food. In the ocean, chum salmon eat a variety of organisms, including herring, pilchards, sand lance, squid, and crustaceans. Adults cease feeding in freshwater.

OTHER NAMES

calico salmon, dog salmon, fall salmon, autumn salmon, chum, keta; French: *saumon keta;* Japanese: *sake, shake.*

Distribution. Chum salmon are the most widely distributed of the Pacific salmon. In North America, they range south to about the Sacramento River in California, and east in the Arctic Ocean to the Mackenzie River in Canada. There, they travel all the way to the mouth of the Hay River and to the rapids below Forth Smith on the Slave River, entering both Great Bear and Great Slave Lakes and traveling through the Northwest Territories to the edge of Alberta.

Salmon, Coho

Oncorhynchus kisutch

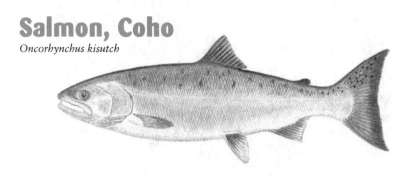

OTHER NAMES

silver salmon, silversides, hookbill, hooknose, sea trout, blueback; French: *saumon coho;* Japanese: *gin-zake.*

Distribution. *The coho salmon is endemic to the northern Pacific Ocean and the rivers flowing into it. In North America it occurs from Point Hope, Alaska, on the Chukchi Sea south to Monterey Bay, California. It has been infrequently reported at sea as far south as Baja California, Mexico. Most sea-run chinook are encountered along the coasts and in spawning rivers.*

A member of the Salmonidae family, the coho salmon is an extremely adaptable fish that occurs in nearly all of the same waters as does the larger chinook salmon, but it is a more spectacular fighter and the most acrobatic of the Pacific salmon. It is one of North America's most important sport- and commercial fish, especially to the Pacific coast of North America.

Identification. The body of the coho salmon is elongate and somewhat compressed, and the head is conical. For most of its life (in saltwater or lake, as well as newly arrived in a spawning river), this species is a dark metallic blue or blue-green above, becoming silvery on the sides and the belly. There are small black spots on the back and on the upper lobe of the caudal fin. It can be distinguished from the chinook salmon by its lack of black spots on the lower lobe of the tail and the white or gray gums at the base of the teeth; the chinook has small black spots on both caudal lobes of the tail, and it has black gums.

Spawning adults of both sexes have dark backs and heads and maroon to reddish sides. The males turn dusky green above and on their heads, bright red on their sides, and blackish below. The females turn a pinkish red on their sides. The male develops a prominent double-hooked snout, called a kype, with large teeth, which makes closing the mouth impossible.

Size. Coho do not attain the size of their larger chinook brethren and in most places are caught around the 4- to 8-pound mark. The all-tackle world record is a 33-pound, 4-ounce specimen from the Great Lakes. Fish to 31 pounds have been caught in Alaska, where the average catch is 8 to 12 pounds and 24 to 30 inches long.

Life history/Behavior. Like all species of Pacific salmon, coho are anadromous. They hatch in freshwater rivers, spend part of their lives in the ocean, and then spawn in freshwater.

Adult male sea-run coho salmon generally enter streams when they are either 2 or 3 years old, but adult females do not return to spawn until age 3. All coho salmon, whether male or female, spend their first year in the stream or river in which they hatch.

The timing of runs into tributaries varies as well. Coho salmon in Alaska, for example, enter spawning streams from July through November, usually during periods of high runoff. In California, the runs occur from September through March, and the bulk of spawning occurs from November through January. Run timing has evolved to reflect the requirements of specific stocks. In some streams with barrier falls, adults arrive in July when the water is low and the falls are passable. In large rivers, adults must arrive early, as they need several weeks or months to reach head-water spawning grounds. Run timing is also regulated by the water temperature at spawning grounds: Where temperatures are low and eggs develop slowly, spawners have evolved early run timing to compensate; conversely, where temperatures are warm, adults are late spawners.

Little is known of the ocean migrations of coho salmon. Evidently, there are more coho salmon in the eastern Pacific and along the coast of North America than in the western Pacific. High-seas tagging shows that maturing southeast Alaska coho move northward throughout the spring and appear to concentrate in the central Gulf of Alaska in June. They later disperse toward shore and migrate along the shoreline until they reach their stream of origin. Although most coho do not seem to migrate extensively, tagged individuals have been recovered up to 1,200 miles from the tagging site.

Food and feeding habits. In the ocean, coho salmon grow rapidly, feeding on a variety of organisms, including herring, pilchards, sand lance, squid, and crustaceans. Like all Pacific salmon, the coho does not feed once it enters freshwater on its spawning run.

Salmon, Pink

Oncorhynchus gorbuscha

OTHER NAMES

humpback salmon, humpy, fall salmon, pink, humpback; French: *saumon rose;* Japanese: *karafutomasu, sepparimasu.*

Distribution. *Pink salmon are native to Pacific and arctic coastal waters from the Sacramento River in Northern California northeast to the Mackenzie River in the Northwest Territories, Canada.*

Pink salmon have been introduced to Newfoundland and to the western coast of Lake Superior and currently maintain populations in these locations; there have been sporadic reports of pink salmon in Labrador, Nova Scotia, and Quebec since their introduction into Newfoundland.

These anadromous fish spend 18 months at sea and then undertake a spawning migration to the river or stream of their birth, although they sometimes use other streams. They tend to migrate as far as 40 miles inland of coastal waters, occasionally moving farther.

An important commercial catch, the pink salmon is the smallest North American member of the Pacific salmon group of the Salmonidae family.

Identification. The pink salmon is known as the "humpback" or "humpy" because of its distorted, extremely humpbacked appearance, which is caused by the very pronounced, laterally flattened hump that develops on the backs of adult males before spawning. This hump appears between the head and the dorsal fin and develops by the time the male enters the spawning stream, as does a hooked upper jaw, or kype.

At sea, the pink salmon is silvery in color, with a bright metallic blue above; there are many black, elongated, oval spots on the entire tail fin and large spots on the back and the adipose fin. When the pink salmon moves to spawning streams, the bright appearance of the male changes to pale red or "pink" on the sides, with brown to olive-green blotches; females become olive green above, with dusky bars or patches, and pale below.

Size/Age. The average pink salmon weighs 3 to 6 pounds and is 20 to 25 inches long, although these fish can grow to 15 pounds and 30 inches. The all-tackle world record is a 14-pound, 13-ounce fish taken in Washington in 2001. Pink salmon live for only 2 years.

Life history/Behavior. Pink salmon are often referred to as "autumn salmon" or "fall salmon" because of their late spawning runs; these occur from July through mid-October in Alaska. Adults die soon after spawning. Almost all pink salmon mature in 2 years, which means that odd-year and even-year populations are separate and essentially unrelated.

Food and feeding habits. At sea, they feed primarily on plankton, as well as on crustaceans, small fish, and squid. They do not feed during the spawning run.

Salmon, Sockeye
Oncorhynchus nerka

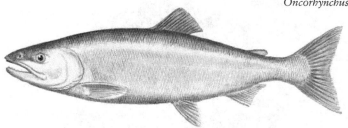

A member of the Salmonidae family, sockeye leave the ocean to spawn in freshwater, as do other Pacific salmon, but they enter only those rivers having lakes at their head-waters. The erection of dams and the alteration of habitat, however, as well as commercial overfishing and other factors, have caused an overall decline in sockeye stocks and the loss of some specific runs.

Identification. The sockeye is the slimmest and most streamlined of Pacific salmon, particularly immature and pre-spawning fish, which are elongate and somewhat laterally compressed. The sockeye is metallic green-blue on the back and the top of the head, iridescent silver on the sides, and white or silvery on the belly. Some fine black speckling may occur on the back, but large spots are absent.

Breeding males develop humped backs and elongated, hooked jaws filled with sharp, enlarged teeth. Both sexes turn brilliant to dark red on their backs and sides, pale to olive green on their heads and upper jaws, and white on their lower jaws. The totally red body distinguishes the sockeye from the otherwise similar chum salmon, and the lack of large, distinct spots distinguishes it from the remaining three Pacific salmon of North America.

Size. Adult sockeye usually weigh between 4 and 8 pounds. The all-tackle world record is an Alaskan fish that weighed 15 pounds, 3 ounces.

Life history/Behavior. Sockeye salmon return to their natal stream to spawn after spending 1 to 4 years in the ocean. They enter freshwater systems from the ocean during the summer months or the fall, some having traveled thousands of miles. Most populations show little variation in their arrival time on the spawning grounds from year to year.

Food and feeding habits. In the ocean, sockeye salmon feed on plankton, plus on crustacean larvae, on larval and small adult fish, and occasionally on squid.

OTHER NAMES

sockeye, red salmon, blue-back salmon, big redfish; French: *saumon nerka;* Japanese: *beni-zake, himemasu.* The landlocked form is called kokanee salmon, Kennerly's salmon, kokanee, landlocked sockeye, kickininee, little redfish, silver trout; French: *kokani.*

Distribution. *The sockeye salmon is native to the northern Pacific Ocean and its tributaries; in North America it occurs from the Sacramento River, California, to Point Hope, Alaska.*

Habitat. *Sockeye salmon are anadromous, living in the sea and entering freshwater to spawn. They mainly enter rivers and streams that have lakes at their source. Young fish may inhabit lakes for as many as 4 years before returning to the ocean.*

Sanddab, Longfin

Citharichthys xanthostigma

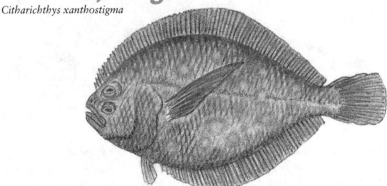

OTHER NAMES

sanddab, soft flounder, Catalina sanddab; Spanish: *lenguado alón.*

Distribution. *Longfin sanddabs occur in the eastern Pacific from Costa Rica to Monterey, California, including the Gulf of California. They are rare north of Santa Barbara.*

Habitat. *These flatfish usually dwell on sand or mud bottoms from 8 to 660 feet deep.*

A member of the Bothidae family of left-eyed flatfish, the longfin sanddab is a small but common bottom-fishing catch by anglers, particularly in Southern California.

Identification. The body of the longfin sanddab is oblong and compressed. The head is deep, the eyes are large and located on the left side, and the mouth is large. The color is uniformly dark with rust-orange or white speckles, and the pectoral fin is black on the eyed side. The blind side is white.

This species can be distinguished from the Pacific sanddab by the length of the pectoral fin on the eyed side, which is always shorter than the head on the Pacific sanddab and longer than the head on the longfin. Sanddabs are always left-eyed and can be distinguished from all other left-eyed flatfish by having a lateral line that is nearly straight along its entire length.

Size. These fish are common to 10 inches in length but are reported to reach a maximum length of 15¾ inches.

Spawning behavior. Females are larger than males and normally mature when 3 years old and roughly 7½ inches long. They produce numerous eggs, and each fish probably spawns more than once a season. The peak of the spawning season is July through September.

Food. The diet of longfin sanddabs is wide ranging and includes small fish, squid, octopus, shrimp, crabs, and worms.

Sanddab, Pacific

Citharichthys sordidus

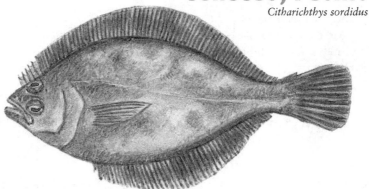

A member of the Bothidae family of left-eyed flatfish, the Pacific sanddab is an excellent food fish that has both commercial significance and a popular sportfishing following. This species is often listed on the seafood menus of California restaurants and is viewed by some as a delicacy.

Identification. The body of the Pacific sanddab is oblong and compressed. The head is deep, and the eyes are large and on the left side. The color is light brown, mottled with yellow and orange on the eyed side and white on the blind side.

The Pacific sanddab can be distinguished from the longfin sanddab by the length of the pectoral fin on the eyed side. It is always shorter than the head of the Pacific sanddab and longer than the head of the longfin. Sanddabs are always left-eyed and can be distinguished from other left-eyed flatfish by their lateral lines, which are nearly straight for their entire length.

Size. These fish may reach 16 inches and 2 pounds but are common to just 10 inches in size and under a half-pound.

Spawning behavior. Females are larger than males and normally mature at age 3, at roughly 8 inches in length. They produce numerous eggs, and each fish probably spawns more than once in a season. The peak of the spawning season is July through September.

Food. The diet of Pacific sanddabs is wide ranging and includes small fish, squid, octopus, shrimp, crabs, and worms.

OTHER NAMES
mottled sanddab, sole, sanddab, soft flounder, megrim; Spanish: *lenguado*.

Distribution. *Pacific sanddabs occur in the eastern Pacific from the Sea of Japan, the Aleutian Islands, and the Bering Sea to Cabo San Lucas, Baja California, Mexico. They are common in shallow coastal water from British Columbia to California.*

Habitat. *These flatfish are found on sand bottoms in water that ranges from 30 to 1,800 feet deep, but they are most abundant at depths of 120 to 300 feet.*

Sand Lance

American sand lance *Ammodytes americanus*
Northern sand lance *Ammodytes dubius*
Pacific sand lance *Ammodytes hexapterus*

OTHER NAMES

Sand launce, sand eel,
launce-fish, sandlance;
French: *lançon*.

Distribution. *Sand lance
occur in temperate and
colder parts of the Atlantic
and Pacific Oceans. On the
western Atlantic coast, sand
lance range from north
Quebec to North Carolina.
Northern sand lance are
believed to inhabit deeper
waters, whereas American
sand lance inhabit inshore
areas. Pacific sand lance
range from the Sea of Japan
to arctic Alaska, the Bering
Sea, and to Balboa Island in
Southern California. The
arctic and the Pacific sand
lance may be separate
species.*

Habitat. *Schools of American sand lance are often
abundant in shallow water
along sandy shores and are
found in salinities of 26 to
32 percent. For protection,
the fish quickly burrow into
the sand, snouts first, to a
depth of about 6 inches.*

Resembling small eels, sand lance are burrowing fish that
are important as food for many gamefish. They are excellent to eat when prepared in the style of whitebait. Quantities of sand lance are often dug up in the intertidal zone by
people seeking clams.

Identification. Sand lance are small, slim, elongated, and
round-bodied fish with no teeth, usually no pelvic fins, no
fin spines, and forked tails. Although the sand lance has a
long soft dorsal fin, it does not have a first dorsal fin. The
body has sloping fleshy folds, and there is a distinct fleshy
ridge along the lower side; the straight lateral line is close to
the base of the dorsal fin.

Fin-ray and vertebral counts distinguish the American
sand lance from the northern sand lance; the American
sand lance has 51 to 62 dorsal fin rays, 23 to 33 anal fin
rays, and 61 to 73 vertebrae, whereas the northern sand
lance has 56 to 68 dorsal fin rays, 27 to 35 anal fin rays, and
65 to 78 vertebrae. Sand lance can be distinguished from
young eels by their separate, rather than continuous, dorsal
and anal fins, and by the rounded caudal fin of the eel.

Size. Sand lance grow to a length of about 6 inches.

Sardine, Pacific

Sardinops caeruleus

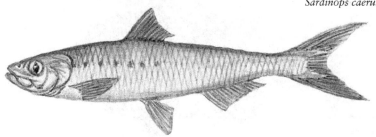

Unlike the young of herring, which are often marketed as sardines, the Pacific sardine is a true sardine. Once one of the most important commercial fish along the Pacific coast, the Pacific sardine population has been depleted by pollution and overfishing. Most commercial fish are canned or processed to make fish meal, fertilizer, or oil; Pacific sardines are not marketed fresh.

Identification. The Pacific sardine has an elongated body, a compressed head, and a small mouth with no teeth. It is silvery with dark blue on the back, shades of purple and violet along the sides, and black spots along both the sides and the back. It can be distinguished from the typical herring by the absence of a sharp ridge of scales (which is found down the midline of the belly of a herring) and by vertical ridges on its gill covers.

Life history/Behavior. In the summer, Pacific sardines migrate northward from California to British Columbia and return in the autumn or the winter. They form large schools of various-size fish. Their eggs are pelagic, and, unlike the eggs of herring, they float. Individuals generally mature in their second year.

Food. The Pacific sardine feeds mainly by filtering zooplankton and phytoplankton.

OTHER NAMES

pilchard, California pilchard, California sardine, sardina; Spanish: *pilchard California, sardina de California, sardina Monterrey.*

Distribution. *In the eastern Pacific, Pacific sardines occur from southeastern Alaska to Cabo San Lucas, and throughout the Gulf of California, Mexico.*

Sargo

Anisotremus davidsonii

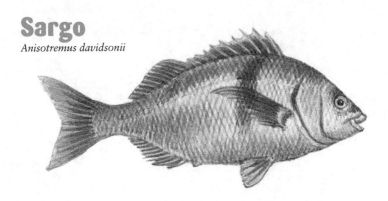

OTHER NAMES

China croaker, blue bass, black croaker, grunt, xantic sargo; Spanish: *burro piedrero*.

Distribution. *Sargo occur in the eastern central Pacific from Magdalena Bay in Baja California, Mexico, to Santa Cruz, California.*

Habitat. *Sargo are found inshore and in bays over rocky and rock-sand bottoms, often near kelp beds, and around pilings or submerged structures. Although they can dwell in up to 130 feet of water, they are most common in water between 8 and 25 feet deep.*

The sargo is the largest of the Pacific grunts and is commonly caught incidentally by anglers fishing for other species, primarily during the summer.

Identification. The body of the adult sargo is a compressed oval shape, and the back is elevated. The head has a steep, straight upper profile and a small mouth. The sargo's coloring is a metallic silver, with a grayish tinge on the back. It is silvery below, and there is a distinguishing dark vertical bar running across the body from the dorsal fin to the base of the pectoral fin. Occasionally, sargo are entirely bright yellow, orange, or pure white.

A young sargo, up to 4 inches, has several dark horizontal stripes. The vertical bar begins to appear when the fish is 2 to 3 inches long.

Size. These fish can reach a maximum length of 22 inches.

Life history/Behavior. Sargo swim close to the bottom in loose schools. The fish spawn in the late spring and the early summer. Spawning first occurs when the fish are about 7 inches long and 2 years old.

Food and feeding habits. Sargo are bottom feeders that primarily forage on small shrimp, crabs, clams, and snails.

Sauries

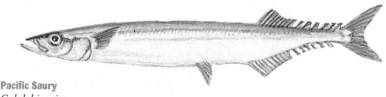

Pacific Saury
Cololabis saira

Abundant offshore fish, sauries are members of the four-species Scomberesocidae family. They have only moderately elongated jaws that are beaklike, and they are easily distinguished from needlefish and halfbeaks by the five to seven finlets behind the dorsal and the anal fins, as in mackerel. Sauries as a group have small scales, relatively small mouth openings, small teeth, and no swim bladders. These relatively abundant fish are heavily preyed upon by tuna, marlin, bluefish, and other predators.

The Atlantic saury *(Scomberesox saurus)* travels in schools containing thousands of fish. They are commonly attacked by a variety of predators that sometimes drive the schools into shallow nearshore waters. Often a whole school will rise simultaneously from the sea and skitter across the surface (for this reason, commercial fishermen refer to them as "skippers"). They are sometimes caught commercially when abundant, but they are not fished for regularly.

The Atlantic saury occurs in the western Atlantic from the Gulf of St. Lawrence south to North Carolina and Bermuda. Atlantic saury are also known as, in French: *balaou;* Italian: *costardella;* Norwegian: *makrellejedde;* Portuguese: *agulhao;* Turkish: *zurna.*

The Pacific saury *(Cololabis saira)* is similar and has a significant commercial interest as well. Also known as mackerel pike and skipper (and *sanma* in Japanese), it occurs in large schools, generally offshore near the surface, and, like the Atlantic saury, feeds on small crustaceans and the eggs and the larvae of fish. The Pacific saury occurs from Japan eastward to the Gulf of Alaska and south to Mexico.

Both species may reach a length of about 14 inches but are usually shorter.

Scorpionfish, California

Scorpaena guttata

spotted scorpionfish, scorpion, rattlesnake, bullhead, scorpene, sculpin; Spanish: *rascacio californiano*.

Distribution. *In the eastern Pacific, this species occurs from Santa Cruz, California, to Punta Abreojos, Baja California, including a cloistered population in the northern Gulf of California and at Guadalupe Island in Mexico.*

Habitat. *California scorpionfish usually live in caves, crevices, and rocky areas of bays along the shore, from just below the surface to 600-foot depths. Resting quietly during the day among rocky reefs and kelp beds, they emerge at night and are often seen by night divers in the open near kelp and eelgrass beds. Some are occasionally found over sand or mud bottoms.*

The California scorpionfish is an excellent food fish and the most venomous member of the scorpionfish family. It has venom glands that are attached to the dorsal, the pelvic, and the anal fin spines, and if these spines penetrate the skin, an intense and excruciating pain in the area of the wound occurs almost immediately. If there are multiple punctures, the wound can induce shock, respiratory distress, or abnormal heart action and sometimes leads to hospitalization of the victim. The California scorpionfish is often called a sculpin but is not a member of the sculpin family.

Identification. The California scorpionfish has a stocky and slightly compressed body, as well as a large head and mouth. Colored red to brown, with dark patches and spots on the body and the fins, this fish is capable of dramatic color changes to blend with its background. It has large pectoral fins, 12 poisonous dorsal spines, and poisonous anal and ventral fin spines.

Size/Age. The California scorpionfish can grow to 17 inches and can live 15 years.

Life history/Behavior. California scorpionfish start spawning at age 3 or 4. Spawning activity occurs from April through August, most likely at night. The eggs are implanted in a single layer on the gelatinous walls of hollow, pear-shaped "balloons" of 5 to 10 inches in length; these are released on the bottom and rise to the surface, and the eggs hatch within the next 5 days.

Food. The California scorpionfish feeds on crabs, squid, octopus, fish, and shrimp.

Cabezon
Scorpaenichthys marmoratus

Staghorn Sculpin
Leptocottus armatus

The Cottidae family of sculpins is made up of more than 300 species, most of which are marine, but many of which also occur in freshwaters throughout the Northern Hemisphere. They are important as food for larger fish and as predators of the eggs and the young of gamefish. Bottom-dwelling fish of cold waters, sculpins live in shelf waters and in rocky tidal pools. A few species of larger sculpins inhabit depths of up to 4,200 feet in saltwater.

Sculpins are characterized by wide bodies that taper to slender, compressed tails. They may be unscaled or may have spiny prickles or platelike scales, although the development of these varies within species, depending on habitat, and is not necessarily useful in identification. All sculpins have a bony support beneath each eye, which connects bones with the front of the gill covers. The dorsal fins are deeply indented between the spiny and the soft-rayed portions, and the pectoral fins are large and fanned. The color and the pattern vary, although they are mainly mottled with various shades and are protectively camouflaged by their mottled pattern. Sculpins are primarily carnivorous, clinging to the bottom and pouncing on small invertebrates, crustaceans, and mollusks for food.

Of the marine species, the cabezon, or great marbled sculpin *(Scorpaenichthys marmoratus),* is the largest and best known, weighing up to 30 pounds. It is good table fare and is a coveted catch in California waters. The staghorn sculpin *(Leptocottus armatus)* inhabits the same waters as does the cabezon and is sometimes caught accidentally by anglers and used for bait. The grunt sculpin *(Rhamphocottus richardsonii)* is so called because of the noises it makes when removed from the water. It is featured in aquariums.

Scup

Stenotomus chrysops

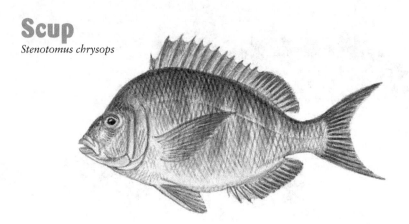

A member of the Sparidae family of porgies, which includes about 112 species, the scup is most commonly known as "porgy" and is a common angling catch along the eastern United States. It is a fine food fish that has had significant commercial interest. Primarily caught through trawling, it was overexploited and at low population levels throughout the 1990s.

Identification. Somewhat nondescript, the scup is rather dusky colored, being brownish and almost silvery, with fins that are mottled brown. It has a deep body, about the same depth all the way to the caudal peduncle, where it narrows abruptly. The fins are spiny. The caudal fin is lunate (crescent-shaped). The front teeth are incisor-form, and there are two rows of molars in the upper jaw.

Size/Age. Scup attain a maximum length of about 16 inches. The all-tackle world record is a 4-pound, 9-ounce Massachusetts fish. Ages up to 20 years have been reported.

Food and feeding habits. The diet of scup consists of crabs, shrimp, worms, sand dollars, snails, and young squid. Although they sometimes eat small fish, scup usually browse and nibble over hard bottoms.

Sea Bass, Black

Centropristis striata

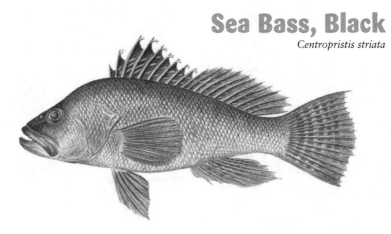

Black sea bass are members of the Serranidae family and are popular sportfish.

Identification. The black sea bass has a relatively stout body that is three times as long (excluding the tail) as it is deep. It also has a noticeably high back, a flat-topped head, a slightly pointed snout, and a sharp spine near the apex of each gill cover. The elongated top ray of the tail sticks out past the rest of the tail and is the most distinguishing feature of this fish.

The body color ranges from black to gray or brownish-gray. The dorsal fins are marked by several slanting white spots, and there also appear to be thin stripes on the sides, with wide vertical bands overlapping the stripes on some fish and a large dark spot on the last dorsal spine. The upper and the lower edges of the tail are white, as are the outer edges of the dorsal and the anal fins.

Size. Big sea bass range from 3 to 8 pounds, and the average fish weighs between 1 and 3 pounds; the all-tackle world record is a 10-pound, 4-ounce fish. Sea bass can grow to 2 feet long, averaging 6 to 18 inches. They are known to live for 10 years.

Life history. Black sea bass are hermaphrodites; most begin their lives as females and later become males. Large fish are males, and females reach reproductive ability in their second year. Transformation from female to male generally occurs between ages 2 and 5. Their protracted spawning season extends from February through May in the southern range and from June through October in their northern range.

Food and feeding habits. Clams, shrimp, worms, crabs, and small fish constitute the diet of the omnivorous black sea bass.

Distribution. *Found in the western North Atlantic Ocean along the United States, the black sea bass ranges as far north as Maine and south to northern Florida, as well as into the Gulf of Mexico. It is most common between Cape Cod, Massachusetts, and Cape Hatteras, North Carolina.*

Habitat. *The black sea bass is a bottom-dwelling species found around wrecks, reefs, piers, jetties, and breakwaters and over beds of shells, coral, and rock. Small fish are found in shallow and quiet waters near the shore, such as in bays, whereas most larger fish prefer offshore reefs, in water ranging from roughly 10 feet deep to several hundred feet deep.*

Sea Bass, Giant

Stereolepis gigas

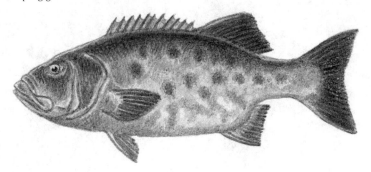

OTHER NAMES

California black sea bass, California jewfish, giant bass, black, black sea bass; French: *bar gigantesque;* Japanese: *kokuchi-ishinagi, ishinagi-zoku;* Spanish: *lubina gigante.*

Distribution. *Giant sea bass occur in tropical and subtropical inshore waters of the northeast Pacific off the California and Mexico coasts, specifically from the Gulf of California southward to Humboldt Bay and Guadalupe Island. In California waters these fish have been in short supply but were rebounding in the 1990s, due to a moratorium on keeping them.*

Habitat. *Inhabiting inshore waters, giant sea bass are bottom-dwelling fish, preferring hard, rocky bottoms around kelp beds. The young occur in depths of about 6 to 15 fathoms, whereas larger specimens usually inhabit depths of 15 to 25 fathoms.*

The giant sea bass, a member of the Serranidae family, is not only a formidable fish in size, it is also renowned for its lengthy life span.

Identification. The body of the giant sea bass is elongate and has dorsal spines that fit into a groove on the back. Greenish-brown or black, the giant sea bass has black or transparent fins, with the exception of the ventral fins, which appear lighter because of a white membrane between the black spines. There is usually a white patch on the throat and underneath the tail, and the membranes between the rays are also light. Young fish are mottled with prominent dark spots and a few pale-yellow blotches on mostly brick-red bodies; these markings are periodically seen on fish up to and exceeding 25 pounds. The first dorsal fin is separated from the second by a single notch; the first is extremely low and has 11 spines, whereas the second is higher and has 10 soft rays.

Size/Age. The giant sea bass reaches maturity by the age of 11 or 12 and weighs roughly 50 pounds, although it has been known to weigh more than 600 pounds and measure more than 7 feet in length. The all-tackle world record is 563 pounds, 8 ounces; the most common catch is in the 100- to 200-pound range, and much smaller fish are seldom caught. Some of the largest specimens are believed to be 75 years or older.

Food and feeding habits. The giant sea bass diet includes crustaceans and a wide variety of fish. Anchovies and croaker are a prominent food source off California; mackerel, sheepshead, whitefish, sand bass, and several types of crabs are also favored. Although these bulky fish appear to be slow and cumbersome, they are reputedly capable of outswimming and catching a bonito in a short chase.

Seabass, White

Atractoscion nobilis (also *Cynoscion nobilis*)

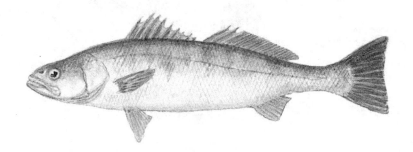

A member of the Sciaenidae family, the popular white seabass belongs to the grouping of weakfish or corvina and is not a true bass or sea bass. White seabass stocks have struggled due to overfishing by commercial gillnets, which are now illegal in California for this species.

Identification. The body of the white seabass is elongate and somewhat compressed. There is a characteristic raised ridge along the middle of the belly, between the vent and the base of the pelvic fins. The head is pointed and slightly flattened. The mouth is large, with a row of small teeth in the roof and a projecting lower jaw. The first dorsal fin has nine spines and the second two spines and 20 soft rays. The anal fin has two spines and 10 soft rays. There are no barbels on the chin. Its coloring is bluish to gray above, with dark speckling, and becomes silver below.

The white seabass can be distinguished from its Atlantic relatives, the weakfish and the spotted seatrout, by its lack of canine teeth. It is most closely related to the California corbina, but it is the only California croaker to exceed 20 pounds. It is most easily separated from other croaker by the presence of a ridge running the length of the belly.

Size/Age. The average weight of a 28-inch fish is 7½ pounds. The all-tackle record is 83 pounds, 3 ounces. White seabass generally live for 5 years.

Life history. Spawning occurs in the spring and the summer. White seabass are schooling fish and are present in California waters all year long. They are especially popular in the spring and also in the winter, when they converge on spawning squid.

Food and feeding habits. White seabass feed on anchovies, pilchards, herring, and other fish, as well as on crustaceans and squid.

OTHER NAMES

Catalina salmon, white corvina, corvina blanca, white weakfish, weakfish, king croaker; French: *acoupa blanc;* Spanish: *corvinata bronzeada.*

Distribution. *White seabass inhabit the eastern Pacific, mainly between San Francisco, California, and Baja California, Mexico, and in the northern Gulf of California. They are found as far north as southern Alaska and as far south as Chile.*

Habitat. *Preferring deep, rocky environments, white seabass usually hold near kelp beds in depths of 12 to 25 fathoms. They are sometimes found in shallow surf or deeper waters. Juveniles inhabit shallow nearshore areas, bays, and estuaries.*

Sea Robin

Northern Sea Robin
Prionotus carolinus

Distribution. *At least 19 species occur in the Atlantic and a few in the Pacific off the coasts of the United States and Canada.*

Sea robins are mostly tropical and subtropical fish of the Triglidae family, characterized by split pectoral fins that consist of stiff separate rays on the lower half and broad, soft, winglike rays on the upper half. The upper rays are not as large as in the similar-looking flying gurnard but are used for the same purpose—swimming. The lower rays are used to find food by sifting through debris and turning over rocks.

Sea robins also use their pelvic and pectoral fins to "walk" across the bottom as they search for fish, shrimp, squid, clams, and crabs to satisfy their insatiable appetites. They are often brightly colored, are capable of making loud noises by vibrating muscles attached to their air bladders, and inhabit moderately deep waters. These fish spawn throughout the summer, their eggs float on the surface, and the young grow quickly during the first year.

One of the more well-known fish of this group is the northern sea robin *(Prionotus carolinus),* which occurs from Nova Scotia to northern South America but is uncommon north of Massachusetts. It averages 12 inches in length and may reach a length of 18 inches. A black, mottled fish with an olive-brown or gray background, the northern sea robin has a large head that is covered with bony plates and spines and has a distinct black chin. It is a bottom-dweller, moving close to shore during the summer and to deeper water in the winter.

Other Atlantic species are the striped sea robin *(P. evolans),* which is distinguished by a few dark bands on its sides, and the leopard sea robin *(P. scitulus),* an almost foot-long species with dark blotches, common in the Gulf of Mexico and the southern Atlantic.

Seatrout, Sand

Cynoscion arenarius

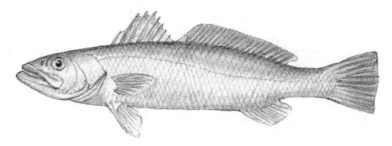

A member of the Sciaenidae family (drum and croaker), the sand seatrout is a small and frequently caught fish. Found primarily in the Gulf of Mexico, it supports a minor commercial and sportfishing industry. It is closely related to the weakfish of the Atlantic coast.

Identification. Its coloring is pale yellow on the back and silver to white below, without any real defined spots. A young sand seatrout has a cloudy back, sometimes forming crossbands. The inside of the mouth is yellow. There are 10 to 12 soft rays in the anal fin. It does not have any chin barbels and can be distinguished from the silver seatrout by the presence of 10 anal rays, the silver seatrout having only 8 or 9.

Size. The average fish is 10 to 12 inches in length and rarely weighs more than a pound. The all-tackle record is a 6-pound, 2-ounce fish caught in Alabama.

Spawning behavior. There is a prolonged spawning season inshore from spring through summer. Fish mature during their first or second year.

Food and feeding habits. The main food sources are shrimp and small fish.

OTHER NAMES

white trout, sand weakfish, white weakfish.

Distribution. The sand seatrout occurs mainly in the Gulf of Mexico from the west coast of Florida through Texas and into Mexico and as far south as the Gulf of Campeche. It also exists on the extreme southeastern Atlantic portion of Florida.

Habitat. The sand seatrout is predominantly an inshore fish found in bays and inlets. The young inhabit shallow bays, particularly in less saline areas. Adult fish move offshore in the winter.

Seatrout, Silver

Cynoscion nothus

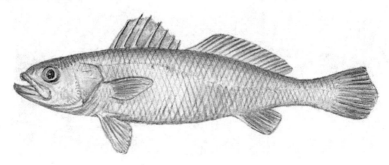

OTHER NAMES

silver trout, silver weakfish.

Distribution. *The silver seatrout occurs mainly throughout the Gulf of Mexico and is also in the Atlantic from southern Florida to Maryland.*

Habitat. *Predominantly an offshore fish, the silver seatrout is usually found over sandy and sandy-mud bottoms. It migrates in bays in the winter months.*

A member of the Sciaenidae family (drum and croaker), the silver seatrout is smaller than other seatrout and generally similar in body shape. It is often misidentified with the spotted seatrout.

Identification. Its coloring is pale straw or walnut on the back and silver to white below, without any real defined spots, although faint diagonal lines may be present on the upper body. There are 8 to 9 rays in the anal fin, distinguishing it from the sand seatrout, which has 10 rays. The silver seatrout has large eyes and a short snout, no chin barbel, and one to two prominent canine teeth usually present at the tip of the upper jaw. The lower half of the tail is longer than the upper half.

Size. Silver seatrout seldom weigh more than a half pound and are usually less than 10 inches long.

Spawning behavior. There is a prolonged spawning season offshore during the spring, the summer, and the fall.

Food and feeding habits. The main food sources are shrimp, small crustaceans, and small fish.

Seatrout, Spotted

Cynoscion nebulosus

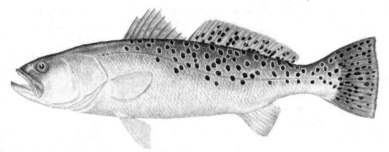

The spotted seatrout is a member of the Sciaenidae family of drum and croaker. It belongs to the genus *Cynoscion* (weakfish and seatrout), which is named for its members' tender mouths, from which hooks tear easily. Considered an exceptionally valuable commercial fish and an even more valuable sportfish to anglers, it is intensely pursued throughout its range, especially in the Gulf of Mexico. Most Gulf and Atlantic coast states have experienced a decline in spotted seatrout populations due to overfishing and exploitation, and fishing is strictly controlled; in some areas, the cessation of gillnetting is leading to stock recoveries and is providing optimism for the future.

The spotted seatrout is also known as an excellent table fish. Its flesh is fine and delicately flavored, but it spoils quickly and should be cleaned or stored on ice when possible after being caught. It usually appears on the menus of southern restaurants as "trout" and can be substituted in recipes for sea bass or redfish.

Identification. The spotted seatrout has an elongated body, with a slightly more regular and even tail fin, with a black margin, than that of a sand or a silver seatrout. Its coloring is dark gray or green on the back, with sky-blue tinges shading to silvery and white below; the dorsal fins are gray-green, and many round black spots speckle the back, the tail, and the dorsal fins. The lower jaw protrudes beyond the upper, which has one or two prominent canine teeth. The first dorsal fin has one spine and 24 to 27 soft rays, and the anal fin has two spines and 10 to 11 soft rays. There are eight or nine short, stubby gill rakers on the lower limb of the first gill arch. There are no barbels, and the interior of the mouth is orange. A very young fish will have a broad, dark lateral band. The presence of spots on the fins can distinguish the spotted seatrout from other seatrout.

OTHER NAMES

trout, speckled trout, speck, spotted weakfish, spotted squeteague, gator trout, salmon trout, winter trout, black trout; Spanish: *corvinata pintada.*

Distribution. *Spotted seatrout occur along the Atlantic and the Gulf of Mexico coasts. They are most abundant along the coasts of Georgia, Florida, Alabama, Mississippi, eastern Louisiana, and Texas but range as far westward as Tampico, Mexico. In the late spring, they can range as far north as Long Island, New York, but are more prominent in the mid-Atlantic in the Carolinas, Virginia, and Maryland.*

Habitat. *An inshore bottom-dwelling species, the spotted seatrout inhabits shallow bays, estuaries, bayous, canals, and Gulf Coast beaches. It prefers nearshore sandy and grassy bottoms and may even frequent salt marshes and tidal pools with high salinity. It also lives around oil*

Seatrout, Spotted (continued)

rigs, usually within 10 miles of shore. Ideal water temperatures are between 58° and 81°F. Cold water is lethal to the spotted seatrout, and although some move into slow-moving or still, deep waters in cold weather, the majority remaining in its normal habitat may be killed by the low temperatures.

Size/Age. Mature spotted seatrout commonly range from 12 to 24 inches and average 4 pounds, although they can reach 48 inches and weigh as much as 16 pounds. The all-tackle record is 17 pounds, 7 ounces, caught at Fort Pierce, Florida, in 1995. They can live up to 10 years; 3-year-old fish in Alabama are generally 12 to 13 inches long, and 4-year-old fish are 14 to 15 inches long. Anglers commonly catch spotted seatrout weighing between 1 and 3 pounds; fish exceeding 7 pounds are considered large, and 10-pounders are definitely trophies.

Life history/Behavior. It is believed that water temperature and salinity levels are more important to spawning than a specific location, because newly hatched spotted seatrout will not survive low salinity and low temperature conditions. Optimum spawning conditions for spotted seatrout exist when salinity is 20 to 34 parts per thousand and temperatures reach 70° to 90°F. Spawning occurs at night in coastal bays, sounds, and lagoons; near passes; and around barrier islands from March through November. A female may lay up to 10 million eggs. The eggs hatch within 20 hours and are transported to estuaries by winds and currents.

Spotted seatrout are schooling fish and are not considered migratory, as they rarely move more than 30 miles, although they do move into deeper waters or deep holes to avoid cold temperatures. Juveniles spend 2 to 4 years in shallow, grassy areas and then tend to move into the nearshore passes and along beaches.

Food and feeding habits. Spotted seatrout are predatory, feeding primarily on shrimp and small fish. When shrimp are scarce, they often consume mullet, menhaden, and silversides. The larger specimens feed more heavily on fish. Juveniles feed on grass shrimp and copepods.

Sennets

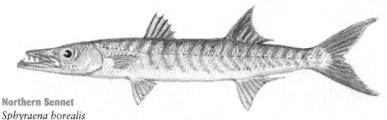

Northern Sennet
Sphyraena borealis

Sennets are members of the Sphyraenidae family of barracuda, although they are smaller and less wide-ranging than barracuda are. Northern sennets *(Sphyraena borealis)* grow to a maximum of 18 inches; they occur in the western Atlantic from Massachusetts to southern Florida and the Gulf of Mexico. Southern sennets *(S. picudilla)* are similar, occurring in Bermuda, Florida, and the Bahamas south to Uruguay; also known as *picuda china,* they have more commercial relevance than the northern sennet and are found near the surface, sometimes in large schools.

These fish are seldom far from the coast, often preferring to be near rocky bottoms. They are good table fare and not known to be poisonous (as barracuda may be). They provide good sport for light-tackle anglers and have been known to take small spoons, plugs, and flies.

Shad, Alabama

Alosa alabamae

OTHER NAMES
Gulf shad, Ohio shad.

Distribution. *This species occurs in the northern Gulf of Mexico, from the Mississippi Delta and Louisiana eastward to the Choctawhatchee River in Florida; it also occurs in rivers from Iowa to Arkansas and across West Virginia.*

Habitat/Life history. *The Alabama shad is a schooling species that spends most of its life in the ocean; when mature, it returns from early spring through summer to rivers and streams to spawn, inhabiting open water of medium to large rivers. Young shad descend rivers in autumn.*

This member of the Clupeidae family of herring and shad is an anadromous species virtually ignored by anglers. It does have some commercial significance, however.

Identification. A silvery fish like its other relatives, the Alabama shad has a large terminal mouth, with upper and lower jaws of almost equal length. Its tongue has a single median row of small teeth, there is no lateral line, the posterior of the dorsal fin lacks an elongated slender filament, and there are 18 or fewer anal rays. In general, it is nearly identical to the larger-growing American shad, but an adult fish has 42 to 48 gill rakers on the lower limb of the first gill arch.

Size. The Alabama shad can grow to just over 20 inches but is usually under 15 inches long.

Food/Angling. The feeding habits of this species at sea are unknown but are presumably similar to those of hickory and American shad. The Alabama shad is anadromous and only a potential angling target during upriver spawning migrations, during which time it does not feed. This smallish shad is a largely incidental catch and a rare deliberate angling target.

Shad, American

Alosa sapidissima

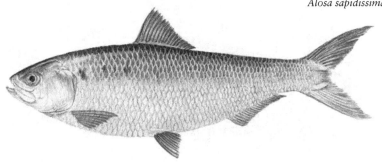

The American shad is an anadromous member of the Clupeidae family of herring and shad and is highly regarded as a gamefish in coastal rivers.

Identification. The laterally compressed, fairly deep body of the American shad is silvery white, with some green to dark blue along the back, frequently with a metallic shine. The coloring darkens slightly when the fish enters freshwater to spawn. There is a large black spot directly behind the top of the gill cover, followed by several spots that become smaller and less distinct toward the tail; sometimes there are up to three rows of these dark spots, one under the other. The American shad has large, easily shed scales, as well as modified scales called scutes, which form a distinct ridge or cutting edge along the belly. The tail is deeply forked, and the fish has weak teeth or no teeth at all.

Size/Age. The normal size of American shad is 2 to 5 pounds. They reach a maximum of 30 inches. The all-tackle world record is an 11-pound, 4-ounce Massachusetts fish. Although American shad can live to age 13, few live past age 7. Females grow more quickly and are generally largest.

Spawning behavior. Most fish spawn for the first time when they weigh 3 to 5 pounds. Males reach sexual maturity at age 3 to 4, females at age 4 to 5. Peak spawning migrations occur when the water temperature is in the 50s. These migrations usually take place in April in southern rivers and through July in northern regions. Post-spawning adults attempt to return to the sea after spawning; many die immediately after spawning, whereas others have been known to live long enough to spawn as many as seven times.

Food and feeding habits. In the ocean, American shad primarily feed on plankton. They cease feeding during upstream spawning migration.

OTHER NAMES

poor man's salmon, common shad, Atlantic shad, Connecticut River shad, North River shad, Potomac shad, Susquehanna shad, white shad, Delaware shad, alose; French: *alose savoureuse*.

Distribution. *The endemic range of this species is east of the Appalachians along the Atlantic coast of North America from Sand Hill River, Labrador, to the St. Johns River, Florida. American shad were introduced into the Sacramento River in California and now occur up and down the Pacific coast from Bahia de Todos Santos in upper Baja California, Mexico, to Cook Inlet, Alaska.*

Habitat. *American shad spend most of their lives in the ocean, ascending coastal rivers to spawn. They are found in freshwater only during their spawning runs and engage in extensive and complex migrations throughout their range.*

Shad, Hickory

Alosa mediocris

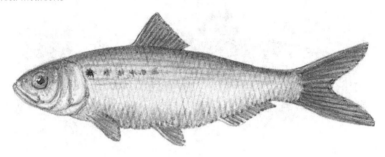

OTHER NAMES

shad herring, hickory jack, freshwater taylor, fall herring, bonejack.

Distribution. *Found only along the Atlantic coast of North America, the hickory shad ranges from the Kenduskeag River, Maine, to the St. Johns River, Florida. It is most common in the Southeast and in the mid-Atlantic regions. This species overlaps with American shad and ascends some of the same rivers when spawning.*

Habitat. *The hickory shad is a schooling species that spends most of its life in the ocean; when mature, it returns in the early spring through the summer to rivers and streams to spawn, inhabiting open water of medium to large rivers. Young shad descend rivers in the autumn.*

A member of the Clupeidae family of herring and shad, the hickory shad is of significant recreational interest, being a friskier, although smaller, cousin of the American shad.

Identification. Gray-green on the back and fading to silver on the side, the hickory shad has clear fins, with the exception of the dusky dorsal and caudal fins, which are occasionally black edged. It has a strongly oblique mouth, a lower jaw that projects noticeably beyond its upper jaw, and a cheek that is longer than or about equal to its depth. There is a blue-black spot near the upper edge of the gill cover, followed by a clump of indistinct dusky spots that extends below the dorsal fin. There are also teeth on the lower jaw and 18 to 23 rakers on the lower limb of the first gill arch.

Size. The hickory shad can reach almost 2 feet in length and averages 1 to 3 pounds in weight. It can weigh as much as 6 pounds.

Life history/Behavior. Hickory shad mature when they are 2 years old and about 12 inches long. Adults ascend coastal rivers during the spring. Preferred water temperatures range from 55° to 69°F, but the lower end of that range seems to trigger the spawning urge. The female lays up to 300,000 eggs. Young fish remain in rivers, estuaries, and backwaters, migrating to the sea by fall or early winter.

Food and feeding habits. At sea, hickory shad feed on small fish, as well as on squid, small crabs, other crustaceans, and fish eggs. In an irony that is common to most anadromous species, they are not pursued or caught by anglers in places where they do feed but are pursued and caught when migrating upriver in natal waters when they do not feed.

Sharks

Today there are at least 370 species of sharks worldwide. Like all fish, sharks are vertebrates, but ichthyologists place them in a separate class from most bony fish because the shark's skeleton is made of cartilage instead of bone. Sharks also have five to seven gill slits on each side of the head, allowing each gill to vent separately into the surrounding water. Bony fish, in contrast, have on each side of their bodies one gill opening that is covered by a bony plate called the operculum.

Sharks also lack the gas-filled swim bladders of most bony fish. Instead, sharks have evolved a different means of maintaining buoyancy: They have extremely large livers that contain oils that are lighter than water. These oils, coupled with the cartilaginous skeleton, make sharks almost neutrally buoyant.

Swimming ability. Not all sharks must swim constantly to force water over their gills for respiration. Some can actively pump water over their gills and occasionally rest motionless on the bottom. Many bottom-dwelling sharks pump water over their gills most of the time. Sharks must literally swim or sink, however, because their bodies are slightly denser than water, and they require forward motion to stay afloat. Sharks have a number of physical adaptations that make them exceptionally efficient swimmers.

Sensory ability. As sharks swim, they constantly sample the water for odors and sounds. They can detect odors at a few parts per million and are attracted by low-frequency vibrations. Feeding is dependent on vision and the detection of electrical fields. Their well-developed visual system functions well in high and low light; a special structure in the eye called the tapetum lucidum increases their sensitivity in low light. At close range, the shark's electroreception system comes into play. Receptors located in pores on the shark's snout and lower jaw can detect tiny electrical fields created by the prey's muscular movement.

Feeding and digestion. A shark swallows its food whole or in chunks. Once the shark is satiated, it may not eat again for several weeks. As the food is digested, it passes through the intestine, which has a spiral valve structure unique to sharks. This valve increases the interior surface

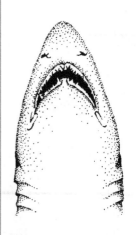

The underside of the head of a sand tiger shark.

Sharks (continued)

area of the intestine for more efficient absorption of nutrients. Sharks are opportunistic feeders and will often eat whatever is available.

Teeth. Shark teeth come in as many shapes and sizes as sharks do. They also say something about the shark's diet.

The upper and lower teeth of a mako shark

Some sharks are specialized predators; their teeth are adapted for efficient capture of their preferred prey. Others eat whatever is available, and their teeth are amply suited for many types of food. The great white uses its triangular, serrated, bladelike teeth for grabbing and biting off chunks of large fish and marine mammals. At the other end of the spectrum, the smooth dogfish uses its flat teeth for crushing the shells of mollusks and crustaceans. Others, like the mako or the sand tiger, have narrow, pointed teeth for impaling and holding onto prey small enough to swallow whole.

Skin. Sharks have placoid scales, or denticles, which are tiny, bony projections implanted in the shark's skin. They come in many shapes and sizes but usually completely cover the shark's skin like a coat of armor. Their main functions are protection and reducing drag as the shark's body slices through the water. Denticles give the shark's hide a rough texture like sandpaper.

Reproduction. Sharks have a number of reproductive strategies. Some enclose fertilized eggs in tough, leathery egg cases that are released into the water for subsequent development and birth. Some females retain eggs within their bodies and hatch the young internally, so they are born alive and fully formed. Others have a sophisticated placental arrangement similar to that of mammals. Many sharks take 10 to 20 years to mature sexually, and they produce as few as one pup at a time. A number of species are estimated to live for 40 or 50 years.

Shark, Atlantic Angel

Squatina dumeril

The Atlantic angel shark is frequently mistaken for a ray because of its flattened, triangular body. This fish is unlike a ray, however, as its gill slits are lateral and create a deep indentation between its head and its pectoral fin.

The Atlantic angel shark is brownish- to bluish-gray on the back and whitish on the belly, and it has a mid-dorsal row of denticles. The large mouth is terminal, and each tooth has a broad base with a long, pointed central cusp. The pectoral fins are not attached to the body at the rear, and Atlantic angels swim without making much use of them.

Growing to 5 feet long, Atlantic angels will bite when captured and can inflict vicious wounds. In the western Atlantic, they range from southern New England to the Gulf of Mexico, also occurring around Jamaica, Nicaragua, and Venezuela; they are rarer off southern Florida and in the Gulf of Mexico. They are common during the summer along the mid-Atlantic states.

OTHER NAME

sand devil.

Shark, Basking

Cetorhinus maximus

The second largest shark in existence today, growing to 45 feet, the basking shark is a member of the mackerel shark family and is basically harmless to humans.

A dark gray or slate-gray fish fading to a paler shade on its belly, the basking shark gets its name from its habit of swimming slowly at the surface. As a plankton feeder, it will not take bait, being too large for sportfishing anyway.

Long gill slits span the sides and nearly meet below, with long, closely set gill rakers that it uses to strain zooplankton. The rakers are shed during the winter, and the basking shark fasts on the bottom while it grows new ones.

Pelagic in cool, temperate waters nearly worldwide, its 3-year gestation period is the longest of any shark's.

Once extensively fished commercially and valued for its liver for oil, the basking shark may be a potential source of anticarcinoma drugs and is used in Chinese medicine.

Shark, Blacktip
Carcharhinus limbatus

The blacktip shark reaches just over 8 feet in length; the all-tackle world record is a 270-pound, 9-ounce fish taken off Kenya in 1995.

It is dark bluish-gray on the back and whitish below, with a distinctive silver-white stripe on each flank; young fish are generally paler. As the name implies, it is black-tipped on the insides of the pectoral fins, as well as on the dorsal, the anal, and the lower lobe of the caudal fins in young fish. This shading may be faint, especially on the first dorsal fin, and it fades with growth.

The blacktip shark has a long, almost V-shaped snout and serrated, nearly symmetrical teeth. It often forms large surface schools and is an active hunter in midwater, responsible for very few attacks on humans but dangerous when provoked.

A wide-ranging species, the blacktip extends along the western Atlantic from Massachusetts to Brazil, and in the east from Senegal to Zaire, Madeira, the Canaries, and the Mediterranean. In the eastern Pacific, it occurs from southern Baja California to Peru and the Galápagos Islands.

OTHER NAMES

blacktip whaler, common blacktip shark, small black-tipped shark.

Shark, Blue

Prionace glauca

A member of the requiem shark family, the blue shark is very slender and streamlined, with a long and pointed snout that is much longer than the width of its mouth. Appropriately, it is a deep, brilliant blue or a dark cobalt to indigo blue above, fading gradually to white below. With up to three rows of functional teeth in each jaw, the larger teeth in the upper jaw are "saber shaped," or broadly convex on one side and concave on the other; the teeth are serrated along the edges, and those in the lower jaw are narrower.

Circumglobal in temperate and tropical waters, blue sharks hardly rate as fighters in comparison to makos and threshers, but they are much more abundant and provide fine sport on appropriate tackle in cooler temperate waters off the northeastern United States, England, and California, where there are large sportfisheries for them.

They usually swim slowly, and yet they can be one of the swiftest sharks. The largest fish exceed 400 pounds and are fairly strong fighters when taken from cool waters.

Viviparous, blue sharks bear live young in large litters, up to 54 at one time (135 have been recorded); they mature at a length of 7 or 8 feet but can reach upward of 13 feet. The all-tackle world record is a 528-pound fish taken off Montauk, New York, in 2001.

Blue sharks are potentially dangerous to humans because they are related to unprovoked attacks on both humans and boats, especially during accidents and disasters at sea when injured people are in the water. They are sometimes called blue whalers because of their habit of trailing whaling ships and feeding off whale carcasses and ship garbage.

Shark, Bonnethead

Sphyrna tiburo

The bonnethead shark is the smallest member of the hammerhead sharks, the family characterized by having eyes located at the far ends of extended lateral lobes.

The bonnethead is particularly distinctive in appearance because it has a smooth, broadly widened head, frequently described as "spade shaped," which has more curve to it than do the heads of any other hammerheads. Also, the front of the head is lacking a median groove, which is present in other hammerheads. Gray to grayish-brown in color, the bonnethead shark seldom exceeds 3 feet in length, maturing at about that length to bear 6 to 12 live young at one time.

Bonnetheads, particularly young fish, are often found over flats, where they can be taken on flies and ultralight tackle. The all-tackle world record is a 23-pound, 11-ounce fish taken off Georgia in 1994.

These fish occur in the western Atlantic from North Carolina (occasionally Rhode Island) to southern Brazil, as well as around Cuba and the Bahamas, and in the eastern Pacific from Southern California to Ecuador.

OTHER NAME
bonnet.

Shark, Bull

Carcharhinus leucas

freshwater whaler, river whaler.

A large member of the requiem shark family, the bull shark is also called the freshwater whaler and the river whaler because it is most common inshore around river mouths and can adapt to life in freshwater.

This is the species that is landlocked in Lake Nicaragua in Nicaragua and has gained fame as a man-eater because it has been repeatedly implicated in attacks on humans. Also known as the Zambezi shark in southern African waters, the bull shark is one of the three most dangerous sharks in that area, along with great white and tiger sharks, due to its relative abundance in inshore habitats where people are more likely to be attacked.

The bull shark gets its name from its bull-like head and is known for its heavy body and short snout, the latter of which appears very broad and rounded from below. Gray to dull brown above and growing pale below, the bull shark has a large first dorsal fin that begins above the midpectoral fin, and the upper lobe of the tail is much larger than the lower.

The bull shark can be sluggish and unwilling to strike a fly or crankbait, but it will hit natural bait readily; unlike other sharks that rise to the surface, the bull shark often stays deep and fights hard. Like the hammerhead, it will frequently attack hooked tarpon.

Usually growing to a length of 6 to 9 feet, the bull shark can reach 12 feet and more than 500 pounds. The all-tackle world record was formerly a 490-pounder taken off Alabama in 1986, but it was superseded by a 697-pounder caught off Kenya in 2001.

Bull sharks are widespread; they inhabit the western Atlantic from Massachusetts to southern Brazil, and the eastern Pacific from southern Baja California, Mexico, to Ecuador and possibly Peru.

Sharks, Hammerhead

Sphyrna species

Hammerhead sharks occur worldwide; the most prominent species include the great hammerhead *(S. mokarran),* the smooth hammerhead *(S. zygaena),* the scalloped hammerhead *(S. lewini,* and the bonnethead shark *(see).*

Hammerheads are easy for even a novice to identify, with eyes located at the ends of two thin lobes and the overall structure resembling a hammer. One possible reason why the head takes on a hammer shape may be that the shape is ideal for turning and locating odors, making the best use of the electroreceptors present in all sharks, which in turn makes detecting food an easier chore.

The largest species is the great hammerhead, which can reach a length of 20 feet and a weight of 1,000 pounds. This shark prefers warm waters and is rarely found outside tropical areas.

The most widely distributed hammerhead is likely the smooth hammerhead, which grows to 14 feet. The front edge of its head is rounded and unnotched at the center, or smooth, and it inhabits shallow, calm coastal waters of bays and harbors.

The scalloped hammerhead is a gray-brown to olive shark that generally grows 5 to 7 feet, usually smaller than the smooth hammerhead but sometimes reaching 15 feet. The front edge of its head is rounded and notched, or scalloped. Both smooth and scalloped hammerheads occasionally school in large numbers.

Stingrays are thought to be the favored food of many hammerheads, and all species are viviparous and prolific, giving birth to many live young at a time. These sharks are exceptionally strong and can make fast, long surface and midwater runs when hooked, fighting hard and thrashing about with a great deal of excitement.

Shark, Lemon

Negaprion brevirostris

A requiem family shark, the lemon shark grows to 11 feet at maximum, although it is usually between 5 and 8 feet long. A potentially dangerous shark, it may rest on the bottom in coastal waters in groups of 4 to 6 and become aggressive when in the vicinity of spearfishing.

It is commonly yellow-brown, although it can also be muddy dark brown or dark gray with olive sides and a paler belly. It has a blunt and broad snout that appears rounded from below. The second dorsal fin is almost equal in size to the large first dorsal fin, and the upper lobe of the tail is much larger than the lower.

Lemon sharks are good inshore, light-tackle sportfish that inhabit western Atlantic waters from New Jersey to Brazil; in the eastern Pacific they extend from southern Baja California, Mexico, and the Gulf of California to Ecuador.

Shark, Leopard
Triakis semifasciata

The leopard shark is a striking fish, so named for its leopardlike black spots, which run in crossbars across its back and sides over a lighter gray background.

It has an elongate body and a short snout that is bluntly rounded. Attaining lengths of up to 7 feet, the leopard shark inhabits inshore sand flats and rocky areas, often in schools with smoothhound sharks. As a smaller, less aggressive species of shark, it is not considered dangerous.

Females bear live young in moderate numbers, between 4 and 29 at each birth. Found in the eastern Pacific from Oregon to the Gulf of California, the leopard shark is good light-tackle game and very good table fare. It is often sought by commercial fishermen.

OTHER NAME

cat shark.

Shark, Porbeagle

Lamna nasus

OTHER NAMES

beaumaris shark, blue dog, bonito shark, herring shark, mackerel shark, porbeagle, salmon shark.

The porbeagle shark is a member of the mackerel shark family, as are the great white and the mako sharks, and bears a resemblance to both species.

The porbeagle has a robust, cobalt blue body with a perfectly conical snout that ends in a point. It is easily identified by its teeth, which are smooth and have little cusps on each side of the base. It often has a distinctive white area at the base portion of the first dorsal fin; this fin is farther forward than it is on mako or white sharks.

There is a large, particularly prominent, flattened keel on both sides of the caudal peduncle, and beneath that but farther back on the tail is a small secondary keel, which mako and white sharks also lack. Its anal fin is directly aligned with the second dorsal fin.

The flesh of the porbeagle is of good quality and texture and is said to taste something like swordfish. Excellent sportfish, porbeagles occur in colder waters than makos or whites, which may explain why they are not implicated in attacks on humans.

A widespread species, it exists in the western Atlantic from Newfoundland to New Jersey, although it rarely ventures south of New England and probably ranges from southern Brazil through Argentina.

Shark, Sandbar

Carcharhinus Plumbeus

The sandbar shark is an inshore fish and a good light-tackle fighter, growing usually to between 5 and 7 feet long. A relatively heavy-bodied fish, it is dark bluish-gray to brownish-gray and has a pale or white belly.

There is a distinct ridge on the back between the first and the second dorsal fins, and the first fin is large and pointed, starting over the middle of the pectoral fin. Its snout is shorter than the width of its mouth, appearing rounded from below.

Sandbar and dusky *(Carcharhinus obscurus)* sharks are coastal migrants that have taken a particularly hard hit from longlining for both their fins and their flesh.

Sandbars are usually called browns by anglers along the east coast of the United States, where they commonly migrate into large bays to spawn. Although basically ground sharks, they are extremely strong fighters. The dusky is almost indistinguishable from the sandbar but grows to more than 700 pounds; the sandbar never exceeds much more than 200 pounds.

Very common along the coast of the Middle Atlantic states, sandbars extend in the western Atlantic from southern Massachusetts to southern Brazil. In the eastern Pacific, they occur around the Hawaiian, Galápagos, and Revillagigedo Islands.

OTHER NAME

brown shark.

Shark, Sand Tiger

Carcharias taurus

Previously called *Odontaspis taurus,* the sand tiger shark is the most common shark sighted along Atlantic beaches.

It grows to about 9 feet and is grayish-brown or tan, with dark brown spots along the sides that grow more numerous toward the tail; although it bears a resemblance to the tiger shark, it has a larger second dorsal fin, a longer snout, and strongly projecting teeth.

Usually caught accidentally by surf casters fishing for other fish, sand tigers are sluggish and offer little resistance when hooked. In the western Atlantic, they occur from the Gulf of Maine to Argentina.

Sharks, Sharpnose

Rhizoprionodon species

There are six sharpnose sharks in the *Rhizoprionodon* genus of the requiem shark family, all sharing a similar external appearance that is characterized by a long, flattened snout.

The best-known member of the family is the Atlantic sharpnose *(R. terraenovae),* which is a very popular small species as an inshore food fish and a small gamefish in the Gulf of Mexico. It grows to between 2 and 4 feet in length and has the characteristic long and flattened snout, as well as a slender brown to olive-gray body with a pale belly. The dorsal and the caudal fins may be edged in black, especially in the young, and often there are small, scattered whitish spots on the sides.

The Atlantic sharpnose is further distinguished by well-developed furrows in the lips at the corners of the mouth and by the second dorsal fin, which begins over the middle of the anal fin. This sharpnose ranges as far north as New Brunswick but is rarely found north of North Carolina. The Caribbean sharpnose *(R. porosus)* may actually be a subspecies of the Atlantic sharpnose but is found mostly in Caribbean waters.

The Pacific sharpnose *(P. longurio)* is fairly common in the Gulf of California and a frequent catch of the shark fisheries there, extending as far south as Peru.

Shark, Shortfin Mako

Isurus oxyrinchus

Distribution. *The shortfin
mako is widely distributed
throughout the oceans. In
the western Atlantic it
ranges from the Gulf of
Maine to southern Brazil; in
the eastern Pacific it ranges
south of the Aleutian Islands
to Hawaii, and from Southern California to Chile.
Although most abundant in
temperate waters (64° to
70°F is considered ideal),
some large makos adapt to
temperatures in the upper
50s, and smaller makos
often prefer waters in the
70s. A similar species, the
longfin mako (I. paucus), is
encountered mainly at night
by anglers fishing great
depths well offshore.*

The shortfin mako is by far the most popular of angling sharks, exceeding 1,000 pounds in weight and 13 feet in length.

The shortfin mako has a streamlined, well-proportioned body that is most striking for a vivid blue-gray or cobalt blue coloring on its back, which changes to a lighter blue on the sides and a snowy white on the belly; this brilliant coloring fades after death to a grayish-brown. Other characteristic features are a conical, sharply pointed snout; a large flat-tened keel on either side of the caudal peduncle; and a lunate (crescent-shaped) tail with lobes of nearly equal size. The large first dorsal fin begins just behind the base of the pectoral fins. The shortfin mako can be easily distinguished from all other sharks by its teeth, which are slender and curved and lack cusps or serrations.

The warm-blooded mako is ovoviviparous, which means the eggs hatch inside the mother and the young are born alive; while in the uterus, the unborn young often resort to cannibalism until just one remains for birth.

Makos have all the characteristics of gamefish, in that they fight hard, have good endurance, and are fast, active, strong swimmers that jump, often spectacularly. Unfortu-nately for makos, they are also very good food fish—a qual-ity that has endeared them to longliners and has led to a sharp decline in abundance.

Because female makos weigh more than 600 pounds before becoming mature, and only a few pregnant speci-mens have ever been recorded, it's something of a miracle that there are any makos left in the oceans at all. The all-tackle world record was a 1,115-pound fish taken off Mau-ritius in 1988, until superseded in 2001 by a 1,221-pounder caught off Massachusetts.

Sharks, Thresher

Alopias species

Known by a variety of names, the thresher shark is characterized by its well-muscled tail, the upper lobe of which is usually as long as the rest of the body. These sharks use their tails to herd baitfish into a mass by slapping or thrashing the water, then stunning or injuring fish before swallowing them.

Grayish to dark charcoal in color, the thresher shark turns abruptly white on the belly and may be mottled on the lower half of the body. The thresher is further identified by the absence of a keel on the caudal peduncle; by its small, pointed, and broad-based teeth; and by its comparatively smooth skin.

Longtail and pelagic threshers have moderate-size eyes, and the first dorsal fin is set almost directly in the middle of their backs and far ahead of the beginning of the pelvic fins. The Atlantic and the Pacific bigeye threshers have much larger eyes, and the rear margins of the dorsal fins are located at least as far back as the origin of the pelvic fins.

Threshers are excellent food fish, comparable to mako and swordfish, and they are outstanding fighters (the longtail has been known to leap out of the water). Thresher sharks were more popular than makos off California until recently and are a relatively rare catch along the U.S. Atlantic coast, although specimens in the 300- to 600-pound class are the most common size encountered from New Jersey to Massachusetts.

The largest threshers have come from New Zealand, where they've been boated in excess of 800 pounds. The all-tackle world record for *A. vulpinus* is a 767-pound, 3-ounce fish taken off New Zealand in 1983.

OTHER NAMES

fox shark, longtail thresher, pelagic thresher, sea fox, swiveltail, thintail thresher, thrasher shark.

Distribution. *All threshers are fundamentally pelagic but will occasionally move in close to shore. There are four species, including the pelagic thresher (A. pelagicus) and the Pacific bigeye thresher (A. profundis), which occur in the northwestern Pacific, and the Atlantic bigeye thresher shark (A. superciliosus), which occurs in the Atlantic. The longtail thresher (A. vulpinus) is cosmopolitan in temperate and tropical waters.*

Shark, Tiger

Galeocerdo cuvier

One of the largest of the requiem sharks, the tiger shark grows to 24 feet. It is infamous as one of the most dangerous sharks.

Although some sharks will attack and kill humans without necessarily eating them, the tiger shark is especially fearsome because it is well-known as a man-eater, often devouring the remains of its victims.

The tiger shark frequents shallow waters where people swim and is circumglobal in tropical and temperate waters. One study has shown that the tiger shark can travel more than 30 miles within a 24-hour period, and that although tiger sharks do revisit the same coastal areas, the time elapsed between visits can vary from a few days to many months.

Dark bluish-gray to brownish-gray above and whitish below, the tiger shark is so called because of its prominent dark brown blotches and bars, or "tiger stripes and leopard spots"; these are especially evident in juveniles and small adults but fade with age.

This fish has an extremely blunt snout that appears broadly rounded from below, and a mid-dorsal ridge is present. The tiger shark is also distinguished by its broad and coarsely serrated teeth, which have deep notches and are the same in both jaws. The first two of five gill slits are located above the pectoral fin, and there is a long, prominent keel on either side of the caudal peduncle, as well as a long upper lobe on the tail.

The tiger shark is an important species for anglers only because it is commonly in the 300- to 800-pound class when encountered and can grow much larger. The long-standing all-tackle record of 1,780 pounds was caught from a pier at Cherry Grove, South Carolina, in 1964. Tigers are famed for eating virtually anything, including metal objects, and are generally poor fighters.

Shark, White

Carcharodon carcharias

Although a relatively uncommon deep-water fish, the white shark occasionally enters shallow waters and will attack, without provocation, humans and small boats alike; because it often lingers near islands and offshore colonies of seals and sea lions, which are some of its preferred foods, it is thought that some attacks on humans occur because the white shark mistakes divers or surfers in wet suits for seals. It is undoubtedly the most dangerous shark, due to a combination of size, strength, ability, and disposition to attack and because of the many recorded attacks that have taken place in the twentieth century.

Growing to 26 feet but usually less than 16 feet in length, the white shark has a stout, heavy body that may be a dull slate blue, grayish-brown, or almost black above, turning dirty white below. There are black edges on the pectoral fins, and often there is a black oval blotch on the body just above or behind the fins.

The large head ends in a point at the conical snout, which accounts for the name "white pointer." There is a large, distinct, flattened keel on either side of the caudal peduncle and a greatly reduced second dorsal fin. A distinguishing feature is its set of large triangular teeth with sharp, serrated cutting edges.

Most whites are found in temperate or even cool waters worldwide and close to a source of the marine mammals they prefer to eat, after growing to large sizes. Actually, there are two much larger sharks, the basking shark of the North Atlantic and the whale shark of the tropics, but these are harmless plankton feeders.

The white shark record—2,664 pounds off South Australia in 1959—continues to be recognized by the IGFA, although a much larger 17-foot specimen of 3,427 pounds was caught on August 6, 1986.

OTHER NAMES

white pointer, white death, man-eater, great white shark.

Sheephead, California

Semicossyphus pulcher

OTHER NAMES

sheepie, goat, billygoat (large), red fish, humpy, fathead; Spanish: *vieja de California.*

Distribution. *California sheephead occur from Cabo San Lucas, Baja California, Mexico, to Monterey Bay, California. An isolated population exists in the Gulf of California, but these fish are uncommon north of Point Conception, California.*

Habitat. *This species is generally taken in rocky kelp areas near shore, in water from 20 to 100 feet deep, although it does occur as deep as 180 feet.*

A member of the Labridae family of wrasses, the California sheephead is a strong bottom-dwelling fish that is a favorite of spearfishing divers. It has some commercial value, although declining numbers caused it to be supplanted commercially by rockfish. Its flesh is white, firm, and mild, and it is preferred in chowder and in salads.

Identification. The body of the California sheephead is elongate, robust, and compressed. This species is a hermaphrodite: It begins life as a female and becomes a male later in life. Females mature at about 8 inches in length and 4 to 5 years of age. Most females transform to males at a length of about 12 inches, or 7 to 8 years of age. This sex change is accompanied by a marked change in appearance. Younger fish (females) are a uniform pinkish-red with white lower jaws. As they age and become males, their heads and the rear thirds of their bodies turn black, the midsections of their bodies remain red, and their lower jaws remain white. In all stages of their development, sheephead have unusually large doglike teeth.

Size/Age. The largest sheephead recorded on rod and reel was 36 inches long and weighed 35½ pounds, although the average fish weighs less than 15 pounds. At least two fish of 40 pounds were speared in the past. A 29-pound, 32-inch-long fish was 53 years old.

Spawning behavior. Spawning takes place in the early spring and the summer.

Food and feeding habits. Crabs, mussels, various-size snails, squid, sea urchins, sand dollars, and sea cucumbers are typical food items. The large caninelike teeth are used to pry food from rocks. A special plate in the throat crushes shells into small pieces for easy digestion. Occasionally, large adults have been observed out of the water in the intertidal zone, hanging onto mussels after a wave has receded.

Sheepshead

Archosargus probatocephalus

This is the most popular member of the Sparidae family of porgies with saltwater anglers in the United States and is a large fish that is commonly caught around barnacle-encrusted structures along shores. It is an excellent food fish and is of commercial value.

Identification. The basic color of the sheepshead is black, including the fins, but the sides and the caudal peduncle are striped alternately with broad bands of silver and black. The stripes are most prominent in young fish. The mouth is small to medium in size, and the teeth are broad and flat for crushing the shells of crustaceans and mollusks.

Size. Sheepshead average about a pound in weight but may attain a weight of 25 pounds and measure as long as 3 feet.

Food and feeding habits. Sheepshead consume mollusks and crustaceans. They are browsing feeders, often in schools, that forage around the pilings of wharves and docks and may be located around jetties, over rocky bottoms, and in other places where they may find oysters and mussels.

OTHER NAMES

convict fish, sheepshead seabream; Portuguese: *sargo;* Spanish: *sargo chopa.*

Distribution. *This species occurs from Nova Scotia to Florida and the northern Gulf of Mexico and south to Brazil, excluding the Bahamas and the West Indies.*

Habitat. *Sheepshead are found in bays and estuaries and along the shoreline, and they commonly enter brackish water in coastal rivers.*

Silversides

California Grunion
Leuresthes tenuis

Silversides are members of the Atherinidae family and occur throughout the world. They are important forage for larger predators along shores, in bays, and in estuaries.

Every silverside lacks a lateral line and has small, almost useless teeth. Its pelvic fins are located well behind the pectoral fins, and the small, spiny dorsal is well separated from the soft dorsal. The body is typically elongated. Some silversides live in freshwater; others are marine, found near shore. They are often called shiners but are more commonly referred to as "smelt," although they are not related to the true osmerid smelt.

One of the most prominent silversides is the California grunion *(see) (Leuresthes tenuis)*, which grows to 7½ inches and is famous for moonlight spawning runs and remarkable beach spawning. A similar fish is the gulf grunion *(L. sardina)*, which is restricted to the Gulf of California.

Also prominent and frequently caught along Pacific piers is the larger (to 17½ inches) jacksmelt *(Atherinopsis californiensis)*, which has small, unforked teeth in bands. This characteristic differentiates the jacksmelt from the California grunion and also from the topsmelt *(Atherinops affinis)*, which grows to 12 inches but generally occupies the same range as the jacksmelt. The topsmelt is most easily distinguished from the jacksmelt by its forked teeth set in a single row, rather than in bands. These species constitute a sizable portion of the Pacific coast "smelt" catch.

Along the Atlantic coast, the tidewater silverside *(Menidia beryllina)*, which grows to only 3 inches long, ranges from Massachusetts to the Gulf of Mexico. Frequently called whitebait and spearing, it is predominantly a saltwater species but is also found in brackish water and freshwater. Several similar species occur in the same general range, including the Atlantic silverside *(M. menidia)* and the Mississippi silverside *(M. audens)*, a freshwater species.

Skipjack, Black

Euthynnus lineatus

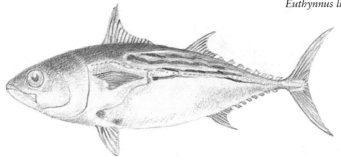

A member of the Scombridae family of mackerel, bonito, and tuna, the black skipjack is commonly caught by anglers, usually while trolling or casting for other pelagic species. It is often used as a bait for big-game fish. Its food value has mixed ratings, although it is of some commercial importance. Its flesh is dark red and the taste is strong.

Identification. The dorsal fin of the black skipjack has 13 to 15 spines and is high anteriorly. This distinguishes it from the bonito *(Sarda)*, which has a relatively long and low first dorsal fin. The anal fin, which has 11 to 13 rays, is similar to the second dorsal fin in size and shape. The body lacks scales, except on the anterior corselet and along the lateral line. This is the only species of *Euthynnus* with 37, instead of the usual 39, vertebrae. Each jaw has 20 to 40 small, conical teeth. Bonito have fewer and larger conical teeth. Mackerel have flat, triangular teeth.

The black skipjack is distinguished from similar species by the four or five broad, straight, black stripes that run horizontally along the back and by its dark spots between the pectoral and the ventral fins. In live specimens, stripes may be visible on the venter, as well as on the back, which has frequently led to confusion with the skipjack tuna *(Katsuwonus pelamis)*. The stripes on the belly rarely persist long after death in the black skipjack, however, whereas they remain prominent in the skipjack tuna.

Size. Black skipjack are reported to attain a maximum length of 33 inches and a weight of 20 pounds, although they are usually encountered weighing several pounds. The all-tackle world record is a 26-pound specimen.

Food. Black skipjack feed predominantly on small surface fish, squid, and crustaceans.

OTHER NAMES

little tuna, false albacore, spotted tuna, mackerel tuna, skipjack; Spanish: *barrilete negro, bonito negro, pataseca.*

Distribution. *This species occurs in tropical and warm temperate waters of the eastern Pacific Ocean from California to northern Peru, including the Galápagos Islands, and rarely the central Pacific.*

Habitat. *Like other pelagic and migratory species, the black skipjack occurs in schools near the surface of coastal and offshore waters. It sometimes forms multispecies schools with other scombrids.*

Sleepers

Bigmouth Sleeper
Gobiomorus dormitor

Sleepers are distributed in tropical and subtropical waters throughout the world. They are so called because of their habit of resting on the bottom as though "sleeping," rarely moving unless disturbed. If not resting on the bottom, they often remain suspended and motionless in the water, diving down to hide when frightened or in danger. Sleepers are closely related to gobies, although they lack the sucking disk that is customary in gobies and instead have separated ventral and pelvic fins. Most sleepers are fairly small, although the larger species have some food value. Sleepers are predatory in their feeding, hiding in weeds and crevices in wait for fish.

The fat sleeper *(Dormitator maculatus)* can reach 2 feet in length but is usually less than a foot long. It inhabits brackish waters and freshwaters through the Caribbean and the warm Atlantic northward to the Carolinas. Usually dark brown and mottled, it has a bluntly rounded head, a large mouth, no visible lateral line, and a rounded caudal fin. It bears a resemblance to a fat mullet, but its second dorsal and anal fins are large and of equal size.

The bigmouth sleeper *(Gobiomorus dormitor)* occurs along the Florida coasts, in the Caribbean, and also in freshwater. It can exceed 2 feet in length and is much thinner than the fat sleeper. It has a large, pikelike mouth and obliquely squared-off second dorsal and anal fins. The bigmouth sleeper has an olive-green body, and its first dorsal fin is outlined in black.

A 4-inch species, the blue sleeper *(Isoglossus calliurus)*, inhabits the deep waters of the Gulf of Mexico; a 6-inch species, the emerald sleeper *(Erotelis smaragdus)*, lives off the southern coasts of Florida and in the Caribbean, where it blends with bright green algae.

Smelt

European Smelt
Osmerus eperlanus

Smelt are small, silvery anadromous fish of the Osmeridae family that live primarily in the sea but make spawning runs into freshwater streams. A few smelt are strictly marine; others live only in large freshwater lakes and spawn in tributary brooks and streams. Some are marine by origin but have adapted to a strictly freshwater environment; populations of some species live both in the sea and in freshwater. In all environments they are extremely important as forage for predators, including many game species.

All smelt inhabit the cool waters of the Northern Hemisphere in the Atlantic, the Arctic, and the Pacific Oceans and their drainages. The family is related to salmonids, contains 11 species in six genera, and is most generously represented in Pacific waters; many smelt species are so similar in appearance that they are difficult to distinguish.

Like the salmon and the trout, the smelt have a stubby adipose fin just in front of the tail. The lower jaw projects slightly beyond the tip of the snout. A lateral line is prominent, and there are no scales on the head. Smelt are generally small (most growing to no more than 8 inches) schooling fish, often found in enormous numbers; in the spring, great numbers move from their marine or freshwater habitats to tributary waters to spawn. Only one species, the anadromous Pacific longfin smelt *(Spirinchus thaleichthys)*, spawns in the late fall and the early winter. All species spawn at night. In North America, the pond smelt *(Hypomesus olidus)* and the rainbow smelt *(Osmerus mordax)* are considered excellent food fish. In quantity, freshly caught smelt have an odor more nearly like cucumbers than like fish.

The rainbow smelt *(see)*, which is also commonly known as the American smelt, is the species most familiar to anglers and most common in North American fish markets. The European smelt *(Osmerus eperlanus)* is similar in size and habits to the rainbow smelt.

Smelt, Rainbow

Osmerus mordax

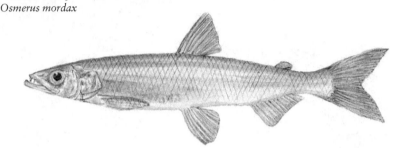

Distribution. *The rainbow smelt is widely distributed throughout eastern and western North America, inhabiting coastal waters, as well as countless inland freshwater lakes. On the Atlantic coast it ranges from New Jersey in the south to Hamilton Inlet, Labrador, in the north. Populations of rainbow smelt also exist on the Pacific coast from Vancouver Island northward around Alaska and eastward along the Arctic coast at least as far as the Mackenzie River.*

Habitat. *The rainbow smelt is a pelagic schooling species, inhabiting inshore coastal regions and the midwaters of lakes. Because it is sensitive to both light and warmer temperatures, schools of rainbow smelt tend to concentrate near the bottoms of lakes and coastal waters during daylight hours.*

One of the most prominent members of the Osmeridae family of smelt, the rainbow smelt is an important forage species for predatory fish and a principal target for inland and coastal commercial fishing. It is a close relative of the eulachon of the Pacific, the pond smelt *(Hypomesus olidus)* of the western Arctic, the capelin of the Atlantic, and the European smelt *(Osmerus eperlanus)*.

Identification. The rainbow smelt is a slender, silver fish, with a pale green or olive-green back. Fresh from the water, the sides of the fish take on a purple, blue, or pink iridescent hue. The scales on the rainbow smelt are large and easily detached, and at spawning time those on the males develop small tubercles, resembling tiny buttons that serve as a mark of their sex. The lower jaw of the fish projects beyond the upper one, and the entire mouth extends beyond the middle of each eye. On the tip of the tongue are large teeth. One large dorsal fin is located about halfway along the back, and behind that is a small adipose fin.

Size/Age. Most rainbow smelt are less than 8 inches long, although some coastal specimens have measured 14 inches. They may live for at least 6 years.

Spawning behavior. In the spring, anadromous adult rainbow smelt migrate upstream to freshwater spawning grounds. Spawners reach the tide head in the main tributaries when the water temperature is only 39° to 41°F. Spawning occurs at night, typically over a gravelly bottom. Rainbow smelt remain at spawning sites for a number of days before migrating downstream. Shortly after spawning, many males die. Some rainbow smelt are mature at 2 years of age, and all are mature at age 3.

Food. Zooplankton, insect larvae, aquatic worms, and small fish constitute the diet of rainbow smelt, with zooplankton being predominant.

Snapper, Cubera

Lutjanus cyanopterus

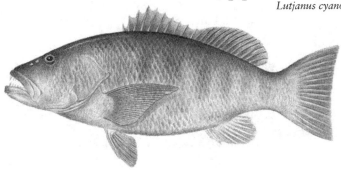

The largest of all the snapper and a member of the Lutjanidae family, the cubera is a hard-fighting gamefish, as well as a fine food fish in smaller sizes.

Identification. The head, the body, and the fins of the cubera snapper are silver or steely gray to dark brown, with an occasional reddish tinge; the body is darker above than below, sometimes with a purplish sheen. Most young fish and some adults have irregular pale bands on their upper bodies. The cubera snapper has dark red eyes, thick lips, and a rounded anal fin. It also has connected dorsal fins that consist of 10 spines and 14 rays and pectoral fins that do not extend as far as the start of the anal fin.

The cubera snapper is often confused with the gray or "mangrove" snapper, although they can be differentiated by the number of gill rakers present on the lower limb of the first branchial arch; there are an average of seven to nine gill rakers on the gray snapper, in contrast to five to seven on the cubera snapper. They can also be distinguished by the tooth patch on the roofs of their mouths; the gray snapper has an anchor-shaped patch, whereas the cubera snapper has a triangular one that does not extend back as the anchor-shaped one does. In general, the canine teeth of the cubera snapper are enlarged and noticeable even when the mouth is closed.

Size. Although the cubera snapper commonly weighs up to 40 pounds, it can weigh more than 100 pounds and reach lengths of 4 or more feet. The all-tackle world record is a 121-pound, 8-ounce Louisiana fish.

Spawning behavior. In the Florida Keys, cubera snapper spawn during the late summer and the early fall during full moon phases.

Food. Cubera snapper feed primarily on fish, shrimp, and crabs.

OTHER NAMES

Cuban snapper; Spanish: *cubera, guasinuco, pargo cabalo, pargo cubera.*

Distribution. *In the western Atlantic, cubera snapper occur from Florida and Cuba southward to the mouth of the Amazon in Brazil. They are very occasionally found north of Florida to New Jersey, are rare in the Gulf of Mexico, and are generally scarce in most of their range.*

Habitat. *Adult fish are found offshore over wrecks, reefs, ledges, and rocky bottoms; young fish sometimes enter freshwater or inhabit mangrove areas and grassbeds. Cubera snapper are solitary and are usually found in 60 feet of water or deeper.*

Snapper, Gray

Lutjanus griseus

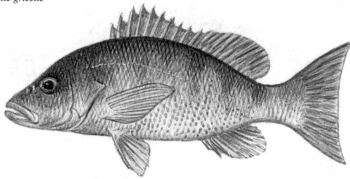

OTHER NAMES

mangrove snapper;
French: *sarde grise,
vivaneau sarde grise;*
Portuguese: *caranha,
castanhola, luciano;*
Spanish: *caballerote, pargo
manglero, pargo prieto.*

Distribution. *In the western Atlantic, gray snapper extend from Massachusetts to Rio de Janeiro, occurring throughout the Caribbean Sea, the Gulf of Mexico, and Bermuda. Although rare north of Florida, they are common off southeastern Florida and around the Antilles.*

Habitat. *Young gray snapper are mostly found inshore over smooth bottoms in such places as estuaries, the lower reaches of tidal creeks, mangroves, and sea-grass meadows; adult fish generally range offshore over irregular bottoms in such places as coral or rocky reefs, rock outcroppings, and shipwrecks, to depths of about 300 feet.*

A member of the Lutjanidae family of snapper and important commercially, the gray snapper is a good gamefish and also an excellent food fish. It is commonly referred to as the mangrove snapper.

Identification. The coloring of the gray snapper is variable, from dark gray or dark brown to gray-green. The belly is grayish tinged with olive, bronze, or red, sometimes described as having reddish or orange spots running in rows on the lower sides. A dark horizontal band occasionally runs from the lip through the eye, and some fish may have dark vertical bars or blotches along the sides. The tail may also have a dark margin, and the anal fin is rounded. There are two conspicuous canine teeth at the front of the upper jaw. The gray snapper can be distinguished from the cubera snapper by the shape of the tooth patch in the mouth, which is triangular in the cubera snapper and anchor shaped in the gray snapper.

Size/Age. The gray snapper averages only about 1 pound, although offshore catches commonly weigh 8 to 10 pounds; it reportedly may grow to 35 inches and 25 pounds, although fish exceeding 15 pounds are rare. The all-tackle world record is a 17-pound Florida fish. The gray snapper may live up to 21 years.

Life history/Behavior. When gray snapper reach age 3 or older and a length of about 9 inches, they begin to spawn, usually at dusk in shallow water during full moon phases and between June and August. The female is courted by one or many males, and fertilized eggs settle to the bottom and remain unattended until they hatch. Gray snapper drift in small schools.

Food and feeding habits. Gray snapper feed primarily at night, leaving reefs late in the day for grassflats, where they consume plankton, small fish, shrimp, and crabs.

Snapper, Lane
Lutjanus synagris

The lane snapper is a member of the Lutjanidae family of snapper and highly regarded as a food fish.

Identification. The lane snapper is silvery pink to reddish, with short, somewhat parallel pink and yellow stripes on its sides; there is often a faint greenish cast to the back and the upper sides, which sometimes highlights a few light olive bands. The pectoral, the pelvic, and the anal fins are often yellowish, and the dorsal and the tail fins are often reddish. The outer margin of the tail is black, particularly toward the center. A black spot about as large as the eye is present just below the rear dorsal fin and just above the lateral line, although it may be missing in rare cases; this spot is what distinguishes the lane from other snapper, in addition to an anchor-shaped tooth patch on the roof of the mouth, 18 to 22 gill rakers on the first arch, and a round anal fin.

Size. Usually weighing less than a pound, the lane snapper is ordinarily 8 to 12 inches long, sometimes reaching a maximum of 15 inches. The all-tackle world record is an 8-pound, 3-ounce Mississippi fish.

Spawning behavior. Becoming sexually mature when they are 1 year old and 6 to 7 inches long, lane snapper spawn from March through September. Spawning activity peaks from June through August. Young fish stay in grass-beds in estuaries, which serve as nursery areas until they reach 5 or 6 inches in length, when they migrate offshore.

Food and feeding habits. Lane snapper are opportunistic carnivores and primarily consume forage that is near or on the bottom, including anchovies and other small fish, crabs, shrimp, worms, and mollusks. They are fast enough to pursue and capture their prey, and they feed at night, moving off reefs and onto grassbeds.

OTHER NAMES

Portuguese: *areocó;* Spanish: *bia-jaiba, chino, machego, pargo biajaiba, pargo guanapo, rayado, villajaiba.*

Distribution. *In the tropical western Atlantic, lane snapper range from North Carolina to southeastern Brazil, including the Caribbean Sea and the Gulf of Mexico. They are commonly found in Florida and only occasionally inhabit waters of the Bahamas and the Caribbean.*

Habitat. *Ranging from depths of 5 to 130 feet, lane snapper are found over all types of bottoms, although they prefer coral reefs and sandy areas with vegetation; young fish stay inshore over grassbeds or shallow reefs, whereas adults move offshore, where they explore deeper reefs. Occurring in turbid, as well as clear, water, lane snapper often drift in schools, especially during the breeding season.*

Snapper, Mutton

Lutjanus analis

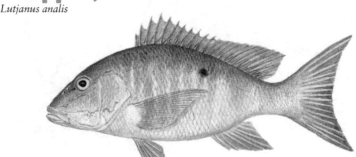

OTHER NAMES

Portuguese: *cioba;*
Spanish: *pargo cebalo,
pargo cebal, pargo col-
orado, pargo criollo, pargo
mulato.*

Distribution. *In the western Atlantic, mutton snapper extend from
Massachusetts to southeastern Brazil, including the
Caribbean Sea and the
northern Gulf of Mexico.
They are most abundant
around the Antilles, the
Bahamas, and off southern
Florida and have been introduced into Bermuda waters.*

Habitat. *Young fish occur
over soft bottoms, such as
seagrass beds, whereas
adults are found over hard
bottoms around rocky and
coral reefs, as well as in
bays and estuaries. They
drift above the bottom at
depths of 5 to 60 feet.*

The mutton snapper is a member of the Lutjanidae family of snapper. It is an excellent food fish, often marketed as "red snapper."

Identification. The mutton snapper can be striking in appearance, varying from orangish to reddish-yellow or reddish-brown, or from silver-gray to olive green on the back and the upper sides. All fins below the lateral line have a reddish cast, and larger mutton snapper take on an over-all reddish color, which causes them to be confused with red snapper. Young fish are often olive colored and may display dark bars. There is a distinct black spot about the size of the eye on the mid-body line below the rear dorsal fin, and of all the snapper with this type of dark spot, the mut-ton is the only one with a V-shaped tooth patch in the roof of the mouth, rather than an anchor-shaped one. There are also small blue lines below and near each eye, and the dor-sal fin has 10 spines and 14 rays. Adults tend to develop high backs, and all fish have pointed anal fins.

The lane snapper is somewhat similar in coloring, except that it has yellow streaks. It also has squarish or even rounded anal and dorsal fins, whereas the mutton snapper has pointed anal and dorsal fins.

Size. Ordinarily 1 to 2 feet in length and 15 pounds in weight, the mutton snapper can reach weights of 25 to 30 pounds and lengths of 30 inches. The all-tackle world record is a 30-pound, 4-ounce Florida fish.

Spawning behavior. Spawning takes place from May through October, with a peak of activity in July and August. Mutton snapper form small groups that disperse during the night.

Food and feeding habits. Mutton snapper feed both day and night on shrimp, fish, snails, crabs, and plankton.

Snapper, Pacific Cubera

Lutjanus novemfasciatus

The Pacific cubera snapper closely resembles the cubera snapper, the "river" or "mangrove red" snapper, and an African snapper; this resemblance involves habitat and behavior but extends as well to a similar appearance; they each have a deep reddish body, four large canine teeth, stubby gill rakers, and almost identical body and fin shapes. This seems to suggest that large cubera-type snappers may be more closely related to each other than are other members of the Lutjanidae (snapper) family. Marketed fresh and frozen, the Pacific cubera snapper is an excellent food fish and is greatly prized as a sport catch.

Identification. The young Pacific cubera snapper is purplish-brown with a light spot in the center of each scale, whereas adults and older fish are almost a deep red. Occasionally, a blue streak is evident under each eye, as are roughly nine shaded bars on the flanks. The tail is very slightly forked or lunate (crescent shaped), the dorsal fin is made up of 10 spines and 14 soft rays, and the anal fin is rounded and has 3 spines and 8 rays. The pectoral fins do not extend to the anal fin or even as far as the vent in adults. The most distinctive feature of the Pacific cubera snapper is four uncommonly large canine teeth, two in the upper jaw and two in the lower, which are somewhat larger than the pupil of the eye. There is also a crescent-shaped tooth patch in the roof of the mouth.

Size. The Pacific cubera snapper is the largest of nine snapper occurring in its range, growing to at least 80 pounds. The all-tackle world record is a 78-pound, 12-ounce fish taken off Costa Rica.

Food and feeding habits. Carnivorous, Pacific cubera snapper prey at night on big invertebrates such as crabs, prawns, and shrimp, as well as fish.

OTHER NAMES

dog snapper, Pacific dog snapper; Spanish: *boca fuerte, huachinango, panza prieta, pargo jilguero, pargo moreno, pargo negro*.

Distribution. Pacific cubera inhabit the eastern Pacific from northern Mexico to northern Peru.

Habitat. Pacific cubera snapper are an inshore species, preferring rocky and coral reefs and caves in shallow waters with depths of 100 feet and possibly deeper. Young fish are found in estuaries near mangroves and the mouths of rivers.

Snapper, Red

Lutjanus campechanus

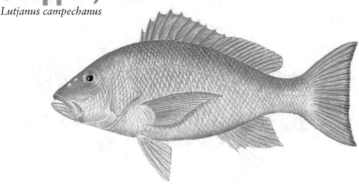

OTHER NAMES

American red snapper, northern red snapper, mutton snapper; Portuguese: *vermelho*; Spanish: *guachinango del Golfo, pargo colorado, pargo de Golfo.*

Distribution. *Red snapper occur in the Gulf of Mexico and along the entire Atlantic coast of the United States as far north as Massachusetts but rarely north of the Carolinas. They are occasionally found in Florida but are absent from the Bahamas and the Caribbean.*

Habitat. *Adult fish are usually found over rocky bottoms at depths of 60 to 400 feet, whereas young fish inhabit shallow waters over sandy or muddy bottoms.*

A member of the Lutjanidae family of snapper, the red snapper is a valued sport and commercial catch; it has been severely overfished in American waters and is now closely protected.

Identification. The red snapper is pinkish, scarlet, or brick red on its head and upper body and silvery whitish below. It has a long triangular snout, a sharply pointed anal fin, and a distinctively red iris. A young fish of under 10 inches in length has a dusky spot below the soft dorsal fin at and above the midline, and the tail sometimes has a dark edge. Although the adult resembles the Caribbean red snapper, there are differences in ray and scale counts; the Caribbean snapper has 8 soft rays in the anal fin, 50 to 51 scales in a row along the flank, and 10 to 11 scales between the beginning of the dorsal fin and the lateral line. The red snapper has 9 soft rays, 47 to 49 flank scales, and 8 to 9 scales between the dorsal fin and the lateral line.

Size/Age. Commonly growing to between 1 and 2 feet in length, the red snapper can reach 3 feet and can weigh more than 35 pounds. The all-tackle world record is a 50-pound, 4-ounce Louisiana fish. Adults can live for more than 20 years.

Life history/Behavior. Red snapper spawn from June through October and sometimes as early as April. They often intermingle with grunts and other snapper in schools. It takes 3 to 4 years for these fish to reach their spawning size of 15 to 16 inches.

Food and feeding habits. Red snapper are opportunistic bottom feeders that prey on fish, shrimp, crabs, and worms.

Snapper, Yellowtail

Ocyrus chrysurus

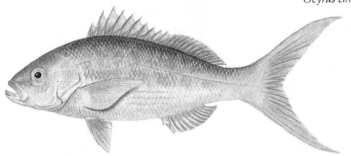

The yellowtail snapper is a member of the Lutjanidae family of snapper, a colorful tropical reef fish, and an excellent sportfish with superb meat.

Identification. The yellowtail snapper has a streamlined body that is olive or bluish-gray above and silver to white below. It has fine yellowish stripes on the belly. Most striking is the prominent mid-body yellow stripe, which runs from the tip of the snout through each eye to the tail, widening as it extends past the dorsal fins. The tail is bright yellow and deeply forked, and the dorsal fins are mostly yellowish. There is no dark lateral spot, and the eyes are red.

Size/Age. The yellowtail snapper usually grows 1 to 2 feet long and commonly weighs up to 3 pounds, although it rarely exceeds 5 pounds. It can reach 30 inches and 7 pounds, and a Florida fish that weighed 8 pounds, 8 ounces is the all-tackle world record. The yellowtail snapper can live for 14 years.

Life history/Behavior. Some yellowtail snapper are sexually mature at age 2; all are mature at age 4. Spawning occurs from April through August, and activity peaks in June and July. Yellowtail snapper move into deeper water, where each female will produce from 11,000 to more than 1.5 million pelagic eggs.

Food and feeding habits. Yellowtail snapper feed mainly at night on benthic and pelagic animals, including fish, crustaceans, and worms. Young fish feed primarily on plankton.

OTHER NAMES

Creole: *colas*; French: *sarde queue jaune*; Portuguese: *cioba, mulata*; Spanish: *rabirrubia*.

Distribution. In the tropical western Atlantic, yellowtail snapper range from Massachusetts and Bermuda to southeastern Brazil, including the Gulf of Mexico. They are abundant in the Bahamas, in southern Florida, and throughout the Caribbean but are rare north of the Carolinas.

Habitat. Inhabiting tropical coastal waters with depths of 10 to 300 feet, yellowtail snapper occur around coral reefs, either alone or in loose schools, and are usually seen well above the bottom. Young fish typically dwell inshore over grassbeds.

Snook

Fat Snook
Centropomus parallelus

Swordspine Snook
Centropomus ensiferus

Tarpon Snook
Centropomus pectinatus

OTHER NAMES

Fat Snook
Portuguese: *robalo;*
Spanish: *robalo chucumite.*

Tarpon Snook
Spanish: *constantino, robalito, róbalos, robalos prieto.*

Distribution. *In the western Atlantic, all three species
are present and are most
abundant in southern
Florida, although sword-
spine and tarpon snook are
rare on Florida's west coast.
Fat and swordspine snook
occur around the Greater
and the Lesser Antilles,
whereas fat snook also
extend down the southeastern coast of the Gulf of
Mexico and the continental
Caribbean coasts to Santos,
Brazil. Swordspine snook
occur down the continental
Caribbean coasts of Central
and South America to Rio de
Janeiro, Brazil. Tarpon
snook are found in the West
Indies and from Mexico to
Brazil. They are also*

These three species of snook are all small, similar-looking
fish with almost identical ranges and habits but are less
prominent than their larger relative the common snook. As
members of the Centropomidae family, which includes the
Nile perch and the barramundi, they are excellent table
fish, with delicate, white, flaky meat, and are good gamefish, despite their small size.

There are believed to be 12 species of snook, 6 of which
occur in the western Atlantic and 6 in the eastern Pacific,
although no single species occurs in both oceans. A good
deal is known about these three smaller Atlantic-occurring
species and about the common snook, but not about the
others, especially those in the Pacific, which include such
large-growing species as the Pacific black snook (*C.
nigrescens;* commonly called black snook) and the Pacific
white snook (*C. viridis*), as well as the smaller Pacific blackfin snook (*C. medius*).

Identification. Snook in general are distinctive in appearance, with a characteristic protruding lower jaw and a particularly prominent black lateral line running from the gill
cover to the tail.

The fat snook has a deeper body than the other snook
have, although it is not strongly compressed. Coloration
varies, depending on the area the fish inhabits, but the fat
snook is frequently yellow-brown or green-brown on the
back and silvery on the sides, and the lateral line is weakly
outlined in black. The mouth reaches to or beyond the center of the eye, and it has the smallest scales of all the snook.
There are 15 to 16 rays in the pectoral fin, 6 soft rays in the
anal fin, and 10 to 13 gill rakers.

The swordspine snook is the smallest snook and is named for its very long second anal spine, which usually extends to or farther than the area below the base of the tail. With a slightly concave profile, it is yellow-green or brown-green on the back and silvery on the belly, and it has a prominent lateral line outlined in black. It has the largest scales of all the snook, as well as 15 to 16 rays in the pectoral fin, 6 soft rays in the anal fin, and 13 to 16 gill rakers.

The tarpon snook is distinctive, having 7 anal fin rays, when all other snook have 6. It also has a distinguishing upturned or tarponlike snout and a compressed, flat-sided body. The prominent black lateral line extends through the tail. The pelvic fin is orange-yellow with a blackish edge, and the tips of the pelvic fins reach past the anus. There are 14 rays in the pectoral fin, 7 soft rays in the anal fin, and 15 to 18 gill rakers.

Size/Age. The fat snook rarely reaches more than 20 inches in length, although it is said to attain a length of 2½ feet. The swordspine and the tarpon snook are usually less than 1 pound in weight or 12 inches in length. The all-tackle world records for the fat and the tarpon snook are, respectively, 9 pounds, 5 ounces and 3 pounds, 2 ounces. Snook have a life span of at least 7 years.

Food. These species feed on fish and crustaceans.

reported on the Pacific coast from Mexico to Colombia.

Habitat/Behavior. *Snook inhabit the coastal waters of estuaries and lagoons, moving between freshwater and saltwater seasonally but always remaining close to shore and to estuaries. Fat and swordspine snook prefer very low salinity water or freshwater, whereas the tarpon snook is most common in shaded lakes with brackish waters. Fat snook occur more often in interior waters than do other snook (instead of estuarine waters), and all three species use mangrove shorelines as nursery grounds. Snook are usually sexually mature by their third year.*

Snook, Common

Centropomus undecimalis

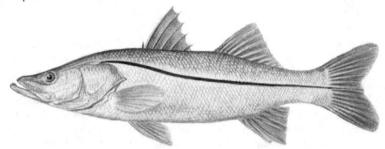

OTHER NAMES

linesider, robalo, sergeant fish, snook; Portuguese: *robalo;* Spanish: *robalo, robalito.*

Distribution. *In the western Atlantic, common snook are found primarily in southern Florida, as well as off the southeastern coast of the Gulf of Mexico. They are also occasionally encountered off North Carolina and Texas. The largest snook in Florida, exceeding 30 pounds, are caught chiefly in east coast bays and inlets from Vero Beach south to Miami, but their most abundant populations are on the west coast from Boca Grande south throughout the Everglades region, including Florida Bay.*

The range of the Pacific black snook is in the eastern Pacific, primarily from Baja California, Mexico, to Colombia. The range of the Pacific white snook is similar, extending from Baja California to Peru.

Habitat. *Snook inhabit warm, shallow coastal*

The common snook is the most abundant and wide-ranging of the snook and is highly sought after because of its strength and acrobatics when hooked. It is a member of the Centropomidae family, which also includes such prized species as the Nile perch, although it is superior to the former as a sportfish, even though it doesn't reach the same monstrous proportions. It is also related to the barramundi, with which it shares some appearance and behavioral traits.

The common snook was once a favored commercial species in Florida; it is now strictly a gamefish there but may be taken commercially in other parts of its range.

Identification. A silvery fish with a yellow-green or olive tint, the common snook has a body that is streamlined and slender, with a distinct black lateral line running from the top of its gills to the end of its forked tail. It has a sloping forehead; a long, concave snout; and a large mouth with brushlike teeth and a protruding lower jaw. The fins are occasionally bright yellow, although the pelvic fin is usually pale, unlike the orange-yellow, black-tipped pelvic fin of the tarpon snook. The common snook has a high, divided dorsal fin, as well as small scales that run from about 70 to 77 along the lateral line to the base of the tail. It has relatively short anal spines that do not reach the base of the tail when pressed against the body; there are usually 6 soft rays in the anal fin. There are also 15 to 16 rays in the pectoral fins and 7 to 9 gill rakers on the first arch.

Size/Age. The common snook grows much larger than other Atlantic-range snook, averaging 1½ to 2½ feet or 5 to 8 pounds, although it can reach 4 feet and 50 pounds. Females are almost always larger than males, although growth rates are variable. The all-tackle world record is a 53-pound, 10-ounce fish, taken off eastern Costa Rica in 1978. Common snook can live for more than 20 years.

Snook, Common (continued)

Life history/Behavior. Common snook congregate at mouths of passes and rivers during the spawning season, returning to the same spawning sites each summer. Spawning grounds include significant passes and inlets of the Atlantic Ocean and the Gulf of Mexico, such as Sebastian, Ft. Pierce, St. Lucie, Jupiter, and Lake Worth inlets on the east coast and Hurricane, Clearwater, and John's passes on the west coast. Common snook also spawn inside Tampa Bay around passes to the secondary embankments of Miquel Bay, Terra Ceia Bay, and Riviera Bay. The season extends from April through November, but activity peaks between May and July; more intense spawning occurs during new or full moon phases. A female may spawn more than 1.5 million eggs every day in the early part of the season, with larvae drifting for 15 to 20 days after hatching. Young fish remain in the quiet, secluded upper reaches of estuaries until they reach sexual maturity, which males attain after 2 to 3 years and females after 3 to 4 years.

Common snook are protandric hermaphrodites—they can change their sex from male to female; this change usually happens between the ages of 2 and 7 and between the lengths of 17 to 30 inches. Within a group of common snook, sex reversal is brought about by a change in the size of individuals; that is, if a group that loses its largest fish has lost females, some males may undergo sex reversal to fill the absence, a process that takes from 60 to 90 days.

Food and feeding habits. Carnivorous predators that ambush their prey as currents sweep food into their vicinity, snook feed on both freshwater and saltwater fish, shrimp, crabs, and larger crustaceans.

waters and are able to tolerate freshwater and saltwater. They are most common along continental shores, preferring fast-moving tides and relying on the shelter of estuaries, lagoons, mangrove areas, and brackish streams, as well as freshwater canals and rivers, usually at depths of less than 65 feet. Occasionally, they occur in small groups over grassy flats and shallow patch reefs and may be found at the mouths of tributaries and along the ocean side of shores near tributaries. Snook cannot tolerate water temperatures below 60°F; in the winter, they stay in protected, stable-temperature areas such as those under bridges and in ship channels, turning basins, warmwater outflows near power plants, and the upper reaches of estuaries.

Sole, Petrale

Eopsetta jordani

OTHER NAMES

sole, round-nosed sole, Jordan's flounder, California sole, brill.

Distribution. *The petrale sole ranges from the Bering Sea and Aleutian Islands throughout the Gulf of Alaska to the Coronado Islands of northern Baja California, Mexico.*

Habitat. *Petrale sole occur on sand and mud bottoms in waters from 60 to 1,500 feet deep, although they are most commonly found between 180 and 400 feet from April through October and deeper in winter. Anglers on party boats are likely to encounter them at such depths on sand bottoms near rocky reefs.*

A member of the Pleuronectidae family of right-eyed flatfish, the petrale sole is an occasional catch by anglers and a good sportfish, in part owing to its moderate size. It is an excellent food fish and is highly sought commercially, primarily by trawlers, and is marketed fresh or as frozen fillets. The livers of large specimens are known to be rich in vitamin A.

Identification. The body of the petrale sole is elongate, moderately slender, and compressed. The head is deep and the mouth large. The eyes are large, and the color on the eyed side is uniformly dark to light brown, with dusky blotches on the dorsal and the anal fins. It is white on the blind side.

The petrale sole is often confused with the California halibut because these species have a similar color and large mouths. The petrale sole, however, has an even, brown coloration and does not have a high arch in its lateral line.

Size. The average commercial catch is between 1 and 2 pounds, but this species can attain lengths to 28 inches and a weight of 8 pounds.

Food. The diet of petrale sole includes crabs, shrimp, and fish such as anchovies, hake, small rockfish, and other flatfish.

Spadefish

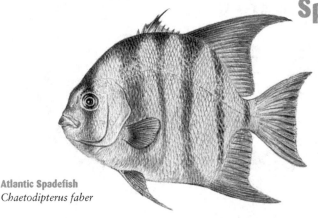

Atlantic Spadefish
Chaetodipterus faber

Spadefish are distinctively shaped members of the Ephippidae family of mainly tropical and subtropical species. Their bodies are very flattened and nearly as deep as they are long. The first, or spiny, dorsal fin is separate from the second, or soft-rayed, dorsal, which has exceptionally long rays at the front and is matched in size and shape by the anal fin directly beneath it. The body is silvery and has four to six black bands that may be absent in older fish. The broad caudal fin has long rays at the tips of the upper and lower lobes so that the fin is concave. The mouth is small. Juvenile spadefish are black and are known to lie on their sides to mimic floating debris.

Species that occur in North American waters and are occasionally encountered by anglers include the Pacific spadefish *(Chaetodipterus zonatus),* which ranges from Southern California to Mexico in the eastern Pacific, and the similar Atlantic spadefish *(C. faber),* which ranges from Massachusetts to Brazil in the western Atlantic and is more abundant in the Caribbean and Florida. The latter is sometimes mistakenly called an angelfish; it is also known in Portuguese as *enxada* and in Spanish as *paguara.*

Spadefish travel in large schools, spawn in the spring and the summer, feed on shrimp and crustaceans, and are found inshore or in nearshore environs, especially around navigational markers, along sandy beaches, in harbors, or over wrecks. They may grow to 15 pounds but usually weigh less than 2 pounds. These fish are good table fare.

Spearfish, Longbill
Tetrapturus pfluegeri

Spearfish, Shortbill
Tetrapturus angustirostris

OTHER NAMES

Longbill Spearfish
longnose spearfish,
Atlantic longbill spearfish;
French: *makaire becune;*
Japanese: *kuchinaga, kuchi-
nagafuura;* Portuguese:
espadim bicudo; Spanish:
aguja picuda.

Shortbill Spearfish
shortnose spearfish;
Arabic: *kheil;* Hawaiian:
a'u; Japanese: *fûraikajiki.*

Mediterranean Spearfish
Tetrapturus belone.
French: *aguglia impériale;*
Italian: *acura imperiale,
aguglia pelerana.*

Distribution/Habitat.
*Spearfish are cosmopolitan,
but nowhere are they abundant. They are pelagic, offshore, deep-water fish that
appear to be available all
year in small numbers but
are infrequently encoun-
tered by anglers in most
parts of their range. The
longbill spearfish is known
to occur in the northwest
Atlantic from New Jersey to
Venezuela, including the
Gulf of Mexico.*

These species are lesser-known and small members of the Istiophoridae family of billfish, which are also referred to as slender spearfish.

Identification. The spearfish can be distinguished from other billfish by a slender, lightweight body; a short bill; and a dorsal fin that is highest anteriorly (higher than in marlin and lower than in the sailfish). The vent is located well in front of the anal fin; in all other billfish, the vent is located close to the anal fin. The bill of the shortbill spearfish is barely longer than its lower jaw, whereas in the longbill spearfish it is about twice as long, but it is still noticeably short when compared to those in other billfish. The pectoral fins of the shortbill and the Mediterranean spearfish barely reach to the curve of their lateral lines. In the longbill spearfish, they extend beyond the curve. The longbill spearfish has more elements (45 to 53) in the first dorsal fin than does any other Atlantic billfish, although it may appear similar to the white marlin. The shortbill spearfish of the Pacific has approximately the same count (47 to 50 elements), but the Mediterranean spearfish has fewer (39 to 46). The lateral line is single and arches above the pectoral fins. The dorsal fin is bright blue and has no spots. The vertical bars on the body are never as prominent as in other billfish and may show only slightly or not at all.

Size/Age. Available data indicate that the longbill spearfish matures by the age of 2 and rarely lives past age 3. The all-tackle world record for the longbill spearfish is a fish of 127 pounds, 13 ounces, and for the Mediterranean spearfish is 90 pounds, 13 ounces.

Food and feeding habits. Spearfish feed at or near the surface, mainly on small and medium-size fish and squid, including on dolphin, sauries, flyingfish, and needlefish.

Spot

Leiostomus xanthurus

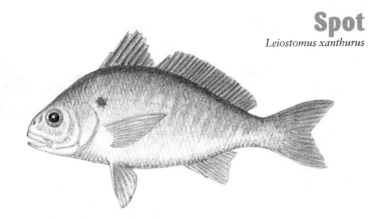

A member of the Sciaenidae family, the spot is an important commercial fish. Its migration habits bring it to shore in schools, enabling both recreational anglers and commercial fishermen to catch spot in large numbers. Much like its cousin, the Atlantic croaker, the spot is a small and flavorful fish.

Identification. The body of the spot is deep and stout, and the tail is slightly forked. The soft dorsal fin has more than 30 rays, and the anal fin has more than 12 rays. Its coloring is gray to silver, with a gold tint on the sides and 12 to 15 dark lines extending from the dorsal fins to the lateral line. There is a round black spot about the same size as the eye above each pectoral fin. The fins are pale yellow, except for the dorsal and the caudal fins, which are milky. The spot's color and lack of chin barbels distinguish it from other sciaenids.

Size/Age. The average spot weighs ½ pound, and these fish rarely reach 2 pounds, making them the proverbial saltwater panfish. They can live for 5 years.

Life history/Behavior. Spawning occurs at sea in the fall and the winter, in water temperatures of 59° to 79°F. A female spot is capable of producing as many eggs as the Atlantic croaker, nearly 1 million. The eggs are pelagic and carried shoreward by wind and currents. Juveniles move into less saline estuary areas, sometimes even to freshwater, until they are old enough to return to saltwater. Growth is rapid for the first few years, due to the abundance of food in estuaries. They reach maturity at age 3. The spot is a schooling fish and travels in groups of 100 or more.

Food and feeding habits. Spot consume small crustaceans, detritus, worms, and small fish.

OTHER NAMES

Norfolk spot, spot croaker; French: *tambour croca;* Spanish: *verrugato croca.*

Distribution. Spot occur from Massachusetts to Mexico, inhabiting roughly the same range as the Atlantic croaker.

Habitat. Spot inhabit estuaries and coastal saltwaters, generally roaming over sandy and muddy bottoms. They may frequent waters as deep as 197 feet but usually remain much shallower.

Steelhead

Oncorhynchus mykiss

OTHER NAMES

steelhead trout, steelie, sea-run rainbow.

Distribution. *The original steelhead range in North America extended from Alaska's Kenai Peninsula to the Baja Peninsula in Mexico, and far inland in coastal rivers. Northern California, Oregon, Washington, southern Alaska, and especially British Columbia have had significant steelhead populations. Overfishing, pollution, dams, other habitat alterations, and additional factors have adversely affected many native runs of steelhead.*

The steelhead is a rainbow trout that migrates to sea as a juvenile and returns to freshwater as an adult to spawn. Steelhead and strictly freshwater-dwelling rainbow trout share the same scientific name. There are no major physical differences between the two, although the nature of their differing lifestyles results in subtle differences in shape and general appearance and a greater difference in color.

Identification. Steelhead are generally slender and streamlined. Coloration on the back is basically a blue-green shading to olive, with black, regularly spaced spots. The black spots also cover both lobes of the tail. The black coloration fades over the lateral line to a silver-white coloration that blends more toward white on the stomach. Steelhead have white leading edges on the anal, the pectoral, and the pelvic fins, and spawners develop a distinct pink to red striplike coloration that blends along the side, both above and below the lateral line.

Size/Age. Steelhead are typically caught from 5 to 12 pounds, and fish exceeding 15 pounds are not uncommon in some waters. Most fish returning to rivers are 5 to 6 years old, and they can live for 8 years. The all-tackle world record is a 42-pound, 2-ounce Alaskan fish caught in 1970.

Life history/Behavior. Most populations appear in rivers in the fall, entering freshwater systems as adults from August into the winter. Spawning takes place in the winter and the spring. The ragged and spent spawners move slowly downstream to the sea, and their spawning, rainbow colors of spring return to a bright silvery hue. Lost fats are restored and adults again visit the feeding regions of their first ocean migration. Generally, juvenile steelhead remain in the parent stream for roughly 3 years before migrating out to saltwater.

Food and feeding habits. Steelhead in the ocean consume squid, crustaceans, and small fish.

Sturgeon, Atlantic

Acipenser oxyrinchus

The Atlantic sturgeon is a member of the Acipenseridae family of sturgeon. It has been used as a high-quality food fish and as a source of caviar since colonial days. It is anadromous, living much of its life in brackish or saltwater and spawning in freshwater rivers. Dam construction, water pollution, and other changes in habitat, in addition to commercial overfishing, caused continued declines throughout the twentieth century. The Atlantic sturgeon is a threatened species today.

Identification. The Atlantic sturgeon is dark brown or olive green with a white belly. The head is protractile and has a long flat snout with four barbels on the underside. Five rows of scutes (bony scalelike plates) extend along the length of the body; one is along the back, and two each are along the sides and the belly. The centers of the scutes along the back and the sides are light, making them stand out in contrast to the darker surrounding color. These scutes are set extremely close together, and the bases of most overlap.

Size/Age. Atlantic sturgeon may live as long as 60 years and can attain a size of 14 feet. An 811-pounder is the largest known specimen. Fish exceeding 200 pounds are rare today.

Life history/Behavior. Spawning migrations last from late winter through early summer. Although it matures late in life, the Atlantic sturgeon is highly fecund, yet has a low reproduction rate, as females spawn only once every 3 to 5 years. Females do not mature until ages 7 to 10 in their southernmost range and ages 22 to 28 in the northernmost range. Tagging studies have demonstrated that Atlantic sturgeon migrate extensively both north and south of their natal river systems.

Food and feeding habits. Juveniles and adults are bottom-feeding scavengers, consuming a variety of crustaceans, bivalves, and worm prey, as well as insect larvae and small fish.

OTHER NAMES

sturgeon, common sturgeon, sea sturgeon, Albany beef; French: *esturgeon noir d'Amerique.*

Distribution. *This species ranges along the northwestern and western Atlantic coast in North America from the Hamilton River in Labrador, Canada, to northeastern Florida. It is currently more populous in the Hudson River, New York, than in other parts of its range, although it is not abundant there.*

Habitat. *The habitats of Atlantic sturgeon are primarily the estuaries and bays of large rivers, and deep pools of rivers when inland; in the ocean it inhabits shallow waters of the continental shelf.*

Sturgeon, White

Acipenser transmontanus

OTHER NAMES
sturgeon, Columbia sturgeon, Oregon sturgeon, Pacific sturgeon, Sacramento sturgeon; French: *esturgeon blanc.*

Distribution. *White sturgeon are limited to the Pacific coast from the Aleutian Islands, Alaska, to Monterey Bay, California, although they move far inland to spawn. It is found in the Fraser River system; the Columbia River above Revelstoke, British Columbia; Duncan Lake, Vancouver Island; and possibly Okanagan Lake and other coastal drainages. In Idaho, the white sturgeon occurs in the Snake River downstream from Shoshone Falls and in the Clearwater and the Salmon Rivers. It is landlocked in some drainages as well.*

Habitat. *White sturgeon primarily inhabit the estuaries and bays of large rivers and the deep pools of rivers when inland.*

A member of the Acipenseridae family of sturgeon, the white sturgeon is the largest fish occurring in freshwater in North America. In some areas, populations have recovered sufficiently since their decline in the early 1900s to support important recreational and commercial fisheries.

Identification. The white sturgeon has a moderately blunt snout as an adult, barbels closer to the snout tip than to the mouth, and no obvious scutes (bony, scalelike plates) behind the dorsal and the anal fins. The fish is gray to pale olive on its upper body and white to pale gray on its ventral side. It has 28 to 30 anal rays, 11 to 14 scutes on its back, and 38 to 48 scutes along the sides.

Size/Age. White sturgeon have been reported at more than 100 years old; most of the oldest individuals of the current era are roughly 40 to 60 years old. Accounts of historic landings of white sturgeon report maximum weights of between 1,300 and 2,000 pounds and a length of 20 feet. Fish under 6 feet long and weighing 60 to 70 pounds are commonly caught today, and fish from 6 to 9 feet long and weighing 200 to 500 pounds are possible.

Life history/Behavior. White sturgeon are anadromous, migrating from the ocean into freshwater to spawn. Spawning typically occurs from April through early July, when water temperatures are 50° to 64°F, during the highest daily flows of the river. Spawning occurs in swift water. When hatched, yolk-sac larvae drift to deep water with slower currents where they grow rapidly, sometimes 15 inches or more in the first year. Females typically mature when 16 to 35 years of age, at roughly 47 inches in fork length.

Food and feeding habits. Adult white sturgeon are piscivorous and do feed in freshwater. Common baits include pile worms, ghost shrimp, grass shrimp, squawfish, and carp.

Sunfish, Ocean

Mola mola

A relative of puffers, triggerfish, and porcupinefish, the giant ocean sunfish is listed in the *Guinness Book of World Records* as the heaviest bony fish and the one with the most eggs. Ocean sunfish are exceptionally strong swimmers, and most records of this fish are based on sick specimens, which are easily captured. Occasionally caught with harpoons, ocean sunfish are utilized fresh and in Chinese medicine.

Identification. Appearing to be all head, the ocean sunfish is characterized by its much-reduced and rudderlike caudal fin, which is gently curved and sturdy; it also has long dorsal and anal fins that it swims with by sculling. It lacks a spinous dorsal fin or pelvic fins, and it is dark brownish-gray or gray-blue. It has no scales, a small terminal mouth, leathery skin, and a poorly developed skeleton.

Size. The ocean sunfish can grow to 10 feet long and 11 feet high (including dorsal and anal fins) and can weigh up to 4,400 pounds.

Food. Ocean sunfish feed on zooplankton, eel larvae, and small deep-sea fish, as well as on jellyfish, crustaceans, mollusks, and brittle stars.

OTHER NAMES

headfish, moonfish; Danish/Swedish: *klumpfisk;* Dutch: *maanvis;* Finnish: *m hk kala;* French: *môle commun, poisson-lune;* German: *mondfisch;* Greek: *fegaró psaro;* Icelandic: *tunglfiskur;* Italian: *pesce luna;* Norwegian: *månefisk;* Polish: *samoglów;* Portuguese: *lua, peixe-lua;* Spanish: *mola, pez cabeza, pez luna, pez sol;* Turkish: *pervane.*

Distribution. *Found in all oceans except polar seas, the ocean sunfish occurs in the eastern Pacific from British Columbia to Peru and Chile. In the western Atlantic it occurs from Canada to northern South America.*

Habitat. *Often drifting at the surface while lying on their sides, ocean sunfish may also swim upright and close to the surface with their dorsal fins projecting above the water. They are sluggish in cold water.*

Surfperch

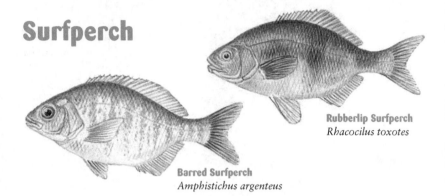

Rubberlip Surfperch
Rhacocilus toxotes

Barred Surfperch
Amphistichus argenteus

OTHER NAMES

Seaperch, surffish.

Distribution. *This group of 21 members of the Embiotocidae family is abundant along the eastern Pacific. Two members of this family occur off Japan and Korea, and the remainder occur along the Pacific coast of North America from Alaska to Baja California, Mexico. All are marine, with the exception of the small tule perch* (Hysterocarpus traski)*, which is found in California's Sacramento and Russian Rivers.*

Habitat. *Most species inhabit the surf along both sandy and rocky coasts, but several species live mainly in bays or in similar shallow inshore waters. One species occurs in relatively deep water (to more than 700 feet), and two smaller species inhabit only tidal pools.*

Surfperch are rare among marine fish for being viviparous, or producing live offspring. Unlike most other fish, female surfperch do not scatter eggs outside their bodies but nourish young fish internally and then spawn them live into the surf. Their maximum size ranges from 4 to 18 inches. They have compressed bodies, more or less oval in shape and generally silvery, and large fleshy lips. The spiny and soft-rayed dorsal fins are joined. They primarily consume small crustaceans, but some also feed on worms, small crabs, shrimp, and mussels.

The shiner surfperch *(Cymatogaster aggregata)* is probably the number one fish caught by youngsters along the California coast. Shiner surfperch range from Baja California, Mexico, to Wrangell, Alaska, and are most abundant around bays and eelgrass beds and the pilings of wharves and piers. They grow to a maximum of 8 inches and are generally greenish or silvery.

The barred surfperch *(Amphistichus argenteus)* grows to a maximum of 17 inches and 4½ pounds, although it is usually much smaller. It occurs along sandy coasts from central California to Baja California. Its sides are marked with a series of dusky, brassy vertical bars with spots between them. The back and the sides are gray to olive. This is among the most popular surfperch with anglers.

The largest member of the surfperch family is the rubberlip surfperch *(Rhacocilus toxotes)*, which reaches 18 inches. Occurring from central to southern California, it is distinguished by thick white to pinkish lips. The whitish background color is usually tinged with a smoky or blackish color, and the pectoral fins are yellow.

Other common species include the redtail surfperch *(A. rhodoterus)*; the calico surfperch *(A. koeizi)*; the walleye surfperch *(Hyperprosopon argenteum)*; the spotfin surfperch *(H. anale)*; the silver surfperch *(H. ellipticum)*; the rainbow surfperch *(Hypsurus caryi)*; the white surfperch *(Phanerodon furcatus)*; the pile surfperch *(R. vacca)*; the black surfperch *(Embiotoca jacksoni)*; and the striped surfperch *(E. lateralis)*.

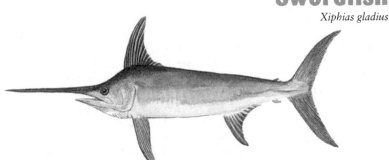

Swordfish
Xiphias gladius

The only member of the Xiphidae family, the swordfish is one of the most highly coveted big-game species in the ocean. Swordfish have been overexploited worldwide, and today fish under 100 pounds—which have likely never had the opportunity to spawn once—are primarily encountered, in some places only rarely, and too few are released alive.

Identification. The swordfish has a stout, fairly rounded body and large eyes. The first dorsal fin is tall, nonre-tractable, and crescent-shaped. The second dorsal fin is widely separated from the first and very small. Both are soft rayed, having thin, bony rods that extend from the base of the fin and support the fin membrane. The anal fins approx-imate the shape of the dorsal fins but are noticeably smaller. Ventral fins, on the underside of the fish, are absent. There is a strong longitudinal keel, or ridge, on either side of the caudal peduncle, which leads to a broad, crescent-shaped tail. Adult swordfish have neither teeth nor scales.

The back may be dark brown, bronze, dark metallic pur-ple, grayish-blue, or black. The sides may be dark like the back or dusky. The belly and the lower sides of the head are dirty white or light brown.

The swordfish snout elongates into a true sword shape. Measuring at least one-third the length of the body, it is long, flat, pointed, and very sharp (especially on smaller fish) and significantly longer and wider than the bill of any other billfish. The lower jaw is much smaller, although just as pointed, ending in a very wide mouth.

The bodies of swordfish fry are quite different from those of adults. Their upper and lower jaws are equally prolonged. Their bodies are long, thin, and snakelike; are covered with rough, spiny scales and plates; and have just one long dor-sal and one anal fin.

Although they are distinctive fish, they do bear some resemblance to the spearfish, which is distinguished from the swordfish by its rounded sword, small teeth, a long continuous dorsal fin, and ventral fins.

OTHER NAMES

broadbill, broadbill sword-fish; Arabic: *kheil al bahar;* French: *espadon;* Hawaiian: *a'u ku;* Italian: *pesce sapda;* Japanese: *dakuda, medara, meka, mekaiiki;* Norwe-gian: *sverdfisk;* Portuguese: *agulha, espadarte;* Spanish: *aja para, aibacora, espada.*

Distribution. *Swordfish occur in tropical, temperate, and occasionally cold waters of the Atlantic, the Pacific, and the Indian Oceans. They generally migrate between cooler waters in the summer to warmer waters in the winter for spawning. In the Atlantic Ocean, swordfish range from Canada to Argentina.*

Habitat. *These are pelagic fish living within the water column, rather than on the bottom or in coastal areas. They typically inhabit waters from 600 to 2,000 feet deep and are believed to prefer waters where the surface temperature is above 58°F, although they can tolerate temperatures as low as 50°F. There seems to be some correlation between larger size and the ability to tolerate cooler*

Swordfish (continued)

temperatures. Few fish under 200 pounds are found in waters with temperatures less than 64°F.

In the western Atlantic, swordfish are summer and fall visitors to New England waters, entering the warming Atlantic coastal waters from far offshore in the Gulf Stream around June and departing in late October. Evidence suggests that such onshore-offshore seasonal migrations are more prevalent than are migrations between the northern feeding areas off Cape Hatteras and the southern spawning grounds off Florida and the Caribbean.

Size/Age. Swordfish are capable of growing to well over a thousand pounds, although fish of this size are unheard of in modern times. In the North Atlantic, a fish weighing more than 400 pounds is extremely unusual, and the average fish caught in the commercial fishery there weighs less than half of this, with reports varying from under 90 pounds to under 200. The all-tackle world record, caught in 1953, weighed 1,182 pounds. The larger fish measure approximately 15 feet in length and have 10-foot-long bodies and 5-foot-long swords.

Female swordfish grow faster, live longer, and are proportionally heavier than their male counterparts. Very large swordfish are always females; males seldom exceed 200 pounds. The maximum longevity of swordfish is unknown, but they do live for at least 9 years. Most swordfish caught in the North Atlantic sportfishery are thought to be immature fish, only up to 2 years old.

Life history/Behavior. Swordfish swim alone or in loose aggregations, separated by as much as 40 feet from a neighboring swordfish. They are frequently found basking at the surface, airing their first dorsal fins. Boaters report this to be a beautiful sight, as is the powerful free jumping for which the species is known. This free jumping, also called breaching, is thought by some researchers to be an effort to dislodge pests, such as remoras or lampreys. It could also be a way of surface feeding by stunning small fish. They reach sexual maturity at about 2 to 3 years of age.

Food and feeding habits. Swordfish feed daily, most often at night. They may rise to surface and near-surface waters in search of smaller fish or prey upon abundant forage at depths to 1,200 feet. Squid is the most popular food item, but they also feed on menhaden, mackerel, bluefish, silver hake, butterfish, herring, and dolphin.

Tarpon
Megalops atlanticus

The largest member of the small Elopidae family, the tarpon is one of the world's premier saltwater gamefish. Also known as the Atlantic tarpon, this species is sometimes scientifically identified as *Tarpon atlanticus;* it is a relative of ladyfish and of a similar but much smaller species, the Indo-Pacific tarpon *(Megalops cyprinoides),* also known as oxeye tarpon or oxeye herring. In prehistoric times, there were many more species of tarpon; today, there are just these two.

Identification. The tarpon's body is compressed and covered with extremely large platelike scales and a deeply forked tail fin. Its back is greenish or bluish, varying in darkness from silvery to almost black. The sides and the belly are brilliant silver. Inland, brackish-water tarpon frequently have a golden or brownish color because of tannic acid.

The huge mouth of the tarpon has a projecting, upturned lower law that contains an elongated bony plate. A single, short dorsal fin originates just behind the origin of the pelvic fin and consists of 12 to 16 soft rays (no spines), the last of which is greatly elongated. The anal fin has 19 to 25 soft rays. The lateral line is straight, with a scale count of 41 to 48.

Size/Age. Most angler-caught Atlantic tarpon are in the range of 40 to 50 pounds, but many from 60 to 100 pounds are encountered. Fish exceeding 150 pounds are rare in the western Atlantic. The all-tackle world record is shared by two 283-pound fish, one caught in 1956 at Lake Maracaibo, Venezuela, and the other in 1991 at Sherbro Island, Sierra Leone. The Florida record for tarpon caught with conventional tackle was a 243-pounder from Key West in 1975.

Some Atlantic tarpon live as long as 55 years. Most of the tarpon caught in the Florida fishery are 15 to 30 years old.

OTHER NAMES

silver king, Atlantic tarpon, cuffum; French: *tarpon argenté;* Italian: *tarpone;* Portuguese: *camurupi, peixe-prata-do-atlântico, tarpao;* Spanish: *pez lagarto.*

Distribution. *Because tarpon are sensitive to cold water, their range is generally limited to temperate climates. Atlantic tarpon have been reported as far north as Nova Scotia and also off the coast of Ireland, although they prefer tropical and subtropical waters. In the western Atlantic, they are most common from Virginia to central Brazil and throughout the Caribbean Sea and the Gulf of Mexico. Atlantic tarpon from the western Atlantic have also emigrated through the Panama Canal and become established in the eastern Pacific; large specimens have been caught along the western Panamanian coast and in the vicinity of some rivers.*

Although scientists believe the western Atlantic

Tarpon (continued)

stock is genetically uniform, they have observed regional differences in behavior and size. Tarpon in Costa Rica, for example, are generally smaller than Florida tarpon, and Costa Rica tarpon spawn throughout the year, rather than seasonally, as Florida tarpon do.

Habitat. Tarpon are most abundant in estuaries and coastal waters but also occur in freshwater lakes and rivers, in offshore marine waters, and occasionally on coral reefs. Adults often patrol the coral reefs of the Florida Keys. In Costa Rica and Nicaragua, anglers frequently catch tarpon in freshwater lakes and rivers miles from the coast. Although tarpon do migrate, little is known about the frequency or the extent of their travels. Tarpon captured in Florida have later been recaptured as far west as Louisiana and as far north as South Carolina.

Life history/Behavior. In May and June, Atlantic tarpon in the western Atlantic begin gathering together in staging areas near the coast in preparation for the journey to their offshore spawning grounds. Here, schools of tarpon may be observed swimming in a circular, rotating motion. This behavior, known as a "daisy chain," may be a prenuptial activity that prepares the fish for spawning. The actual exodus to the offshore spawning areas is probably triggered by lunar phases and tides. Although no one knows exactly where tarpon spawn, tarpon larvae only a few days old have been collected as far as 125 miles offshore in the Gulf of Mexico. Spawning in Florida occurs mainly in May, June, and July.

The eggs hatch into larvae called leptocephali. These bizarre-looking creatures have transparent, ribbonlike bodies and slender, fanglike teeth. The leptocephali drift with the currents toward the shore, reaching estuarine areas within about 30 days. By the time the larvae reach these inshore areas, they are about an inch long. At this point, they begin an amazing transformation in which they lose their teeth and begin shrinking in length, winding up as miniature versions of the behemoths they will eventually become.

One particularly remarkable facet of tarpon physiology is the fish's ability to breathe both underwater and out of the water. When dissolved oxygen levels in the water are adequate, tarpon breathe like most fish, through their gills. When oxygen levels are depleted, however, they can also breathe by gulping air, which is then passed along to their highly specialized swim bladders. The swim bladder functions as an accessory lung and even resembles that organ, with its spongy, highly vascular tissue. The swim bladder can also be filled with air as needed to help the fish maintain its desired depth in the water.

Although tarpon can tolerate water of various salinities, they are vulnerable to cold snaps and become stressed when water temperatures fall below 55°F. Adults can often seek refuge from the cold in deep holes and channels.

Food. Tarpon often travel in schools with other tarpon and are opportunistic eaters that feed on a variety of fish and crabs.

Tautog
Tautoga onitis

Primarily known as blackfish, the tautog is a member of the Labridae family of wrasses, which includes some 500 species in 57 known genera, and is a popular inshore sport-fish.

Identification. Blunt-nosed and thick-lipped, the tautog has a high forehead and a heavy body. It is brownish on the back and the sides and lighter below, and it has blackish mottling over the entire body. The belly and the chin are white or gray, and there may be spots on the chin. The female develops a white saddle down the middle of each side during spawning. The caudal fin is rounded on the corners and squared across the tip; the soft-rayed dorsal and the anal fins are rounded.

The first dorsal fin has 16 to 17 spines. The short second dorsal fin consists of 10 somewhat longer soft rays. The anal fin has 3 spines and 7 to 8 soft rays. There is a detached area of small scales behind and beneath each eye but none on the opercle. The lateral line is arched more or less following the contour of the back and has a scale count of 69 to 73. There are 9 gill rakers on the first branchial arch, 3 on the upper limb, and 6 on the lower limb. A number of small teeth are present along the sides of the jaws, and there are 2 to 3 large canine teeth in the tips.

Size. This fish averages 3 pounds or less in weight. Specimens weighing 6 to 10 pounds are caught with some regularity, however, and the all-tackle world record is a New Jersey fish that weighed 25 pounds.

Food and feeding habits. The diet of the tautog is mainly mollusks and crustaceans, with blue mussels being especially favored. It uses the flat, rounded, stout teeth located in the rear of its mouth to crush the shells.

OTHER NAMES

blackfish, tog, Molly George, chub, oysterfish; French: *tautogue noir.*

Distribution. *The tautog occurs in the western Atlantic from Nova Scotia to South Carolina, and the greatest abundance is between Cape Cod, Massachusetts, and Delaware Bay. It overlaps in range with the smaller and more northerly relative the cunner.*

Habitat. *Tautog are known to move in and out of bays or inshore and offshore according to the water temperature, but they do not make extensive migrations up and down the coast. Preferred environs include shallow waters over rocky bottoms, shell beds, inshore wrecks, and the like, which they often inhabit year-round.*

Tilefish

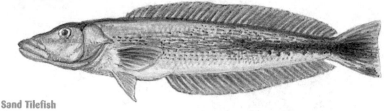

Sand Tilefish
Malacanthus plumieri

Tilefish are members of the Branchiostegidae and Malacan-thidae families, which include roughly 50 species that are distributed worldwide. Most have little to no significance to anglers but are popular food fish, with firm, white flesh, and are found in fish markets.

Most tilefish are less than 2 feet long and slender. The anal and the dorsal fins are long and low; the pelvic fins are located far forward, directly under the pectorals. Some exist in temperate waters, but most are tropical.

A well-known species is the great northern tilefish *(Lopho-latilus chamaeleonticeps)*, which inhabits the outer conti-nental shelf from Nova Scotia to northern South America and is relatively abundant from southern New England to the mid-Atlantic coast at depths of 44 to 240 fathoms. Tile-fish are generally found in and around submarine canyons, where they occupy burrows in the sedimentary substrate and feed on crustaceans, shrimp, squid, and small fish.

This species is relatively slow growing and long lived, with a maximum age and length of 35 years and 43 inches in females, and 26 years and 44 inches in males. Both sexes are mature at ages 5 to 7. The back and the sides are bluish- or greenish-gray, sprinkled with yellow spots. The belly and the cheeks are rose, grading into white at the midline. The dorsal fin is marked with yellow spots. The pectoral fins are dark and margined with black, as is the anal fin.

The sand tilefish *(Malacanthus plumieri)*, averaging 12 inches in length and occasionally reaching 24 inches, is a slim, almost eel-like fish found in reefs and sandy areas of warm Caribbean and Florida waters, rarely deeper than 50 feet. A similar species is *M. hoedtii* of the western Pacific. The ocean whitefish *(Caulolatilus princeps)*, found from British Columbia to Peru (but rare north of California), is found in eastern Pacific waters.

Tomcod, Atlantic

Microgadus tomcod

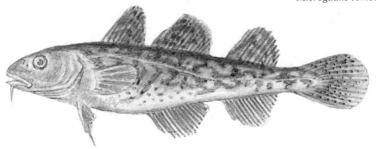

A member of the Gadidae family (codfish), the Atlantic tomcod is a small, hardy fish, resembling its relative the Atlantic cod. Able to adapt to salinity changes and sudden cold spells, the tomcod can survive in both saltwater and freshwater. It is a delicious fish, sometimes taken in large quantities by anglers, and is caught commercially in small numbers due to its size.

Identification. Characteristic of the cod family, the Atlantic tomcod has three dorsal and two anal fins, which are rounded, as is the caudal fin. The body is heavy and has a large, subterminal mouth. Its eyes are small. The coloring is olive brown on the back, fading lighter below, and the sides are heavily blotched with black. The fins have wavy or mottled designs.

The Atlantic tomcod can be distinguished from the Atlantic cod by its long, tapering ventral fins and smaller body.

Size/Age. A generally small species that might be considered a saltwater panfish, the Atlantic tomcod averages 6 to 12 inches in length. It can weigh up to 1 pound.

Spawning behavior. The spawning season of the Atlantic tomcod is from November through February. It spawns in brackish water or saltwater. The eggs sink to the bottom and attach to algae and rocks.

Food. The Atlantic tomcod uses its chin barbel and ventral fins to detect and inspect food. It consumes small shrimp, amphipods, worms, clams, squid, and small fish.

OTHER NAMES

tomcod; French: *poulamon atlantique;* Spanish: *microgado.*

Distribution. *The Atlantic tomcod inhabits waters along the North American coast from Labrador and the Gulf of St. Lawrence south to Virginia. It is common locally north from Long Island.*

Habitat. *Primarily dwelling along the coast, the Atlantic tomcod is known to enter freshwater rivers during the winter. It is also landlocked in some Canadian lakes. The tomcod lives close to the bottom and is usually found in depths of 2 to 3 fathoms.*

Tomcod, Pacific

Microgadus proximus

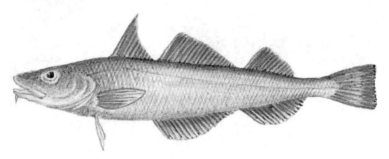

OTHER NAMES

tomcod, piciata, California tomcod.

Distribution. *This species occurs from central California, at roughly Point Sal, to Unalaska Island, Alaska.*

Habitat. *Inhabiting depths from 60 to 720 feet, the Pacific tomcod prefers the shallower end of this range and locations with a sandy bottom.*

A member of the Gadidae family, the Pacific tomcod is a small fish with minor commercial importance, due to its small average size. In central California, it is a popular recreational sportfish, usually taken incidentally by anglers pursuing larger-growing species. Its flesh is tasty, and it might be considered a saltwater panfish.

Identification. The body of the Pacific tomcod is elongated and slender. It has a small barbel on the chin. Characteristic of the cod family, the Pacific tomcod has three dorsal fins, two anal fins, a large head, and a large mouth with fine teeth. The body is covered with small, thin scales. Its coloring is olive green above and creamy white below, and the fins have dusky tips.

Three spineless dorsal fins and the small chin barbel separate the Pacific tomcod from any similar-appearing fish, except its cousin the Pacific cod. The Pacific cod has a barbel as long as the diameter of the eye, whereas the Pacific tomcod has a barbel less than one half the diameter of the eye.

Size. The Pacific tomcod can reach up to 1 foot in length.

Food. The Pacific tomcod primarily consumes anchovies, shrimp, and worms.

Tomtate

Haemulon aurolineatum

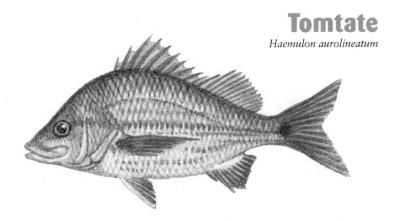

The tomtate is the widest-ranging member of the grunts, a small species and one that is fairly tolerant of colder water. It is not often caught by anglers, but it is important as a forage fish for larger species and may be used as bait.

Identification. Slim-bodied, the tomtate is silver-white overall and has a yellow-brown stripe along the length of its body, ending in a dark blotch on the caudal peduncle. The pelvic and the anal fins are yellowish. The inside of the mouth is red. It has 13 dorsal spines and 14 to 15 dorsal rays, 9 anal rays, and 17 to 18 pectoral rays.

Age/Size. The maximum length is 10 inches but seldom exceeds 8 inches. Tomtate are reported to live up to 9 years.

Behavior. Like other grunts, this species is a schooling fish often found in large groups around natural and artificial reefs. Fish are sexually mature at about 5½ inches, and spawning takes place in the southeastern United States in the spring.

Food and feeding habits. Tomtate are bottom feeders that forage on worms, snails, shrimp, crabs, and amphipods; they are, in turn, food for various snapper, grouper, and mackerel.

OTHER NAMES

tomtate grunt; Spanish: *ronco jeníguano.*

Distribution. *The tomtate exists in the Western Atlantic from Massachusetts and Bermuda to Brazil, including the Caribbean and the Gulf of Mexico.*

Habitat. *Tomtate prefer shallower water, from nearshore to outer reef areas, and rocky and sandy bottoms. Schools are commonly seen congregated around piers or docks.*

Tope

Galeorhinus galeus

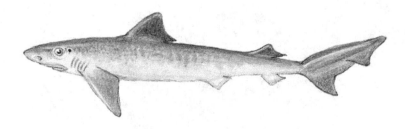

One of the smallest members of the requiem shark family, the tope is an active and highly sought species within its extensive range.

The tope has a slender body; a prominent, long, pointed snout; long pectoral fins; and a large and strong tail fin with a large lower lobe. It is a bottom-roaming inhabitant of inshore environs that commonly weighs from 20 to 40 pounds but may grow as large as 75 pounds and can exceed 5 feet in length. It is reported to live as long as 55 years. Despite its size, it is favorably regarded by anglers for its vigorous fight.

Tope occur in all oceans. In the eastern Pacific, they range from British Columbia to southern Baja California, Mexico, including the Gulf of California, and also Peru and Chile.

Torpedo, Atlantic

Torpedo nobiliana

A member of the electric ray family, the Atlantic torpedo can generate a shock of 170 to 220 volts. The electricity-generating organs are located in the front half of the body, one on each side, making up about one-sixth of the fish's total weight. The Atlantic torpedo may use these to stun prey, to protect itself from predators, and to identify or attract members of the opposite sex.

Identification. The Atlantic torpedo has a broad disk squared off in front and a short snout. It is uniformly dark olive to brown or black, occasionally with black blotches and small white spots, and whitish underneath. The Atlantic torpedo can be distinguished from its relatives by its large size.

Size. The average fish weighs roughly 30 pounds and has been known to reach 200 pounds in weight and 6 feet in length.

Life history. Reproduction takes place in deeper waters in warm areas, and the young are born alive.

Food. Atlantic torpedoes are sluggish bottom dwellers and feed on such fish as flounder and eels, although they are able to capture fast-swimming prey, such as sharks and salmon.

OTHER NAMES

torpedo, electric ray, dark electric ray; French: *torpille noire;* Spanish: *tremolina negra.*

Distribution. *Strictly an Atlantic Ocean species, it ranges from Nova Scotia and the Bay of Fundy to the Florida Keys and Cuba, but it is absent from the Gulf of Mexico.*

Habitat. *Atlantic torpedoes live on sandy or rubble bottoms, ranging from beaches to sounds, and appear to be more common in the cooler parts of their range. They are believed to be most prevalent in waters 60 to 240 feet deep.*

Triggerfish

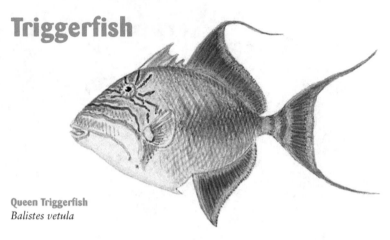

Queen Triggerfish
Balistes vetula

Triggerfish are members of the Balistidae family, which includes 40 species in 11 genera that inhabit coral reefs in the Atlantic, the Indian, and the Pacific Oceans. They are more common to divers than to anglers, although some are occasionally caught incidentally, and they have been associated with poisoning.

This fish has a compressed body, and the stout first spine of the dorsal fin is locked into place when erect by the much shorter second dorsal spine, which slides forward. The long first spine can be lowered again only by sliding the second spine back. This can be done by depressing the third spine—the "trigger"—which is attached by a bony base to the second spine. By erecting the first spine and locking it in place, the triggerfish can lodge itself immovably in crevices.

The second dorsal and the anal fins are the same size and shape. Pelvic fins are lacking, and the belly has a sharp-edged outline, with its greatest depth just in front of the anal fin.

The triggerfish is covered with an armor of bony plates. Its leathery skin lacks slime or mucus, and it is capable of rotating each eyeball independently. It normally swims by undulating its second dorsal and its anal fins but will use its tail for rapid bursts.

The queen triggerfish *(Balistes vetula)* occurs in warm western Atlantic waters northward to the Carolinas and also in the Caribbean. It usually travels alone or in pairs but is occasionally seen in small groups. It has been caught to 12 pounds.

The gray triggerfish *(B. capriscus)* is widely distributed in the warm Atlantic and the Gulf of Mexico, ranging farther north than most triggerfish. It has been caught at more than 13 pounds. The ocean triggerfish *(Canthidermis sufflamen)* may also weigh more than 13 pounds and is found off the Florida coasts and in the Caribbean.

Tripletail
Lobotes surinamensis

The tripletail gets its name from its second dorsal and anal fins, which extend far back on the body so that the fish appears to have three tails. A member of the Lobotidae family, it is an excellent food fish.

Identification. The tripletail is characterized by its rounded dorsal and anal fins, which reach backward along the caudal peduncle, giving the fish the appearance of having a three-lobed, or triple, tail. It has a deep, compressed body that resembles the body shape of the freshwater crappie, and it has a concave profile. The eyes are far forward on the snout, and the edge of the preopercle is strongly serrated.

Compared with other saltwater fish, the tripletail probably most resembles the grouper but lacks teeth on the roof of the mouth. The color is drab, various shades of yellow-brown to dark brown, with obscure spots and mottling on the sides.

Size/Age. The tripletail may reach a length of 3½ feet and weigh as much as 50 pounds, although 1½- to 2½-foot lengths and weights of less than 20 pounds are more common. The all-tackle world record is 42 pounds, 5 ounces. The tripletail may live as long as 7 to 10 years.

Life history/Behavior. Although little is known about their spawning behavior, tripletail are believed to be sexually mature by the end of their first year. Spawning occurs in the spring and the summer, and although some fish may move inshore to spawn, young tripletails have been found in estuaries and in patches of offshore sargassum. Tripletail swim or float on their sides in the company of floating objects.

Food and feeding habits. Tripletail feed almost exclusively on other fish, such as herring, menhaden, and anchovies, as well as on eels and benthic crustaceans like shrimp, crabs, and squid.

OTHER NAMES
Atlantic tripletail, brown tripletail, dusky tripletail, sleepfish, buoy fish, buoy bass, chobie, triplefin, flasher; Afrikaans: *driestert;* Bengali: *samudra koi;* French: *croupia roche;* Japanese: *matsudai;* Malay/Indonesian: *ikan tidur, kakapbato, pelayak, sekusong;* Portuguese: *furriel, prejereba;* Spanish: *dormilona.*

Distribution. *Inhabiting tropical and subtropical waters of all oceans, tripletail are found in the western Atlantic from Massachusetts and Bermuda to Argentina. In the eastern Pacific they occur from Costa Rica to Peru.*

Habitat. *Tripletail occur in coastal waters and enter muddy estuaries, commonly in depths of up to 20 feet. There is some suggestion of a northerly and inshore migration into warm waters in the spring and the summer.*

Tuna, Bigeye

Thunnus obesus

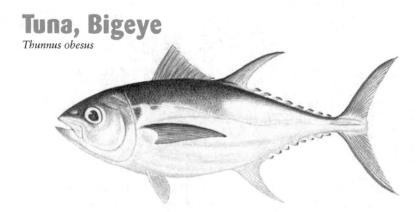

OTHER NAMES

bigeyed tuna, bigeye
tunny; French: *patudo,
thon obèse*; Hawaiian: *ahi;*
Indonesian: *taguw, tongkol;*
Italian: *tonno obeso;* Japanese: *mebachi, mebuto;*
Portuguese: *albacora
bandolim, atum patudo,
patudo;* Spanish: *albacora,
atún ojo grande, patudo.*

Distribution/Habitat.
*Found in warm temperate
waters of the Atlantic,
Indian, and Pacific Oceans,
this schooling, pelagic, seasonally migratory species is
suspected of making rather
extensive migrations.
Schools of bigeye tuna generally run deep during the
day, whereas schools of
bluefin, yellowfin, and some
other tuna are known to
occasionally swim at the
surface, especially in warm
water.*

Like other tuna, the bigeye is a member of the Scombridae family and a strong-fighting species that is equally revered for sport as for its flesh.

Identification. A stocky body and large eyes characterize this species. Generally, there are no special markings on the body, but some specimens may have vertical rows of whitish spots on the venter. The first dorsal fin is deep yellow. The second dorsal fin and the anal fin are blackish brown or yellow and may be edged with black. The finlets are bright yellow with narrow black edges. The tail does not have a white trailing edge like that of the albacore.

The pectoral fins may reach to the second dorsal fin. The second dorsal fin and the anal fins never reach back as far as those of large yellowfin tuna. It has a total of 23 to 31 gill rakers on the first arch. The margin of the liver is striated. The two dorsal fins are close-set, the first having 13 to 14 spines and the second 14 to 16 rays. The anal fin has 11 to 15 rays. On either side of the caudal peduncle is a strong lateral keel between two small keels that are located slightly farther back on the tail.

Size. Bigeyes are normally found from 16 to 67 inches in length but may attain 75 inches. The all-tackle world record is a 435-pound fish caught off Peru in 1957.

Spawning behavior. Bigeye tuna reach sexual maturity at about 40 to 50 inches in length and spawn at least twice a year. This occurs throughout the year in tropical waters, peaking during the summer months.

Food. The diet of bigeyes includes squid, crustaceans, mullet, sardines, small mackerel, and some deep-water species. They frequent the depths, particularly during the day, and, unlike other tuna, are rarely seen chasing baitfish at the surface.

Tuna, Blackfin

Thunnus atlanticus

A member of the Scombridae family and one of the smaller tuna, the blackfin is primarily a sportfish, with minor commercial interest.

Identification. The pectoral fins of the blackfin tuna reach to somewhere between the twelfth dorsal spine and the origin of the second dorsal fin, but they never extend beyond the second dorsal fin, as in the albacore *(see)*. There are a total of 19 to 25 (usually 21 to 23) gill rakers on the first arch (15 to 19 are on the lower limb), which is fewer than in any other species of *Thunnus*. The finlets are uniformly dark, without a touch of the bright lemon yellow usually present in those of other tuna, and they may have white edges. Light bars alternate with light spots on the lower flanks. The first dorsal fin is dusky; the second dorsal and the anal fins are also dusky, with a silvery luster. The back of the fish is bluish-black, the sides are silvery gray, and the belly is milky white. A small swim bladder is present. The ventral surface of the liver is without striations, and the right lobe is longer than the left and the center lobes.

Size. Blackfin tuna may attain a maximum length of 40 inches, although they are common at about 28 inches and weigh in the 10- to 30-pound range. The all-tackle world record is a 45-pound, 8-ounce Florida fish.

Spawning behavior. The blackfin's spawning grounds are believed to be well offshore. Off Florida, the spawning season extends from April through November, with a peak in May; in the Gulf of Mexico, it lasts from June through September.

Food and feeding habits. The diet of blackfin tuna consists of small fish, squid, crustaceans, and plankton. Blackfin often feed near the surface, and they frequently form large mixed schools with skipjacks.

OTHER NAMES

Bermuda tuna, blackfinned albacore, deep-bodied tunny; French: *bonite, giromon, thon nuit;* Japanese: *mini maguro, monte maguro, taiseiyo maguro;* Spanish: *albacora, atún aleta negra.*

Distribution/Habitat.

The blackfin is a pelagic, schooling fish that occurs in the tropical and warm temperate waters of the western Atlantic from Brazil to Cape Cod, including the Caribbean and the Gulf of Mexico. It is most common from North Carolina south and is Florida's most abundant tuna.

Tuna, Bluefin

Thunnus thynnus

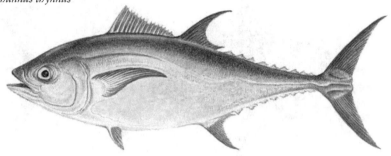

OTHER NAMES

Atlantic bluefin tuna, northern bluefin tuna, tunny fish, horse-mackerel; Arabic: *tunna;* Chinese: *cá chan, thu;* French: *thon rouge;* Italian: *tonno;* Japanese: *kuromaguro;* Norwegian: *sjorjf, thunfisk;* Portuguese: *atum, rabilha;* Spanish: *atún aleta azul, atun rojo;* Turkish: *orkinos.*

Distribution/Habitat.

Bluefin tuna occur in subtropical and temperate waters of the north Pacific Ocean and the North Atlantic Ocean and in the Mediterranean and the Black Seas. They are widely distributed throughout the Atlantic. Distribution in the western Atlantic occurs along Labrador and Newfoundland southward to Tobago, Trinidad, Venezuela, and the Brazilian coast; they are especially encountered by anglers off Nova Scotia and Prince Edward Island; Cape Cod; Montauk, New York; the canyons offshore of New York and New Jersey; the North Carolina region; and

The bluefin tuna is the largest member of the Scombridae family and one of the largest true bony fish. A pelagic, schooling, highly migratory species, it has enormous commercial value, especially in large sizes, and is of significant recreational interest.

High demand for its dark red flesh has made the bluefin tuna the object of intense commercial and recreational fishing efforts and has resulted in a dwindling population of adult fish. This species, as well as its cousin the southern bluefin tuna, is gravely overfished. According to some estimates, the population of the species in the western Atlantic has declined by roughly 87 percent since 1970.

Because bluefin tuna are slow to mature, they are especially vulnerable to overexploitation. Although some catch quotas have been established, the continued landing of small bluefins, as well as large ones (called giants), in some regions; the failure to restrict harvest in others; the ignorance of restrictions by commercial fishermen of some countries; the lack of punishment or enforcement; and the managerial treatment of bluefins on a separate two-stock basis, instead of on one interpolar migratory one, are leading reasons for both species of bluefin tuna to be further troubled, if not endangered. In 1996, scientists warned that existing worldwide catch quotas would have to be cut by 80 percent for populations to recover in 20 years, but these were raised instead.

Identification. The bluefin tuna has a fusiform body, compressed and stocky in front. It can be distinguished from almost all other tuna by its rather short pectoral fins, which extend only as far back as the eleventh or twelfth spine in the first dorsal fin. There are 12 to 14 spines in the first dorsal fin and 13 to 15 rays in the second. The anal fin has 11 to 15 rays. The bluefin has the highest gill raker count of any species of *Thunnus,* with 34 to 43 on the first arch. The ventral surface of the liver is striated, and the middle lobe is usually the largest.

The back and the upper sides are dark blue to black, with a gray or green iridescence. The lower sides are silvery, marked with gray spots and bands. The anal fin is dusky and has some yellow. The finlets are yellow and edged with black. The caudal keel is black at the adult stage but is semi-transparent when immature.

Size/Age. Bluefin tuna can grow to more than 10 feet and are commonly found at lengths from 16 to 79 inches. Adults weigh from 300 to 1,500 pounds, although fish exceeding 1,000 pounds are rare. The all-tackle world record is a fish from Nova Scotia that weighed 1,496 pounds when caught in 1979. The species reportedly can live for 40 years.

Life history/Behavior. Bluefin tuna are warm blooded and able to maintain their body temperatures up to 18°F above the surrounding water, which makes them superbly adapted to temperate and cold waters. They retain 98 percent of muscular heat, may have the highest metabolism of any known fish, and are among the fastest and most wide-ranging animals on earth. When hunted or hunting, they can accelerate to 35 miles per hour.

Bluefins are schooling fish and do congregate by size, although the largest schools are formed by the smallest individuals, and the smallest schools are composed of the largest fish. They swim in a single file, side by side (soldier formation), or in an arc (hunter formation). Extensive migrations appear to be tied to water temperature, spawning habits, and the seasonal movements of forage species.

Bluefins in the western Atlantic are sexually mature at approximately age 8 (80 inches curved fork length) and in the eastern Atlantic at about age 5 (60 inches).

Food. The diet of bluefin tuna consists of squid, eels, and crustaceans, as well as pelagic schooling fish such as mackerel, flyingfish, herring, whiting, and mullet.

the Bahamas. Distribution in the eastern Atlantic extends as far north as Norway and Iceland and as far south as northern West Africa. Atlantic bluefin tuna spawn in the Gulf of Mexico between April and June and in the Mediterranean Sea in June and July.

Tuna, Skipjack

Katsuwonus pelamis

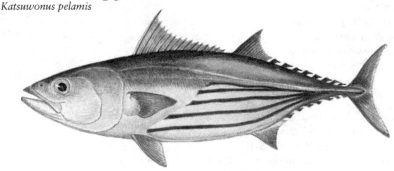

OTHER NAMES

skipjack, ocean bonito, arctic bonito, striped tuna, watermelon tuna; French: *benite à ventre raye;* Hawaiian: *aku;* Italian: *tonnetto striato;* Japanese: *katsuo;* Portuguese: *gaiado, listão, listado;* Spanish: *bonito ártico, barrilete, listado.*

Distribution/Habitat.

Skipjack tuna are cosmopolitan in tropical and subtropical seas, usually in deep coastal and oceanic waters. They are common throughout the tropical Atlantic south to Argentina and may range as far north as Cape Cod, Massachusetts, in the summer months. A pelagic, migratory, deep-water species, the skipjack tuna may form schools composed of 50,000 or more individuals, which makes it a prime target for commercial fishermen using purse seines.

Although commonly called arctic bonito, the skipjack tuna is not a bonito and does not venture into arctic waters. This member of the Scombridae family is an esteemed light-tackle species and has great commercial value.

Identification. The presence of stripes on the belly and the absence of markings on the back are sufficient to distinguish the skipjack tuna from all similar species. The top of the fish is a dark purplish-blue, and the lower flanks and the belly are silvery and have four to six prominent, dark, longitudinal stripes. The first dorsal fin has 14 to 16 spines, and the pectoral and the ventral fins are short. The body is scaleless, except on the corselet and along the lateral line.

This fish has no swim bladder. On each side of the caudal peduncle is a strong lateral keel. There are roughly 30 to 40 small conical teeth in each jaw. The teeth are smaller and more numerous than those of bonito and are unlike the triangular, compressed teeth of the mackerel. There are 53 to 63 gill rakers on the first arch, more than in any other species of tuna except the slender tuna (*Allothunnus*).

Size/Age. Skipjack tuna can attain a maximum of 40 to 45 inches in length but are commonly between 16 and 28 inches long and weigh from 5 to 15 pounds. The all-tackle world record is 45 pounds, 4 ounces. They may live for 12 years.

Life history/Behavior. In the western Atlantic, skipjack tuna frequently school with blackfin tuna. Skipjack tuna reach sexual maturity at about 18 to 20 inches in length. Spawning occurs in spurts throughout the year in tropical waters and from spring to early fall in subtropical waters.

Food and feeding habits. This gregarious, fast-swimming fish feeds near the surface, and its diet consists of herring, squid, small mackerel and bonito, lanternfish, shrimp, and crustaceans.

Tuna, Yellowfin

Thunnus albacares

Preferring warm waters, the yellowfin is the most tropical species of tuna in the Scombridae family. It is highly esteemed both as a sportfish and as table fare. Anglers throughout the world are familiar with the yellowfin, and it is heavily targeted commercially. The meat of the yellowfin is light in color compared to that of most other tuna, with the exception of the albacore and the dogtooth tuna, which have white meat.

Identification. This is probably the most colorful of all the tuna. The back is blue-black, fading to silver on the lower flanks and the belly. A golden yellow or iridescent blue stripe runs from each eye to the tail, although this is not always prominent. All the fins and finlets are golden yellow, although in some very large specimens the elongated dorsal and the anal fins may be silver edged with yellow. The finlets have black edges. The belly frequently shows as many as 20 vertical rows of whitish spots. Many large yellowfins become particularly distinguishable, as they grow very long second dorsal and anal fins.

Overall, the body shape is streamlined and more slender than that of the bluefin or the bigeye tuna. The eyes and the head are comparatively small. Just as the albacore has characteristically overextended pectoral fins, the yellowfin has overextended second dorsal and anal fins that may reach more than halfway back to the tail base in some large specimens. In smaller specimens under about 60 pounds, and in some very large specimens as well, this may not be an accurate distinguishing factor, as the fins do not appear to be as long in all specimens. The pectoral fins in adults reach to the origin of the second dorsal fin but never beyond the second dorsal fin to the finlets, as in the albacore.

The bigeye tuna and the blackfin tuna may have pectoral fins similar in length to those of the yellowfin. The yellowfin

OTHER NAMES

Allison tuna, albacore, autumn albacore, yellowfinned albacore; French: *albacore, thon à nageoires jaunes;* Hawaiian: *ahi, ahimalai-lena;* Italian: *albacore, tonno albacora;* Japanese: *kihada, kiwade, kiwada maguro;* Portuguese: *alba-cora, atum amarello;* Spanish: *atún de aleta amarilla, atún de Allison, rabil.*

Distribution/Habitat.

This species occurs worldwide in deep, warm, temperate oceanic waters. It is both pelagic and seasonally migratory but has been known to come fairly close to shore where there are warm currents. The largest yellowfins have been encountered by long-range party boats fishing in the Revillagigedo Islands off the coast of Baja California, Mexico. Specimens exceeding 200 pounds are common during many winter trips, and some in the 300-plus-pound class are boated.

can be distinguished from the blackfin by the black margins on its finlets; blackfin tuna, like albacore, have white margins on the finlets. The yellowfin can be distinguished from the bigeye tuna by the lack of striations on the ventral surface of the liver. The yellowfin tuna has a total of 25 to 35 gill rakers on the first arch, and it has an air bladder, as do all species of *Thunnus* except the longtail tuna. There is no white, trailing margin on the tail.

Previously, large yellowfins with long second dorsal and anal fins were called Allison tuna or long-finned yellowfin tuna, and the smaller specimens were called short-finned yellowfin tuna, in the mistaken belief that they were a separate species. It is now the general consensus that there is only one species of yellowfin tuna.

Size/Age. Yellowfins are commonly caught under 100 pounds in size but may grow to more than 400 pounds. Their maximum length is 75 inches, and the all-tackle world record is a 388-pound, 12-ounce Mexican fish.

Life history/Behavior. Yellowfins are fairly abundant in tropical waters. Young fish are known to form large schools near the surface. Adults inhabit fairly deep water but also live near the surface, and they are caught close to the surface by anglers. They often mix with other species, especially skipjack and bigeye tuna. Yellowfin are sexually mature when they reach a length of approximately 40 inches, and they spawn throughout the year in the core areas of their distribution, with peaks occurring in the summer months.

Food. The diet depends largely on local abundance and includes flyingfish, other small fish, squid, and crustaceans.

Tunny, Little

Euthynnus alletteratus

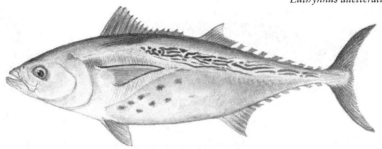

Although not part of the *Thunnus* genus like many tuna, the little tunny is a member of the same Scombridae family and is one of the finest small gamefish available. It is frequently misnamed "false albacore" and "bonito."

Identification. The little tunny has a scattering of dark spots resembling fingerprints between the pectoral and the ventral fins, as well as wavy, "wormlike" markings on the back. These markings are above the lateral line within a well-marked border and never extend farther forward than about the middle of the first dorsal fin. The spots and the markings are unlike those of any other Atlantic species. The pectoral and the ventral fins are short and broad, and the two dorsal fins are separated at the base by a small space. The body has no scales except on the corselet and along the lateral line, and there is no air bladder. Unlike the black skipjack, it has no teeth on the vomer.

The little tunny is often confused with the Atlantic bonito, the skipjack tuna, the frigate mackerel, and the bullet mackerel. There are, however, differences among these species. The Atlantic bonito has a lower, sloping first dorsal fin. The frigate and the bullet mackerel have the dorsal fins set apart. The skipjack tuna has broad, straight stripes on the belly and lacks markings on the back.

Size. Little tunny may attain a length of 40 inches but are most common to 25 inches. The all-tackle world record is an Algerian fish that weighed 35 pounds, 2 ounces.

Spawning behavior. Little tunny reach sexual maturity at approximately 15 inches in length. Spawning occurs from about April through November.

Food and feeding habits. Little tunny are common in inshore waters near the surface, where they feed on squid, crustaceans, fish larvae, and large numbers of smaller pelagic fish, especially herring.

OTHER NAMES

little tuna, Atlantic little tunny, false albacore, bonito; French: *thonine de l'Atlantique;* Italian: *tonnetto dell' Atlantico, tonnella sanguinaccio, alletterato;* Japanese: *yaito, suma-rui;* Portuguese: *merma;* Spanish: *bacoreta del Atlántico, merma, barrilete, carachana pintada.*

Distribution/Habitat.
This species occurs in tropical and warm temperate waters of the Atlantic Ocean; in the western Atlantic, it ranges from the New England states and Bermuda south to Brazil. It is not as migratory as other tuna species are and is found regularly in inshore waters, as well as offshore, usually in large schools.

Wahoo
Acanthocybium solandri

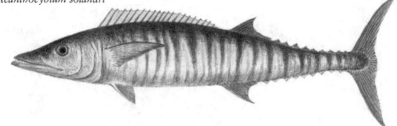

Distribution. *In North America, wahoo occur in tropical and subtropical waters of the Atlantic and the Pacific. Seasonal con-centrations exist off the Pacific coasts of Panama, Costa Rica, and Baja Cali-fornia; off Grand Cayman Island; and near the west-ern Bahamas and Bermuda.*

Habitat. *An oceanic species, wahoo are pelagic and seasonally migratory. They are frequently solitary or form small, loose group-ings of two to seven fish. They associate around banks, pinnacles, and even flotsam and are occasionally found around wrecks and deeper reefs, where smaller fish are abundant.*

The wahoo is a popular gamefish and a close relative of the king mackerel. It is reputedly one of the fastest fish in the sea, attaining speeds of 50 miles per hour and more.

Identification. A long, slender, cigar-shaped mackerel with a sharply pointed head and a widely forked tail, the wahoo is a brilliant or dark blue color along its back. It has 25 to 30 bright or dusky blue vertical bands, or "tiger stripes," that extend down the bright silver to silvery gray sides and sometimes join into pairs below.

A distinguishing feature is the movable upper jaw, which has 45 to 64 teeth, of which 32 to 50 are on the lower jaw; these teeth are large, strong, and laterally compressed. The gill structure resembles that of the marlin, but it lacks the characteristic gill rakers of the latter fish. The lateral line is well defined and drops significantly at the middle of the first dorsal fin and extends in a wavy line back to the tail. The first dorsal fin is long and low and has 21 to 27 spines. It is separated from the second dorsal fin, which has 13 to 15 rays; the anal fin has 12 to 14 very small rays. There are a series of 9 dorsal finlets, both above and below the caudal peduncle.

Size. The wahoo grows so rapidly that both sexes reach sexual maturity during the first year of life. They average 10 to 30 pounds, and 4- to 5-foot lengths are common. The maximum size is 7 feet and more than 180 pounds. The all-tackle world record is a 158-pound, 8-ounce fish taken off Baja California, Mexico, in 1996.

Food. Wahoo feed on such pelagic species as porcupine-fish, flyingfish, herring, pilchards, scad, lanternfish, and small mackerel and tuna, as well as on squid.

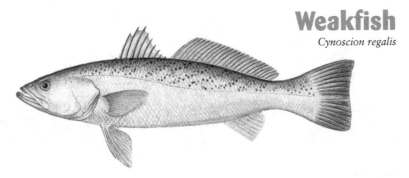

Weakfish

Cynoscion regalis

The weakfish is a member of the Sciaenidae family (drum and croaker), and its name refers to the tender, easily torn membrane in the fish's mouth.

Identification. The body of weakfish is slim and shaped somewhat like a trout's. The lower jaw projects beyond the upper jaw. There are two large, protruding canine teeth in the upper jaw and no chin barbels. Its coloring is dark olive or greenish to greenish-blue on the dorsal surface and blue, green, purple, and lavender with a golden tinge on the sides. Numerous small black spots speckle the top, occasionally forming wavy diagonal lines. There is sometimes a black margin on the tip of the tongue.

The weakfish is distinguished from the closely related spotted seatrout because its spots do not extend onto the tail or the second dorsal fin and are not as widely spaced. The scales also do not extend onto the fins on the weakfish.

Size/Age. In southerly waters, weakfish average 1 to 4 pounds. In the upper mid-Atlantic, they typically weigh 4 to 7 pounds. The all-tackle record is 19 pounds, 2 ounces, and the maximum possible growth is believed to be higher. The average life span is roughly 10 years, but some reportedly live twice that long.

Life history/Behavior. Mature weakfish are 3 to 4 years old. Spawning occurs in the nearshore and estuarine zones along the coast from May through October. A schooling species, weakfish migrate northward in the spring, spending the summer inshore, then moving southward again in the late autumn.

Food and feeding habits. Weakfish feed on crabs, shrimp, other crustaceans, and mollusks, as well as on herring, menhaden, silversides, killifish, and butterfish. Because of their varied diet, weakfish forage at different levels and adapt to local food conditions.

OTHER NAMES

squeteague, common weakfish, northern weakfish, common seatrout, northern seatrout, gray trout, summer trout, tiderunner, yellowfin, weakie; French: *acoupa royal;* Portuguese: *pescada-amarela;* Spanish: *corvinata real.*

Distribution. Weakfish inhabit the western Atlantic Ocean from Florida to Massachusetts, and records show isolated populations occurring as far north as Nova Scotia. They are most abundant from North Carolina to Florida in the winter and from Delaware to New York in the summer.

Habitat. Preferring sandy and sometimes grassy bottoms, weakfish are usually found in shallow waters along shores and in large bays and estuaries, including salt marsh creeks and sometimes into river mouths, although they do not enter freshwater. They can be found in depths of up to 55 fathoms in the winter.

Wolffish

Atlanitc Wolffish
Anarhichas lupus

Eel-like in body shape, wolffish are blenny relatives that live in the cold to arctic waters of the Atlantic and the Pacific. They are members of the Anarhichadidae family, which encompasses seven species. The wolffish lacks pelvic fins, and the dorsal fin, which begins just behind the head, extends to the caudal fin but is not joined to it. The anal fin extends about half the length of the ventral surface. Wolffish have powerful jaws and numerous broad teeth that are used to crush the shells of mollusks and crustaceans. They also have sharp canine teeth.

The Atlantic wolffish *(Anarhichas lupus)* inhabits the western Atlantic from southern Labrador and western Greenland to Cape Cod, rarely occurring as far south as New Jersey. The sides of its brownish-gray to purplish body are crossed by as many as a dozen vertical black bars. It is sedentary and rather solitary and is commonly found at depths of 45 to 65 fathoms. Populations tend to be localized. Although it appears sluggish, it is easily provoked, can move rapidly for short distances, and gives severe bites.

Individuals can attain a length of 5 feet and a weight of 40 pounds. They prey on mollusks, crabs, lobsters, and sea urchins. The Atlantic wolffish is seldom caught by anglers and is usually taken commercially by otter trawls. It is overexploited and depleted in the western Atlantic.

Also in the North Atlantic and with similar ranges are the spotted wolffish *(A. minor)* and the northern wolffish *(A. denticulatis)*. In the North Pacific, the very similar Bering wolffish *(A. orientalis)* occurs from the Aleutian Islands in Alaska southward to central California. The wolf-eel *(Anarrichthys ocellatus)* has a similar range; it reaches a length of 6½ feet. These species are also caught by commercial trawlers.

Wreckfish

Polyprion americanus

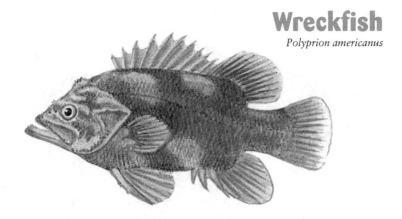

A member of the Polyprionidae family and related to the giant sea bass, the wreckfish is a very deep-dwelling and large-growing species occasionally caught by heavy-tackle anglers probing extreme depths. It is marketed fresh or frozen, sometimes as a sea bass or a stone bass, although it is susceptible to overfishing and is regulated in U.S. federal waters.

Identification. The wreckfish has a deep, strongly compressed body and a very bumpy head, with a ridge and bony protuberances above each eye. Adult fish are uniformly dark brown or bluish-gray, and the young are mottled. The second dorsal, as well as the caudal and the anal fins, are often edged in black, although the rounded caudal fin is otherwise edged in white, as are the pectoral fins. The spinous and soft parts of the dorsal fins are notched, and the lower jaw projects past the upper jaw.

Size. The wreckfish grows slowly but can eventually reach 7 feet or more in length and can weigh 100 or more pounds. The all-tackle world record is a 106-pound, 14-ounce fish taken off Portugal.

Food. Wreckfish feed on crustaceans, mollusks, and deep-dwelling fish found around wrecks or underwater objects.

OTHER NAMES

bass, stone bass, wreck bass, hapuku; Afrikaans: *wrakvis;* Danish: *vragfisk;* Dutch: *wrakbaars;* Finnish: *hylkyahven;* French: *chernier commun, mérot gris;* Greek: *vláchos;* Icelandic: *rekaldsfiskur;* Italian: *cherna di fondale;* Norwegian and Swedish: *vrakfisk;* Portuguese: *cherne;* Spanish: *cherna;* Turkish: *iskorpit hanisi.*

Distribution. *In the western Atlantic, the wreckfish ranges from Newfoundland to North Carolina.*

Habitat. *Found in the deep part of the continental shelf, at up to 2,000-foot depths, wreckfish prefer rocky ledges, pinnacles, and outcroppings around shipwrecks. They are solitary fish and are sometimes found drifting with floating timber or other objects.*

Yellowtail

Seriola lalandi

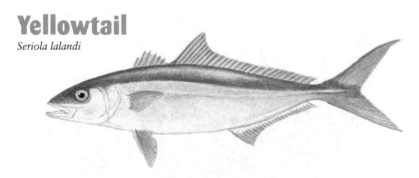

OTHER NAMES

kingfish, yellowtail king-fish, king yellowtail, kingie, amberjack.

Distribution. *The California yellowtail ranges throughout the Gulf of California and along the Pacific coast of North America from Baja California, Mexico, to Los Angeles, California. On occasion, it is found as far north as Washington.*

Habitat. *Yellowtail are primarily coastal schooling fish found in inshore waters and out to the continental shelf. In addition to schooling in and around offshore reefs and rocky shores, they frequent deep water around wharves, jetties, and man-made structures such as sunken vessels or artificial reefs, where baitfish are common. Occasionally, they will venture along ocean beaches and into larger estuaries. Large specimens, especially of the southern variety, are encountered in deep water around rocky pinnacles.*

Yellowtail are members of the Carangidae family and are closely related to amberjack. Although they are commonly referenced as three separate species—California yellowtail *(Seriola lalandi dorsalis)*, southern yellowtail *(S. lalandi lalandi)*, and Asian yellowtail *(S. lalandi aureovittata)*—it is currently believed that the worldwide yellowtail pool consists of one species, *S. lalandi*. The three varieties are recognized distinctly, however, because they are isolated from each other and do not appear to interact; there are also size differences with some populations, the southern variety growing larger than the others.

These are fast-swimming, hard-striking, strong-pulling fish that give anglers a great struggle and are a commercially important species.

Identification. Yellowtail are readily identifiable by their deeply forked, bright yellow caudal fins. Their body coloring graduates from a purple blue on their backs to a silvery white on their bellies. The yellowtail's body is elongate and moderately compressed, and a brass-colored stripe runs the length of the body from mouth to tail. There is a small keel on either side of the caudal peduncle.

Size. The southern yellowtail is believed to grow to a maximum weight of 154 pounds and a length in excess of 6½ feet. A 114-pound southern yellowtail from New Zealand holds the all-tackle world record. The world record for the California yellowtail is nearly 79 pounds, but the average fish is much smaller.

Behavior. Yellowtail can form large schools around reefs and will rise to the surface en masse to feed on schools of baitfish, as well as to drive baitfish up against the shore. Their migratory habits are not well known, but large individuals are believed to be less migratory.

Food and feeding habits. Yellowtail will eat whatever is available, but they feed predominantly on small fish, squid, and pelagic crustaceans. Large specimens will tackle bluefish, salmon, and small tuna.

Glossary

ADIPOSE EYELID
A translucent tissue partially covering the eyeballs of some species of fish.

ADIPOSE FIN
A small fleshy fin without rays found on the backs of some fish, behind the dorsal fin and ahead of the caudal fin. Only a small percentage of fish have an adipose fin; among gamefish, these include various trout, salmon, grayling, whitefish, and piranhas.

ALGAE
The term "algae" refers to a large, heterogenous group of primitive aquatic plants whose members lack roots, stems, or leaf systems and range from unicellular organisms to large networks of kelp. Algae exist in both freshwater and saltwater. They can be blue-green, yellow, green, brown, and red; there are more than 15,000 species of green algae alone. All species of algae photosynthesize.

As the primary or lowest plant forms, algae are important in sustaining marine and freshwater food chains. In freshwater, algae occur in three different types often encountered by anglers: plankton, filamentous, and muskgrass. Plankton is a diverse community made up of suspended algae (phytoplankton), combined with great numbers of minute suspended animals (zooplankton). Filamentous algae consist of stringy, hairlike filaments, often erroneously described as moss or slime because of their appearance when they form a mat or a furlike coat on objects. Muskgrass, or stonewort, algae are a more advanced form that has no roots but attaches to lake or stream bottoms.

ALIEN SPECIES
A species occurring in an area outside of its historically known natural range as a result of intentional or accidental dispersal by human activities. These are also known as exotic or introduced species.

AMPHIPODS
A large group of crustaceans, most of which are small, compressed creatures (such as sand fleas and freshwater shrimp). These may be of food importance to juvenile fish.

ANADROMOUS
Fish that migrate from saltwater to freshwater in order to spawn. Fish that do the opposite are called catadromous.

Literally meaning "up running," anadromous refers to fish that spend part of their lives in the ocean and move into freshwater rivers or streams to spawn. Anadromous fish hatch in freshwater, move to saltwater to grow to adulthood or sexual maturity, and then return to freshwater to reproduce. Salmon are the best-known anadromous fish, but there are many others, including such prominent species as steelhead trout, sturgeon, striped bass, and shad, and many lesser-known or less highly regarded species. Around the world there are approximately 100 species of anadromous fish.

Complicating an understanding of anadromy is the fact that some anadromous species have adapted, either naturally or by introduction, to a complete life in freshwater environments. These species, which include salmon, striped bass, and steelhead, make spawning migrations from lakes, where they live most of their lives, into rivers to spawn. In such instances, these fish are originally saltwater in origin. They remain anadromous when moved into purely freshwater, although they use the lake as they would the ocean. There are also species of freshwater fish that are native to freshwater and that migrate from lake to stream or river to spawn. These are not technically anadromous but adfluvial.

Fish that originate in saltwater but have freshwater forms are often called "landlocked," whether or not they have a clear path to and from the sea. Sometimes these fish are physically blocked from reaching the ocean. Fish in a reservoir or a lake may be unable to leave. Fish in some streams, like those in high-mountain areas, have a clear passageway to the sea but no means of returning because of waterfalls. Coldwater species may be effectively landlocked in the colder headwaters of a stream because temperatures are too high for them in the lowland parts of that stream or in the ocean in that area. Dolly Varden, for example, are landlocked in the southern tip of their range, but anadromous forms are common farther north.

ANAL FIN
The median, unpaired, ventrally located fin that lies behind the anus, usually on the posterior half of the fish.

AXILLARY PROCESS
A fleshy flap, which is usually narrow and extends to the rear, situated just above the pectoral or the pelvic fins on some fish.

BAITFISH
A generic term used by anglers for any fish species that are forage for predators, although it often specifically pertains to smaller fish; this term also references fish that are used in live bait angling.

BARBEL
A whiskerlike feeler on the snouts of some fish that contains taste buds and is used for touching and tasting food before ingesting it. One or more barbels may be present on either side of the mouth of a fish that is primarily a bottom feeder and is attracted by food odor. Catfish, carp, and sturgeon are among the species with such appendages.

BASS
Many species of fish, in both freshwater and saltwater, are referred to as "bass." Some are truly bass and some are not, but all have a physique and a profile that are generally similar. Three of the most prominent freshwater sportfish with this name include the largemouth bass and the smallmouth bass, both of which are actually sunfish, and the peacock bass, which is actually a cichlid.

True bass are members of the Serranidae family of sea bass, which in freshwater includes the white bass and the yellow bass, and in saltwater includes the black sea bass, the striped bass, the giant sea bass, the kelp bass, and many other species that do not carry the name "bass."

BENTHIC
The bottom layer of the marine environment and the fish or the animals that live on or near the bottom.

BILLFISH
The term "billfish" refers to members of two families of marine fish: Xiphidae, which has only one genus and one species, the swordfish; and Istiophoridae, which numbers 11 species in three genera and includes marlin, sailfish, and spearfish. Of the latter family, the term "marlin" is used for the larger species, "spearfish" for the smaller species, and "sailfish" for the species with a high dorsal fin. All are good sportfish, and some—especially swordfish, blue marlin, and black marlin—are among the largest and most coveted angling quarries.

A billfish is characterized by a long spearlike or swordlike upper jaw or beak that may be used to stun prey during feeding; although this bill has been employed in apparent aggression to spear objects, including boats, it is not deliberately used to spear prey. These species are pelagic, migratory, and found in all oceans. They are related to tuna and mackerel and, like those fish, are able to swim at great speeds; the sailfish is considered the fastest of all fish, having been clocked at 68 miles per hour over short distances. Billfish also have complex air (or swim) bladders that enable them to compensate rapidly for changes in depth and thus can move without difficulty from deep water to the surface.

Billfish grow fairly rapidly and feed on various pelagic species. When alive, they are generally ocean blue above and silvery below. They spawn in the open sea and are usually solitary or travel in pairs or small groups. Sportfishing interest in these big-game species is high, although due to their migratory and pelagic nature they are seldom accessible to large numbers of anglers and rarely to those who fish from small boats and inshore. Fishing in offshore bluewater environments is the norm.

Most billfish, particularly swordfish, have good to excellent food value and are of significant commercial interest. As a whole, and especially in certain parts of their range, billfish stocks are overexploited and have seriously declined, due to commercial longlines and gillnets. Sportfishing has not adversely impacted billfish stocks; only a small percentage of the world's billfish are caught by recreational anglers, and a still smaller percentage of those are killed. Angler tagging of released billfish has contributed significantly to scientific knowledge about this species. Nevertheless, worldwide, commercial fishermen kill millions of billfish annually. The Billfish Foundation, a research and conservation organization, reports that more than 500,000 billfish in the Atlantic Ocean alone were killed each year from the 1970s through 1990s by longlining. Furthermore, its data show that for every porpoise killed by commercial tuna fishermen, 10 tons of billfish were killed during the same period. Although efforts to save porpoises from commercial destruction have been widely reported and awareness has triggered some success, no organized international effort has emerged to prevent the commercial overharvesting and destruction of the world's billfish stocks.

BIOLUMINESCENCE

The emission of visible nonthermal light by chemical reaction in living organisms. Bioluminescence is a highly developed characteristic of species in the deepest parts of the ocean and a less highly developed characteristic of many near-surface ocean creatures, including species of bacteria, phytoplankton, metazoans, marine invertebrates, and fish. It occurs when luciferin, a compound found naturally in the luminescing organism, combines with oxygen and the enzyme luciferase to form oxyluciferin, water, and energy. Thus, chemical energy is transformed into light energy, and the resulting light is often used to attract prey. Some species have daily light cycles; others have seasonal ones. Individual luminescing organisms are difficult to see, but a large population of organisms glowing together becomes visible in darkness.

Saltwater anglers who fish at night and boaters traveling at night sometimes observe an eerie glow in the water caused by luminescent organisms being displaced by the movement of the boat.

BLUE WATER

That portion of the open ocean that is blue in color and usually many miles from shore. Blue-water fishing is synonymous with offshore fishing.

The water in the open ocean appears deep blue in a manner similar to the blue color of the sky. Particulate matter in the open ocean is relatively scarce, and marine life has a low concentration in comparison with coastal waters, causing the water to appear blue due to the size of the water molecules and the fact that they disperse solar radiation in such a way as to mostly scatter wavelengths for blue light. Coastal waters are usually greenish in color, partly because of yellow-green microscopic marine algae in coastal waters but mostly because they have more large particulate matter, dispersing solar radiation so as to mostly scatter wavelengths for greenish or yellowish light.

BONY FISH

Fish that have a bony skeleton and belong to the class *Osteichthyes*. Basically, this includes all fish except sharks, rays, skates, hagfish, and lampreys.

BREAM

Many species of both freshwater and saltwater fish around the world are referred to as bream, particularly in Australia, the United Kingdom, and the United States. In the United States, "bream" (pronounced "brim") is a colloquial expression for various freshwater panfish species, particularly sunfish and especially bluegills.

In Europe, the bream pursued by anglers are members of the Cyprinidae family and are relatives of carp, barbel, and tench. These primarily small or midsize fish (less than 8 pounds) are bottom feeders and are widely distributed. They are also a popular coarse (non-gamefish) species. The primary quarry is the bronze bream, which is also known as the common bream or the carp bream.

In saltwater, various members of the Sparidae family are known as sea bream and are related to porgies. Sea bream occur in temperate and tropical waters worldwide.

CANINE TEETH

Pointed canine teeth are found in some carnivorous fish; they are usually larger than the surrounding teeth.

CATADROMOUS

Fish that migrate from freshwater to saltwater in order to spawn. Fish that do the opposite are called anadromous and are more numerous. Freshwater eels are typical of catadromous fish; they are born at sea, migrate upstream to live and grow to adulthood, and then return to the sea to migrate to their spawning grounds.

CAUDAL FIN

The tail fin, or the fin at the rear of the fish. The fleshy section connecting the caudal fin to the end of the body is called the caudal peduncle (see).

CAUDAL PEDUNCLE

The fleshy tail end of the body of a fish between the anal and the caudal fins. On some fish, the caudal peduncle is rigid and provides a convenient "handle" of sorts for holding the fish.

CRUSTACEAN

A group of freshwater and saltwater animals having no backbone, with jointed legs and a hard shell made of chitin. In saltwater this group includes shrimp, crabs, lobsters, and crayfish, all of which may be used as bait when angling but are not targeted by anglers or deliberately sought with sporting equipment. Freshwater crustaceans also include crayfish, as well as scuds, sowbugs, and shrimp.

DEMERSAL

A term used for fish or animals that live on or near the seabed or the water bottom. Examples include flounder and croaker. Demersal is often used synonymously with groundfish.

DETRITUS

Waste from decomposing organisms, which provides food for many other organisms.

DIADROMOUS

Fish that migrate between freshwater and saltwater.

DINOFLAGELLATE

Unicellular microscopic organisms, classified as plants or animals, depending on the presence of chlorophyll or the ingestion of food, respectively. Found in two main groups, armored and naked, dinoflagellates have flagella (whiplike extensions) that provide locomotion, and they move vertically in response to light. Many dinoflagellates are phosphorescent, and some greatly increase in number periodically, occasionally resulting in toxic red tides. Some dinoflagellate blooms are toxic to shellfish and can cause gastroenteritis in the organisms that feed on them, including humans. As a component of phytoplankton (microscopic organisms that photosynthesize), dinoflagellates are an important basis for marine life.

DORSAL FIN
A median fin along the back, which is supported by rays. There may be two or more dorsal fins, in which case they are numbered, with the fin closest to the head called the first dorsal fin.

ENDANGERED SPECIES
In the United States, a species is classified as endangered if it is in danger of extinction throughout all or a significant portion of its range. Elsewhere, a species is classified as endangered if the factors causing its vulnerability or decline continue to operate, as defined by the International Union for the Conservation of Nature and Natural Resources.

EXOTIC SPECIES
Organisms introduced into habitats where they are not native are called exotic species. They are often the agents of severe worldwide, regional, and local habitat alteration. Also referred to as nonindigenous, nonnative, alien, transplant, foreign, and introduced species, they can be the cause of biological diversity loss and can greatly upset the balance of ecosystems.

Exotic species have been introduced around the world both intentionally and accidentally; occasionally, exotic species occur in new places through natural means, but usually the agent is some action of humans. That includes transportation of fish or larvae via the ballast of ocean freighters and the bait buckets of small-boat anglers, passage of new species via newly constructed canals, the introduction of plants by using them in packing shellfish that are shipped transcontinentally, the dumping of aquarium plants and fish into local waterways, the experimental stocking of predator and prey species by scientists and nonscientists, and many other means. Exotic species can be transported by animals, vehicles, commercial goods, produce, and even clothing.

While some exotic introductions are ecologically harmless, many are very harmful and have even caused the extinction of native species, especially those of confined habitats. Freed from the predators, the pathogens, and the competitors that have kept their numbers in check in their native environs, species introduced into new habitats often overrun their new home and crowd out native species. In the presence of enough food and a favorable environment, their numbers explode. Once established, exotics rarely can be eliminated.

FIN
An organ on different parts of a fish's body that may be used for propulsion, balance, and steering.

FINFISH
An alternative collective term for all species of fish, used to separate true fish from crustaceans and mollusks, which are collectively termed shellfish. The term is rarely used in reference to freshwater species but is commonly used to refer to saltwater and anadromous fish, particularly by fisheries managers.

FINGERLING
A young fish about 2 to 4 inches long.

FISHERY
In a biological sense, all the activities involved in catching a species of fish or a group of species; the place where a species or a group of species is caught. In common usage by the general public, fishery also refers to fishing opportunity or species availability in either a recreational or a commercial sense, as in "the fishery for coho salmon does not commence until the annual migration run." This term is used interchangeably with fisheries.

FISHKILL
The die-off of fish, usually in numbers. Fishkills may occur as the result of chemical pollution, especially from pesticides in agricultural runoff, but most often happen as a result of insufficient oxygen in the water.

A winter fishkill occurs when ice and snow cut off the transfer of oxygen from the air to the water; the oxygen in the water gets used up, and fish die. This does not happen if there is enough oxygen in the water to last throughout the winter until the ice and snow melt.

A summer fishkill usually occurs when inadequate amounts of oxygen exist in the water during extended periods of hot, calm, and cloudy days. Warm summer water temperatures, high demands for oxygen, and days with no sunlight or wind to mix the surface water may lead to oxygen demands exceeding oxygen production. When this happens, distressed fish may be seen as they rise to the surface and gasp for oxygen, and dead fish may be seen floating on the surface.

FLATFISH

The term "flatfish" broadly refers to a group of more than 500 species of unique, compressed fish that have developed special features for living on the bottom, the most interesting of which is that both eyes are on one side of the head. They are capable of excellent camouflaging and are widespread, ranging from cold, boreal habitats to warm, tropical environments. The flatfish group includes some of the world's most important commercial, recreational, and food fish, such as sole, flounder, halibut, dab, plaice, and turbot—names that often apply to species in different families.

FRESHWATER

Water with less than 0.5 gram per liter of total dissolved mineral salts.

GILL

A breathing organ with much-divided thin-walled filaments for extracting oxygen from the water. In a living fish, the gills are bright red feathery organs that are located on bony arches and are prominent when the gill covers of the fish are lifted.

GILL RAKERS

Toothlike extensions, located along the anterior margin of the gill arch, that project over the throat opening and strain water that is passed over the gills. These protect the gill filaments and, in some fishes, are used to sieve out tiny food organisms. The number of gill rakers on the first gill arch is sometimes used as an aid in identifying or separating species that closely resemble one another.

GRILSE

A salmon, usually male, that returns to freshwater rivers after 1 year at sea. These are small fish, generally weighing from 2 to 4 pounds.

GROUNDFISH

A species or a group of fish that lives most of its life on or near the seabed. The term may be used synonymously with demersal. Groundfish refers to Atlantic cod, haddock, pollock, American plaice, white hake, redfish, and various flounders.

HYBRID

The offspring of two individuals of different species. The offspring of two individuals belonging to different subspecies of the same species are not hybrids.

Hybridization may occur in the wild or under artificial conditions. Some species that have been known to cross-breed naturally, although not frequently, include lake trout and brook trout (splake), northern pike and muskellunge (tiger muskie), and walleye and sauger (saugeye). Hybrid fish have been cultivated in hatcheries by fisheries managers for stocking purposes; hybrid striped bass (known as whiterock bass, wiper, and sunshine bass), which result from a cross of pure-strain striped bass and white bass, have been extremely popular for stocking and are widely spread in freshwater lakes and reservoirs. Most hybrid fish are sterile (although some, like whiterock bass, are not), so the stocking of these fish is attractive because they can be controlled fairly well; if the initial stocking experiment does not achieve the desired results, the population of hybrids can be extinguished by discontinuing stocking.

INSHORE

The waters from the shallower part of the continental shelf toward shore. In saltwater fishing parlance, inshore is a loose and variable term referring to that portion of the water from which land is visible or is nearly visible, usually on the shoreward side of major currents or shelves, and is populated by nonpelagic species. This term is seldom used by freshwater lake anglers.

INTERTIDAL ZONE

The shallow area along shore and in an estuary between high- and low-water marks that is exposed at low tide and covered at high tide; also known as the littoral zone.

KRILL

Small pelagic shrimplike crustaceans with bristled tails. Krill range from about ½ inch to 3 inches long. Most are transparent, and many have light-producing organs. They migrate vertically and are plentiful enough to be a major food source for seabirds, fish, and whales.

LACUSTRINE

Having to do with, or living in, a lake.

LANDLOCKED

A term for anadromous fish that have adapted to a completely freshwater existence, spending the greater portion of their lives in a lake and returning to natal rivers or streams to spawn. Any fish—usually salmon but also striped bass—with such behavior and without access to saltwater is landlocked.

LARVAE

The early life forms of a fish or other animal between the time of hatching and transforming to a juvenile.

LATERAL LINE

A series of sensory cells, usually running the length of both sides of the fish's body, that performs an important function in receiving low-frequency vibrations.

LITTORAL

Living in or related to nearshore waters; the intertidal zone of the marine environment that is exposed at low tide and covered at high tide.

LUNATE

Used to describe a caudal fin that is shaped like a crescent moon.

MARINE

Pertaining to the sea and saltwater environs, from the open oceans to the high-water mark and into estuaries; also used to refer to seawater or saltwater.

MIDWATER

In or near the middle layer of water. This term is generally used by biologists to describe the habitat of fish that are not surface or bottom (benthic or demersal), dwellers.

MIGRATION

A regular journey made by a particular species of fish, on an annual or a lifetime basis, usually associated with propagation patterns but also associated with the seasonal availability of food. Most migrations are mass movements and involve travel over a particular route, usually at the same time annually. Migration is not to be confused with the relocation of fish because of pollution, sedimentation, storms, or the temporary relocation of food sources. Anglers, for example, often refer to fish as making migrations from deep water to shallow water to feed, an action that is really a localized movement. The periodic movement of fish in a water body is not necessarily a migration, although the movement of a fish species to and from breeding grounds (such as walleye in the spring moving from a spawning river back to the main lake) is a migration.

Migrations occur in various species and in both freshwater and saltwater. All freshwater fish that move from lake or river environs to a tributary in order to spawn will migrate to and from the spawning grounds at or around the same time each year. All anadromous and catadromous fish undertake spawning migrations, the former from saltwater to freshwater and the latter from freshwater to saltwater, also around the same time annually. Pelagic ocean species migrate from winter to summer grounds, both for spawning and for food procurement, also around the same time annually.

Migrations occur in north-south, south-north, offshore-inshore, and inshore-offshore patterns, and in combinations of these (some sea organisms migrate up and down in the water column). Some fish migrations cover great distances, even thousands of miles, and some are extremely short, perhaps just a short distance up a river.

MOLLUSK
A group of freshwater and saltwater animals with no skeleton and usually one or two hard shells made of calcium carbonate. This group includes the oyster, the clam, the mussel, the snail, the conch, the scallop, the squid, and the octopus. Mollusks may be used as bait when angling, but they are not targeted by anglers or deliberately sought with sporting equipment.

NATIVE
A species of fish that is endemic to a region, a watershed, or a specific body of water. A native species is distinguished from an introduced or exotic species, which occurs outside its endemic range and has been placed there by unnatural means (usually deliberate but sometimes accidental planting by humans). The term "native" is particularly applied in North America to endemic trout, especially brook trout.

NEARSHORE
The shallow portion of inshore saltwaters adjacent to the shoreline. In fishing parlance, inshore is a more common term than nearshore, and they are generally interchangeable, although nearshore is more specific.

NEST
A visible bed, often circular, made by egg-laying fish on the bottom of a body of water for spawning. Eggs are laid in the nest, and sometimes they are guarded by one or more of the parents.

NURSERY
The part of a fish's or an animal's habitat where the young grow up.

OFFSHORE
Although this term practically signifies the direction away from land, in fishing parlance it generally means that portion of the water from which land is not visible, and to most saltwater anglers it pertains to deep-water areas, on the edge of ocean currents or shelves, where big-game species, particularly billfish and tuna, are pursued.

ONSHORE
Waters abutting a coastline. This word is also used synonymously with ashore, meaning physically on the land adjacent to water, but is even more specific than nearshore. It is not the opposite of offshore in common angling usage.

OPERCULUM
The largest and uppermost bone that forms the gill cover of a fish.

PALATINE TEETH
Teeth located on the palatine bones inside the upper jawbone, usually behind the vomerine tooth patch.

PANFISH
This term is used widely by anglers and fisheries managers to collectively describe a variety of small fish of several species. There is no individual species called a panfish. The term is used almost universally in freshwater, seldom in saltwater; although common to anglers, it may be unfamiliar or even confusing to nonanglers.

The term "panfish" often refers to fish that, when fried whole, can fit into a pan, but it is also frequently understood to mean species that are not technically classified as gamefish and that are usually abundant and as valued for their tasty flesh as for the enjoyment of catching them.

Although panfish are commonly linked by these factors, the species that fit under this umbrella are not all linked biologically. Many "panfish" are members of the sunfish family, perch family, bass family, catfish family, and sucker family. These include, but are not limited to, such sunfish as green, longear, orangespotted, spotted, and redear varieties; plus bluegill, Sacramento perch, rock bass, warmouth bass, black crappie, white crappie, yellow bass, white bass, yellow perch, and white perch. In some areas, people include suckers, bullhead, pickerel, and even carp in this category.

PARR
Small, young anadromous fish, particularly salmon and trout, living in freshwater prior to migrating out to sea. During this life stage, parr develop large vertical or oval rounded spots (sometimes called bars) on the sides. Called parr marks, these help camouflage the fish and also identify it; they will gradually disappear as the fish becomes silvery, regardless of whether the fish goes to sea (some do not). In the silvery phase, the fish is known as a smolt. Migration to sea occurs between 2 and 8 years.

PECTORAL FIN
The fin usually found on each side of the body, directly behind the gill opening.

PELAGIC FISH
Free-swimming fish that inhabit the open sea and are independent of the seabed or the water bottom.

PELVIC FIN
The pair of adjoining fins ventrally located beneath the belly and in front of the anus; also called ventral fins.

PHARYNGEAL
Bones in the throat of certain fish that are used like teeth to crush food. These bones are hard and strong and will crush such objects as clams, mussels, and snails. Carp have pharyngeal teeth, which play an important role in their forage habits.

PHYTOPLANKTON
Microscopic suspended algae in the surface waters of seas and lakes, where there is enough light for photosynthesis to occur.

PISCIVOROUS
Fish eating. Most predatory fish, and most of those considered sportfish, are piscivorous.

PLANKTON
Passively floating or weakly swimming organisms in a body of water. Planktonic organisms may drift and float freely, range widely in size, and include the larval stages of many fishes. Some are invisible without magnification, and others are visible to the unaided eye.

POD
A small, tight group of fish swimming together.

POTAMADROMOUS
Fish that migrate within rivers or streams to spawn.

PREDATOR
A species that feeds on other species. Most of the fish species that are pursued by anglers are predators at or near the top of the food chain.

PREY
A species that is fed upon by other species.

ROE
The eggs of a female fish; also a term for a female fish with eggs.

SALTWATER/SEAWATER
Commonly used terms for water with many dissolved salts in or from the ocean, as well as in connected seas, bays, sounds, estuaries, marshes, and the lower portion of tidal rivers.

SCHOOL
A closely spaced collection of fish whose members swim in association with each other. Fish in a school are often of the same species and of similar size, but species may intermingle and may vary in size. Some species are noted for their tendency to school, while other species are more solitary.

SCHOOLING

(1) The behavioral grouping of fish, usually of the same or related species, which move together as a unit and exhibit a specific geometrical relationship. Similar to herding, schooling may be a natural means of reducing predation and ensuring the survival of some individuals. Many species of fish school throughout their lives, and young fish, as well as prey species, are especially likely to school. Fish of different species seldom intermingle, although related species (such as white bass and striped bass, for example) may do so.

Schools are composed of many fish of the same species moving in more or less harmonious patterns throughout the oceans. A very prevalent behavior, schooling is exhibited by almost 80 percent of all fish species during some phase of their life cycles. Many of the world's commercial fishing industries rely on this behavior pattern to produce their catch, especially for species like cod, tuna, mackerel, and menhaden.

SEA-RUN

Another term for anadromous, referring to fish that move from the sea to freshwater to spawn.

SHOAL

A school of fish, usually at the surface or in shallow water (a term used in Europe and sometimes in South America).

SMOLT

A young silvery salmon migrating from freshwater to the sea.

THREATENED SPECIES

In the United States, a species is classified as threatened if it is likely to become endangered within the foreseeable future throughout all or a significant portion of its range. Elsewhere, a species is classified as vulnerable rather than threatened, according to the International Union for the Conservation of Nature and Natural Resources.

TUBERCLE

A small hard knob on the skin that appears seasonally on some breeding male fish.

VERMICULATIONS

Short, wavy, wormlike lines on the backs and sides of some fish.

VOMERINE TEETH

Teeth located on the vomer, a median bone in the front of the roof of the mouth of a fish.

ZOOPLANKTON

Minute suspended animals in the water column of seas and lakes.

CPSIA information can be obtained
at www.ICGtesting.com
Printed in the USA
BVHW010832200619
551296BV00023B/1/P

9 781630 261269